AF796099

CIAL PROPERTY

NE 9120753 3

COMMERCIAL PROPERTY

Peter Luxton, Solicitor
Lecturer in Law, University of Sheffield

and

Margaret Wilkie, Solicitor
Principal Lecturer in Law, University of Westminster

University of East London Library

BLACKSTONE
PRESS LIMITED

8297. PB

First published in Great Britain 1994 by Blackstone Press Limited,
9-15 Aldine Street, London W12 8AW. Telephone 081-740 1173

© P. Luxton and M. Wilkie, 1994

ISBN: 1 85431 351 7

British Library Cataloguing in Publication Data
A CIP catalogue record for this book is available from the British Library.

Typeset by Style Photosetting Limited, Mayfield, East Sussex
Printed by WM Print Limited, Walsall, West Midlands

All rights reserved. No part of this book may be reproduced or transmitted in any form or by any means, electronic or mechanical, including photocopying, recording, or any information storage or retrieval system without prior permission from the publisher.

CONTENTS

PREFACE

This book is designed for students taking an option in commercial property or business leases in the Legal Practice Course. It is written with a practical bias, with particular regard to the drafting and amending of leases and other documents, such as assignments of leases. Precedents for clauses are provided where appropriate in order that the student may more easily appreciate the significance of choosing particular words or clauses. It is not, however, intended to be a precedent book, and for this the student is referred to such standard works as the *Encyclopaedia of Forms and Precedents*. Our book contains two complete model leases in Appendix 1, these being the two model forms of business lease prepared by the Law Society. They are both fairly short and informal, and will generally be more appropriate for shorter leases of smaller properties. The student will find it helpful to compare some of the clauses set out in the text with their counterparts in these model leases.

Although primarily concerned with the law relating to commercial landlord and tenant, this book looks at commercial property from a broad practical perspective. We therefore examine the ways in which other areas have a practical impact on commercial property, as, for instance, planning law and taxation. The current recession has shifted bargaining power towards the tenant, and we consider the tactics that the parties might employ in negotiating leases and assignments. The recession has also led to the insolvency or risk of insolvency of many tenants, and we have therefore included a fairly detailed coverage of insolvency as it relates to commercial property.

As is readily evident, this book contains a great deal of the law relating to commercial leases. We make no apology for this. We firmly believe that a fundamental grasp of the law is the only secure foundation for the practical skills of negotiating and drafting, and this is nowhere more evident than in the case of commercial leases, where practitioners must constantly update their precedents to take account of the latest decisions of the courts, of which there is an unending stream.

We have tried to state the law as at 1 January 1994. This enabled us to take in the judgment of the European Court in *Lubbock Fine & Co.* v *Commissioners of Customs and Excise*, which has important consequences for VAT on the surrender of leases.

Finally our acknowledgments. We have referred to our sources in the text, but we would mention here one work in particular. Everyone writing in the field of insolvency affecting commercial leases must be indebted to Patrick McLoughlin's work, *Commercial Leases and Insolvency*, Butterworths, 1992, and we found it of invaluable assistance in preparing our chapters on insolvency and secured lending. For individual help, we thank Robert Abbey, June Hood and Alan Moran. We are also grateful to everyone at Blackstone Press Ltd, but particularly to Mandy Preece, for the speed and efficiency with which, having received the typescript from us at almost the eleventh hour, they swiftly turned it around to produce the finished product which you are now holding. We, the authors, are responsible for any errors that remain.

Peter Luxton and Margaret Wilkie
March 1994

TABLE OF CASES

TABLE OF CASES

ONE

LEASES GENERALLY

1.1 The Nature of a Lease — its Essential Requirements

A lease is a contract which creates an estate in land for a definite period. The person who grants the estate is called the 'lessor' or 'landlord'. The person to whom the estate is granted is called the 'lessee' or 'tenant'. A lease is often called a 'demise'. The estate created by a lease is called a 'term of years'. It is the only estate of less than freehold. There has been an increasing tendency in the cases to emphasise the contractual nature of a lease rather than to regard it simply as an estate in land, and in *National Carriers Ltd* v *Panalpina (Northern) Ltd* [1981] AC 675 the House of Lords was prepared to accept that circumstances could arise in which the contractual doctrine of frustration could apply to a lease.

1.1.1 FIXED AND DEFINITE DURATION

Whereas a freehold estate is an estate in land of indefinite duration, an estate of less than freehold (a leasehold estate) is of a fixed and definite duration. In order to create a valid lease, therefore, the duration of the term granted must be fixed and definite. In *Lace* v *Chantler* [1944] KB 368 a lease for the duration of the war was held to be invalid, and the House of Lords confirmed this principle in *Prudential Assurance Co. Ltd* v *London Residuary Body* [1992] 2 AC 386 where a council had purported to grant a lease of land until such time as it was required for road widening. The wording of the lease was:

> **The tenancy shall continue until the said land is required by the Council for the purposes of the widening of Walworth Road . . . and the Council shall give two months' notice to the tenant at least prior to the day of determination when the said land is so required.**

It was held to be bad for uncertainty of the term.

A lease is not invalid for uncertainty just because it can be ended by notice, or the usual proviso for re-entry and forfeiture should the tenant default on payments of rent or be in breach of covenant, (Law of Property Act 1925, s. 205(1)(xxvii)). Moreover, provided that a maximum duration is stated, it will not matter that it is made terminable on some event, such as the death of the tenant, within that maximum time.

Although the maximum duration of a lease must be certain, it will still be valid if its commencement is uncertain but dependent upon some event, provided that the event has occurred at the time when it is sought to enforce the lease (*Brilliant* v *Michaels* [1945] 1 All ER 121).

The technical legal name for a leasehold estate is a term of years, but the Law of Property Act 1925, s. 205(1)(xxvii) specifically provides that this shall include also a term for less than a year or for a fraction of a year, so that it would be possible to have a lease for a term of one day only.

A person who has a leasehold estate can 'sublease' or 'subdemise' the land to a subtenant for a shorter term.

1.1.2 EXCLUSIVE POSSESSION

A tenant has an estate in the land and so has the right to exclude anyone else, including the landlord, from the land during the subsistence of that estate. For this reason, a lease will usually expressly reserve rights of entry to the landlord for certain purposes, such as viewing the state of repair of the property. A contract giving a right to be on land without exclusive possession is not a lease but a licence. So in *Clore* v *Theatrical Properties Ltd* [1936] 3 All ER 483 a right to sell refreshments in a cinema did not create a lease but a licence.

1.1.3 REVERSION EXPECTANT UPON THE TERM

A leasehold estate for a particular term can be granted only by someone who has an estate in the land for a longer term, either a freehold estate for an indefinite term or a longer-term lease. When the tenant's term ends the land reverts to the landlord's longer-term estate. The time, either indefinite (freehold) or a term of years (leasehold), for which the landlord can expect to hold the land after it reverts is called the landlord's 'reversion'. The term and the immediate reversion must be vested in different persons. In *Rye* v *Rye* [1962] AC 496 the two tenants in common of freehold premises were in partnership together. The premises were used for the partnership business and a sum of money allowed to them both for this. It was held that this arrangement could not have created a lease. Viscount Simonds said '. . . it is meaningless to say that a man accepts from himself something which is already his own'. Exclusive possession entitles the tenant to exclude everyone else, including the landlord, from the premises, and this was obviously impossible in this situation. There must, essentially, be two parties to a lease.

1.1.4 LEASES AND LICENCES

Many landlords have been anxious to grant licences of their premises rather than leases in order to avoid the effect of various statutes which operate on leases. Landlords have wanted to avoid legislation giving security of tenure and controlling rents, and legislation giving business tenants a right to renewal of their leases. The courts have therefore had to deal with various agreements purporting to grant a licence rather than a lease by providing that the licensee shall not have exclusive possession, although in reality the purported licensee did have exclusive possession. Thus in *Addiscombe Garden Estates Ltd* v *Crabbe* [1958] 1 QB 513 a document which called itself a licence gave trustees of a tennis club the exclusive use of tennis courts for a fee. Many of the terms, such as the obligation to repair, to allow the licensor to enter to view the state of repair of the property and to re-enter on non-payment of the fee, were entirely consistent with a lease, however, and the court held that a lease had in fact been created.

In *Street* v *Mountford* [1985] AC 809 the House of Lords warned the courts to be aware of 'sham' agreements, and indicated that the factor determining whether a lease or a licence had been created was the true intention of the parties rather than what was stated in the agreement between them. Lord Templeman said that wherever premises are granted for a term at a rent, there will prima facie be a tenancy, and that what the parties state in the agreement is irrelevant if it does not reflect the reality of the situation. He did, however, concede that there might be some circumstances, such as where the parties did not intend to create legal relations at all, or services were provided which made the status of the occupier a lodger, in which a tenancy would not arise, even though the occupier had exclusive possession of the premises. These considerations are unlikely to arise in the case of business tenancies, however, and it would seem therefore that occupation of business premises for a term at a rent will be very strong evidence of a tenancy in most cases.

There may, nevertheless, still be some cases where occupation is not under a tenancy agreement, even though there may be exclusive possession. One example would be the circumstances mentioned by Lord Templeman in *Street* v *Mountford* where a person occupies premises by agreement with the landlord pending completion of a lease. The type of agreement to use rooms for trading as in *Clore* v *Theatrical Properties Ltd* [1936] 3 All ER 483 would also be a licence, lacking the element of exclusive possession essential for a lease.

The agreement which the court has to interpret may not always be clearly a lease or a licence and may include characteristics of both. For example, in *Shell-Mex and BP Ltd* v *Manchester Garages Ltd* [1971] 1 WLR 612 a petrol company gave a licence of a filling station to a garage company which undertook to use its best endeavours to promote the sale of the petrol company's products. The employees of the petrol company frequently visited the filling station as they pleased and rights of access to the licensor were assumed and not expressly reserved in the licence. It was held that the agreement was in substance a licence. In *Dresden Estates Ltd* v *Collinson* [1987] 1 EGLR 45 a builder was granted the use of storage space. Some of the terms of the agreement, such as the right of the owners to enter and carry out repairs, were similar to the terms of a lease, but the owner reserved the right to require the builder to transfer his belongings to other storage space of the owner's, and it was held that this was inconsistent with the grant of exclusive possession which is necessary for a lease.

In *Vandersteen* v *Agius* (1993) 65 P & CR 266, CA, the goodwill of an osteopathic practice was sold and the purchaser was allowed to occupy two rooms in the premises where the practice was previously carried on. The purchaser was to make monthly payments for the goodwill over eight years. The vendor's executor argued that the occupation was referable to the sale of the goodwill and was therefore an exception to the rule that exclusive possession normally indicated a tenancy. The court rejected this because the purchase of goodwill did not necessarily require occupation of two rooms. The occupation was therefore referable to a separate transaction which, since it transferred exclusive possession, created a tenancy.

1.1.5 SERVICE TENANCIES AND SERVICE OCCUPANCIES

A service tenancy or a service occupancy will arise where the consideration given for the premises is the tenant's services. The former is a lease and an interest in the property, whereas the latter gives the occupier merely a licence. It may therefore be important to determine which type of arrangement has been created.

Where the occupation of the accommodation is essential for the performance of an employee's duties, such as a surgeon required to live in a hospital or a caretaker in part of a building, then it will be only a service occupancy. In these cases, the occupation of the employee is deemed to be that of the employer (*Glasgow Corporation* v *Johnstone* [1965] AC 609). Even if it is not essential that the employee occupies the premises for the purpose of the employment, but occupying them will enable the duties to be better performed, there may still be merely a service occupancy (*Norris* v *Checksfield* [1992] 1 EGLR 159).

Where the accommodation is provided as part, or all, of an employee's remuneration, but it is not essential to live there in order to do the work, the employee will be a tenant. No tenancy will be created, however, if the services which the employee is required to perform are uncertain and incapable of being quantified in money. In *Barnes* v *Barratt* [1970] 2 QB 657 an agreement giving a right to occupy rooms in a house in return for shopping, cooking and cleaning was only a licence.

1.2 Different Types of Tenancies

Although all tenancies must have the basic characteristics set out above, and the absence of any of these may mean that a licence and not a tenancy has been created, there are many different kinds of tenancies.

1.2.1 FIXED-TERM TENANCIES

Most business leases are for a fixed term, often for 20 or 25 years, and the contractual term expires automatically at the end of the period. On the expiry of a lease of business premises, the tenant can insist on a new lease being granted and may apply to the court if no agreement is reached, unless the parties have agreed that the Landlord and Tenant Act 1954, Part II, shall not apply and their agreement to opt out of the provisions of the Act has been authorised by the court under s. 38(4).

From the landlord's point of view, a long term provides a continuing investment income, but there should be provisions for reviewing the rent from time to time to keep up with inflation. Rent review clauses, which are dealt with in **9.4**, usually provide for a recalculation of the rent every three or five years.

The tenant, who may be uncertain about how his business venture will go, may want some flexibility in a long fixed-term lease. It may be possible to achieve this by a break clause which allows either party to serve notice on the other determining the lease after certain periods, such as seven years and 14 years in a 21 year lease (see **12.3**).

A tenant who is taking a long term should also ensure that it will be easily assignable to an alternative tenant, and that any restrictions on how the premises may be used will not make this difficult. A tenant may also wish to have the right to sublet.

If the landlord wishes to retain a strict control over who occupies the premises, then it may be more appropriate to provide that before assignment the tenant will first offer to surrender the term to the landlord. This will cause problems, however, if the tenancy is within the Landlord and Tenant Act 1954, Part II (see **12.4.4.1**).

When a tenant assigns the lease to a new tenant there is no direct contractual relationship — known as privity of contract — between the landlord and the new tenant. The landlord's contract is still with the original tenant, and the landlord can still require the original tenant to pay the rent if the new tenant does not. The government has proposed reform of this position (see **6.1.1**) but meanwhile, a tenant should favour a short-term lease in order to limit possible liability after assignment. The short term may be extended by giving the tenant an option to renew, and the tenant may in any case apply for a new lease under the Landlord and Tenant Act 1954.

1.2.1.1 Option to renew

An option to renew a lease is a covenant which touches and concerns the land, and the benefit of it therefore passes to an assignee of the term. To bind an assignee of the reversion, however, it must be registered as a class C(iv) land charge (unregistered title) or a minor interest (registered title, unless binding as an overriding interest under the Land Registration Act 1925, s. 70(1)(g)).

Terms of an option to renew a lease, such as provisions for agreeing a rent, should be drafted as clearly as possible and care should be taken to avoid the possibility of inadvertently creating a perpetually renewable lease (see **1.2.4**). The tenant will only be able to exercise the option if he has complied strictly with the terms of the lease (*West Country Cleaners (Falmouth) Ltd* v *Saly* [1966] 1 WLR 1485), where the tenant was unable to exercise an option to renew because he had not redecorated every three years as the lease provided, although the premises were well kept). In *Bairstow Eves (Securities)* v *Ripley* [1992] 2 EGLR 47 a tenant who had not repainted the premises in the last year of the term as covenanted was unable to exercise an option to renew, even though the premises were in good decorative repair and the landlord could only have recovered nominal damages.

1.2.1.2 Commencement of term

The date on which a tenancy commences may not be the date of execution of the lease. Although the term cannot come into existence before the execution of the lease, the lease may backdate the term so that it starts at an earlier date than the date of the lease. The earlier date will apply for the calculation of the term, break clauses and rent reviews. The tenant's solicitor should ensure that the tenant is not made liable for rent and service charges for any period before the execution of the lease during which the tenant was not in occupation of the premises.

Subject to indications to the contrary, a lease specified to commence 'from' a particular day will commence at midnight at the end of that day. To avoid doubt, it is therefore better to state that the term commences 'on' a particular day.

1.2.2 PERIODIC TENANCIES

A periodic tenancy is one for a period, such as a year, a quarter, a month or a week, which automatically continues from one period to the next unless it is terminated by either party giving notice to quit to the other (see **15.2.2.1** and **15.2.2.4**). The period of a periodic tenancy is the period for which the rent is payable not the frequency of payment. Thus a tenancy which reserves a quarterly rent payable monthly in advance will be a quarterly tenancy and not a monthly one (*Adler* v *Blackman* [1953] 1 QB 146).

As well as arising by express agreement between the parties, a periodic tenancy may arise also by implication where a tenant occupies premises and pays a rent. In these circumstances, the type of periodic tenancy will be according to the periods of rent payments.

Part II of the Landlord and Tenant Act 1954 applies to periodic tenancies and the tenant may therefore obtain a new lease.

1.2.3 TENANCIES AT WILL

A tenancy at will usually arises by implication where a tenant holds over at the end of a lease, or where a purchaser occupies premises before completion. It is not always easy to distinguish this type of tenancy from a licence, although it may be important to do so as time may run under the Limitation Act 1980 to extinguish a landlord's title in the case of a tenancy at will, whereas it will not do so if the occupier is merely a licensee (*Heslop* v *Burns* [1974] 1 WLR 1241).

A tenancy at will may also arise by express agreement between the parties, and in these circumstances it may be difficult to distinguish it from a periodic tenancy. Thus in *Manfield and Sons Ltd* v *Botchin* [1970] 2 QB 612 the owner of a shop had made unsuccessful applications to develop the premises. He agreed to allow someone to occupy them until such time as he was able to develop them, and the occupier did so, paying a yearly rent. It was held that the agreement had created a tenancy at will and not an implied yearly tenancy.

It was held in *Wheeler* v *Mercer* [1957] AC 416 that a periodic tenancy which arose by implication from occupation of the premises and payment of rent was not a 'tenancy agreement' upon which the Landlord and Tenant Act 1954 could operate. In *Hagee (London) Ltd* v *AB Erikson and Larson* [1976] QB 209 this was extended to an express tenancy at will which was held not to be a 'tenancy agreement' for the purposes of the Act, and a tenant at will does not therefore have any right to a new tenancy under the Act (see **15.1.1**). However, Lord Denning MR warned the courts to look carefully at any such agreement for a tenancy at will, which might in reality be an implied periodic tenancy within the Act disguised as a tenancy at will.

1.2.4 PERPETUALLY RENEWABLE LEASES

A perpetually renewable lease arises where a tenant is granted a lease for a fixed term with an option to renew the lease on exactly the same terms, including the option to renew. Such a lease effectively gives the tenant the right to renew the lease indefinitely.

These leases are converted by the Law of Property Act 1922, sch. 15, into leases for 2,000 years, terminable by the tenant only on giving 10 days' written notice to expire on a date when the lease would have expired had it not been converted to a term of 2,000 years.

There is always a possibility that a perpetually renewable lease may have been created inadvertently, but the present attitude of the courts is to construe an agreement if possible in a way that does not create such a lease. Thus in *Marjorie Burnett Ltd* v *Barclay* (1980) 258 EG 642 the relevant terms of the lease were:

> **If the tenant shall be desirous of taking a new lease of the demised premises after the expiration of the term hereby granted . . . then the landlord will at or before the expiration of the term hereby granted . . . grant to the tenant a new lease of the premises hereby demised for a further term of seven years . . . at a rent to be agreed between the parties. . . . And such lease shall also contain a like covenant for renewal for a further term of seven years on the expiration of the term thereby granted.**

It was held that the provision for the rent to be agreed between the parties, which was effectively a rent review, was inconsistent with a lease for 2,000 years and that the parties had failed to create a perpetually renewable lease.

The tenant of a perpetually renewable lease enjoys one advantage which other tenants do not have. On assignment of the term, the tenant is no longer liable to the landlord under privity of contract.

1.2.5 REVERSIONARY LEASES

A lease, or a contract for a lease, will be void if the term which it purports to create is not to take effect in possession until more than 21 years later (Law of Property Act 1925, s. 149(3)). This provision does not affect an option to renew a lease contained in a lease for more than 21 years if the tenant will go into possession under the new lease within 21 years of exercising the option (*Re Strand and Savoy Properties Ltd* [1960] Ch 582).

1.2.6 CONCURRENT LEASES

A landlord who has granted a lease and then grants another longer lease of the same premises has effectively disposed of part of the reversion, and the lessee of the longer term becomes entitled to possession at the termination of the shorter term. From the moment that the longer lease is granted, the longer-term tenant becomes the landlord of the tenant with the shorter term. Such a lease is sometimes referred to as a 'reversionary' lease, being, in effect, a lease of part of the landlord's reversion, although it is in reality a concurrent lease and is not related to the reversionary lease described in **1.2.5**.

1.3 Formalities for Creating a Lease — Legal and Equitable Leases

A lease is one of the two estates capable of subsisting at law after 1925 (Law of Property Act 1925, s. 1(1)). It will not subsist as a legal estate, however, unless the formalities required for the creation of a legal estate have been complied with. It may nevertheless subsist in equity in certain circumstances. There are important differences between legal and equitable leases.

1.3.1 FORMALITIES REQUIRED FOR A LEGAL LEASE

In order to create or convey a legal estate in land, a deed must be used (Law of Property Act 1925, s. 52). This means that generally a deed must be used to create a legal lease. There is an exception for leases not exceeding three years contained in s. 54(2), which provides that such a lease may be legal even if parol, provided that it takes effect in possession and is at the best rent obtainable (a market rent) without a fine (a premium).

Because all periodic tenancies are regarded as leases for the period (week, month, quarter or year), they fall within s. 54(2) (if the period is three years or less) and will be legal leases even though created orally. Similarly, all periodic leases which arise impliedly from occupation and payment of rent will also be legal leases.

It should be noted that s. 52 requires a deed not only to create a legal estate but also to convey one. The assignment of a lease must also therefore be made by deed, even if the lease is a legal lease not exceeding three years within s. 54(2) (*Crago* v *Julian* [1992] 1 WLR 372).

1.3.2 REQUIREMENTS FOR AN EQUITABLE LEASE

Even though the formalities necessary to create a legal lease have not been complied with, it is possible that there is a valid and enforceable contract to create a lease. In certain circumstances, equity will grant specific performance of an enforceable contract to create a lease, so that it may be regarded as an equitable lease — one enforceable in equity. It is necessary then to consider in what circumstances a contract for a lease, enforceable in equity, may be made.

As regards leases created after 26 September 1989, such a contract must be in writing and signed by both parties, or alternatively it may be in two parts, one part signed by each party, and the parts exchanged (Law of Property (Miscellaneous Provisions) Act 1989, s. 2).

A contract with two parts which are exchanged is the usual way of conducting conveyancing transactions, and in order to avoid the unintentional creation of a binding contract before exchange has taken place, pre-contract correspondence is usually expressly made 'subject to contract'. Negotiations for a lease should similarly be made 'subject to contract' or 'subject to lease'. In *Longman* v *Viscount Chelsea* (1989) 58 P & CR 189 correspondence expressly stipulated that any agreement between the parties was 'subject to lease'. It was held that this meant that there would be no binding agreement until the lease and counterpart lease had been exchanged. Furthermore, the signing and sealing of the lease did not constitute delivery of it as an escrow unless it was specifically stated to do so.

It seems that s. 2 will only apply to an executory agreement relating to land. In *Tootal Clothing Ltd* v *Guinea Properties Ltd* (1992) 64 P & CR 452 an agreement for a lease stated that it was the entire agreement between the parties, but the parties had in fact signed another agreement on the same day whereby the landlord was to give the tenant £30,000 towards the cost of fitting out a shop. Subsequently, and after the lease had taken effect, the landlord refused to pay and pleaded s. 2 as a defence to the tenant's action. It was held that s. 2 only applies to an executory agreement, and the collateral contract was not a land agreement caught by the section. Scott LJ took the view that the separate agreement, not being an agreement relating to the disposition of land, would have been enforceable anyway.

Section 2(5) exempts from these requirements a contract for a lease within the Law of Property Act 1925, s. 54(2), so that the contract for such a lease, like the grant, may be purely oral.

Contracts for a lease created on or before 26 September 1989 were governed by the Law of Property Act 1925, s. 40 (repealed by the 1989 Act), and were enforceable if merely evidenced in writing, or if they were purely oral but there was a sufficient act of part performance. It is possible of course that some of these equitable leases may still survive. It is also possible that the courts might be prepared to grant specific performance of a lease which does not comply with the 1989 Act if the plaintiff seeking to enforce it is able to invoke the equitable doctrine of proprietary estoppel. In *J.T. Developments Ltd* v *Quinn* (1990) 62 P & CR 33 the landlords of a shop entered into negotiations with the tenants for a new lease on different terms. On the strength of the negotiations, the tenants spent money on the property. The landlords then sold the reversion to a third party. The events preceded the 1989 Act and it was argued by the tenants that there was an oral agreement of which they could claim specific performance by reason of part performance. This argument was rejected by the Court of Appeal as no agreement had ever been concluded. It was held, however, that an estoppel had arisen, as the tenants had effectively been assured that a new lease would be granted, and had acted to their detriment on this assurance. Moreover, the lease which arose from the estoppel was binding on the purchasers of the reversion.

1.3.3 ENFORCEABILITY AND EFFECT OF AN EQUITABLE LEASE

The equitable remedy of specific performance will be available to enforce a contract for a lease only in accordance with the normal rules for equitable intervention. Equity will not assist a plaintiff who is at fault and is in breach of a term of the agreement (*Coatsworth* v *Johnson* (1886) 55 LJ QB 220, where a plaintiff in breach of a covenant was unable to obtain specific performance of a contract for a lease). In *Warmington* v *Miller* [1973] QB 877 the court refused to grant specific performance of a contract for a sublease where there was a covenant against subletting in the head lease as to do so would have necessarily involved the tenant in a breach of covenant with a third party.

Moreover, as the interest created by the enforceable contract is an equitable lease only, it will only bind a purchaser of the reversion if it is registered as a class C(iv) estate contract (unregistered title) or a minor interest (registered title, although it may become overriding under the Land Registration Act 1925, s. 70(1)(g)).

On assignment, there is no privity of estate and although the benefit of covenants may be assigned, the burden of covenants touching and concerning the land will not pass to an assignee (*Purchase* v *Lichfield Brewery Co.* [1915] 1 KB 184).

Finally, the Law of Property Act 1925 s. 62, which operates to transfer rights appurtenant to the land in certain circumstances, will not apply to an equitable lease as it is not a 'conveyance' of the legal estate, although the section does apply to the creation of a legal lease within s. 54(2) of that Act if it is in writing (*Wright* v *Macadam* [1949] 2 KB 744) and possibly even if it is purely oral (see **3.2.4**).

It will be recalled that a legal periodic tenancy may arise where someone occupies premises and pays a rent (see **1.2.2**). A person with an equitable lease who occupies the premises and pays rent will therefore have a legal periodic tenancy as well as an equitable lease, and will have two concurrent leases in the land. The legal periodic tenancy will be binding as a right *in rem* against a purchaser of the reversion in unregistered title, and binding as an overriding interest under the Land Registration Act 1925, s. 70(1)(k), in registered title.

1.4 Conditional Agreement for a Lease

An agreement for a lease may be made conditional upon some event, such as the vacation of the premises by another tenant. This will not infringe the requirement of certainty of term (*Brilliant* v *Michaels* [1945] 1 All ER 121).

The Landlord and Tenant Act 1954, s. 38(4), provides a mechanism for the landlord and the tenant to agree that the provisions of the Act shall not apply to a business tenancy, but this agreement has to be approved by the court to be effective. A contract to grant a lease may be made conditional upon such approval, or it may be possible to infer from the circumstances that an agreement is conditional upon this (see **15.1.5**). In *Cardiothoracic Institute* v *Shrewdcrest Ltd* [1986] 1 WLR 368 the court had approved agreed short-term tenancies outside the Act and the parties began negotiations for a third agreement. This was not concluded before the end of the previous agreement and the tenant, who remained in possession of the premises, claimed to have an implied periodic tenancy which was protected under the Act. It was held that there was an inference that the third agreement would also be conditional upon the court's consent to the exclusion of the Act.

In both of these cases, the conditions were precedent to the formation of a contract. The true interpretation of some conditions, however, is that there is a binding contract which is avoided in certain circumstances. Examples of this type of agreement are a contract subject to planning permission being obtained (*Batten* v *White* (1960) 12 P & CR 66) or subject to the reversioner's consent being obtained to the assignment of a lease (*Property and Bloodstock Ltd* v *Emerton* [1968] Ch 94). Any such agreement should be made as clear as possible and a time specified for the condition to be fulfilled. If no time is specified, then it will be a reasonable time. If the condition is too vague (such as 'subject to a satisfactory mortgage' — *Lee-Parker* v *Izzet (No. 2)* [1972] 1 WLR 775) then the term may be void for uncertainty.

Because the true construction of this type of contract is that there is a valid agreement which may be avoided if certain conditions are not fulfilled, any such condition may be waived by the party who benefits from it. So, in *Batten* v *White* where the vendor repudiated an agreement to sell subject to the purchaser's obtaining planning permission, the purchaser was able to waive the condition and sue for specific performance even though planning permission had not been obtained.

1.5 Covenant for Quiet Enjoyment

A lease confers exclusive possession on the tenant, and a landlord's covenant for quiet enjoyment is designed to protect such possession, as well as to prevent substantial interference by the landlord on those claiming under the landlord with the tenant's ordinary lawful enjoyment of the premises.

A landlord's covenant for quiet enjoyment is implied into all leases, but it will often be expressed in a form such as the following:

> **That the tenant paying the rent and observing and performing the tenant's covenants herein contained shall be permitted peaceably to hold and enjoy the premises herein demised without interruption or disturbance by the landlord or any person claiming under or in trust for the landlord.**

The wording of an express covenant for quiet enjoyment may extend the covenant to the acts of a subtenant's head lessor, as well as those of the sublessor itself (*Queensway Marketing Ltd* v *Associated Restaurants Ltd* (1984) 271 EG 1106). This can be done, for instance, by adding the words '**or by title paramount**' to the foregoing covenant.

If, however, the covenant is not so extended, or if it is merely an implied covenant, it will cover the acts only of the landlord, but not the landlord's superiors in title (*Celsteel Ltd* v *Alton House Holdings Ltd (No. 2)* [1986] 1 WLR 666; affirmed [1987] 1 WLR 291).

The tenant's remedies for breach of the covenant are damages and an injunction. The damages may cover loss of income because the tenant is unable to sublet at a rent due to interference by the landlord's construction operations (*Mira* v *Aylmer Square Investments Ltd* (1990) 22 HLR 182).

TWO

CONVEYANCING AND PLANNING CONSIDERATIONS

It is assumed that you will have acquired a basic knowledge of the format of a conveyancing transaction and how this operates in relation to leasehold property. As far as conveyancing is concerned, therefore, this chapter does no more than to highlight some of the main considerations which should additionally be borne in mind when dealing with leasehold property. Some of these may already have been mentioned in your conveyancing course.

A person taking leasehold premises will be either a tenant under a new lease, an assignee of an existing lease, or an underlessee of part of a term of an existing lease. Each of these possibilities will be considered in turn.

2.1 A New Lease

2.1.1 PRELIMINARY CONSIDERATIONS

Where the tenant is taking a new lease, there should be some scope for negotiation over terms, particularly in the current economic climate where the tenant is in a much stronger bargaining position than for many years.

The tenant should consider carefully the extent of the demised premises and their physical state in relation to any repairing covenants. A survey may be necessary to discover any latent defects for which the repairing covenant may make the tenant liable, and to ensure that the premises comply with any statutory safety requirements bearing in mind the proposed use of the premises. The lease may also include a covenant to comply with statutory requirements, in which case the survey should discover what work, if any, needs to be done to comply with this.

The tenant should also consider if any easements necessary for enjoyment and use of the premises will be properly granted (**3.2.3** and **3.2.4**), and what easements or rights will be reserved over the demised premises to the landlord or other tenants (**3.2.5**). If the demised premises are a unit in a larger block, service charges are important, and the tenant should enquire what services will be included, who will be responsible for administering them and how the charges are to be apportioned.

The tenant will also want to know how insurance is to be effected and what risks this will cover. If there is a block policy, a copy should be obtained and there should be an undertaking that notice of the tenant's interest will be given to the insurers and noted on the policy.

All these matters should be dealt with in the preliminary enquiries, and many of them are covered in the standard form of preliminary enquiries applicable to leasehold property.

Planning matters may also be raised in the preliminary enquiries as well as on the local search. These will be referred to in more detail in **2.6**. The fact that a use of property is authorised under a lease does not imply that it is a lawful use for planning purposes (*Hill* v *Harris*) [1965] 2 QB 601).

2.1.2 CONTRACT

The usual commercial lease, which will be at a full market rent and no premium, will mostly be entered into without any prior contract. This is because the lease itself is the important document, which will determine in detail the legal relations between the parties. Any contract will merely provide that a lease is to be in the terms of the draft lease attached, and indeed Standard Condition 8.2.3 provides for this.

There will usually be three copies of the draft lease — one to be kept by each of the parties and the third to be the 'travelling draft lease' on which they may both suggest amendments.

Nevertheless, a contract will be necessary if the grant of the lease is to be delayed at all. This could arise where it is to be conditional upon planning permission being obtained, or if it is to be subject to the court's authorisation of an agreement to exclude the Landlord and Tenant Act 1954, Part II. Any agreement must comply with the Law of Property (Miscellaneous Provisions) Act 1989, s. 2, unless it is an agreement for a short-term or periodic tenancy within the Law of Property Act 1925, s. 54(2), in which case it is exempted by s. 2(5) of the 1989 Act.

A contract for a lease may be registered as a class C(iv) land charge in unregistered title or protected as a minor interest in registered title.

The Costs of Leases Act 1958 provides that neither party to a lease shall be bound to pay the other's costs, unless there is an agreement in writing to the contrary. It is not unusual for the landlord's solicitor to provide that the tenant shall pay the landlord's costs in connection with the lease and the tenant will usually pay the costs of engrossing the lease. Standard Condition 8.2.6 provides that the landlord (or 'seller') is to engross both the lease and the counterpart. A limitation to the effect that the tenant will pay 'reasonable' costs, and an estimate of what these are likely to be, is obviously a cautionary measure that a tenant's solicitor should take. The solicitor should be wary of giving any undertaking to pay such costs unless first put in funds by the client. Even then, consideration should be given to what is to happen if, for any reason, the lease is not completed.

2.1.3 THE LANDLORD'S TITLE

The law with regard to the tenant's right to call for deduction of the landlord's title is most unsatisfactory. Unless expressly stipulated, the tenant has no right to call for deduction of the freehold title at all, either in unregistered or registered land (Law of Property Act 1925, s. 44(2)). The tenant's solicitor should resist this state of affairs wherever possible, particularly where the tenant is to pay a premium, or intends to spend sums of money on alterations or fitting out the premises.

In any event, it leaves the tenant uncertain as to what restrictive covenants there may be affecting the property which will, of course, be binding on the tenant. It will also mean that the tenant will not be able to use the lease as security for a loan. Even if this does not concern the tenant, it may affect an assignee who requires a loan, thereby making the premises less easily disposable. If the landlord's freehold title is mortgaged, then the mortgagee's consent to a lease may be required, and the tenant should be assured that this has been granted.

The standard form of preliminary enquiries asks for information on the reversionary title, whether the lease is a head lease or a sublease, and the names and addresses of any superior lessors.

Where the lease will exceed 21 years, it will be registrable substantively at HM Land Registry, and Standard Condition 8.2.4 provides that the 'seller' landlord is to deduce a title which will enable it to be registered with title absolute. The Land Registry will make a note of any lease in the charges register of the freehold title, and the tenant's solicitor should require that the landlord deposits his land certificate with the Registry on completion of the lease so that a corresponding note may be made on the land certificate.

A lease of 21 years or less will be an overriding interest under the Land Registration Act 1925, s. 70(1)(k), and additionally under s. 70(1)(g) if the tenant is in occupation or in receipt of the rents and profits of a sublease.

2.1.4 THE LEASE

The effect of the various clauses in a lease is dealt with in detail in the relevant chapters of this book. It should not be forgotten that the privity of contract between the original landlord and the original tenant makes the tenant liable on the covenants in the lease throughout the term (see **6.1.1**). In the current economic climate, the tenant's solicitor should consider a clause that the tenant's liability under the lease should cease on assignment to a tenant of whom the landlord has approved and given consent to assign. This might well have the effect of discharging the liability of any surety also (depending upon the wording of the surety's covenant) and ideally should be expressly extended to the surety in any event. Legislation to mitigate the harshness of the continuing liability of the tenant under a lease has been suggested for some time, but does not seem to be imminent at the time of writing.

2.1.5 COMPLETION OF THE LEASE

Before the lease is finally completed, the usual pre-completion conveyancing searches should be made. These include a Land Charges search in bankruptcy (or a full Land Charges search if the freehold title is unregistered), a search at HM Land Registry if the title is registered, and a company search if the landlord is a company. Both the lease and the counterpart should be executed by the landlord and the tenant respectively, and dated on completion, when the lease is handed over to the tenant and the counterpart to the landlord. Care should be taken to insert the date on which the term is to commence, and from which rent is to be payable, if these are different from the date of the lease itself.

After completion, the lease and the counterpart will require stamping, and the lease may require registration with the Land Registry. It may also be necessary under the terms of the lease to give notice of the lease to any mortgagee of the landlord's interest.

2.2 Assignment of a Lease

The assignor and assignee of a lease cannot, upon an assignment, themselves vary the terms of the lease. The lessor will need to be a party to any deed varying such terms; and, of course, may demand consideration, and will invariably require to be indemnified for costs. An assignment will follow closely the usual purchase procedure and will usually be preceded by exchange of contracts. The usual preliminary enquiries and local searches should be made. If planning permission is required, then the contract should be made conditional upon this being granted. In this event, it might also be prudent to make the contract conditional on there being no unacceptable conditions attached to planning consent.

2.2.1 TITLE

Like a lessee under an open contract, an assignee cannot call for the freehold title to be deduced. An assignee is entitled to see only a copy of the lease which is being assigned and all assignments for the last 15 years. If the leasehold title is registered with title absolute, however, this means that the registrar has seen, and approved, the freehold title out of which the lease is granted, so that the assignee has no cause for concern. Otherwise the disadvantages of not seeing the freehold title are much the same as those of the lessee outlined above in **2.1.3**.

The assignor should furnish a copy of the lease with the draft contract and provide specifically that the assignment is subject to its terms. Standard Condition 8.1.2. provides that an assignee who has been provided with the documents embodying the terms of the lease is deemed to know of and to accept them.

A breach of covenant by the assignor will amount to a defective title, to which the assignee may object unless the right to do so is negated by a special condition in the contract of sale. To avoid the objection that a repairing covenant may not have been strictly complied with, Standard Condition 8.1.4 provides that the assignor shall not be liable for any breach of covenant as to the condition of the premises, even though the assignee assigns as beneficial owner.

The standard form of preliminary enquiries asks about any breach of covenants by either the lessor or the lessee.

The lease will almost certainly require that the landlord's consent must be obtained to any assignment. Standard Condition 8.3.2 provides that the assignor is to apply for this at his expense, and to use all reasonable efforts to obtain it, whilst the assignee is to furnish references and information reasonably required in this connection. Standard Condition 8.3.4 provides that either party may rescind the contract if the landlord's consent to the assignment is not forthcoming three days before the date for completion. This applies even if there is doubt about the reasonableness of the landlord's refusal of consent.

2.2.2 THE ASSIGNMENT

Even if the lease itself is within the Law of Property Act 1925, s. 54(2), and so may be created by word of mouth, any assignment of it must be made by deed (*Crago* v *Julian* [1992] 1 WLR 372). If the title to the lease is registered, then the assignment may simply be a transfer of the whole of the registered title.

If the assignor assigns as beneficial owner, there are implied covenants with the assignee for quiet enjoyment, that the assignor has a right to convey and for further assurance. If the assignment is for value, it is also implied that the lease is valid and in force and that all the tenant's covenants have been performed. This is limited as regards the physical state of the property by Standard Condition 8.1.4 (see **2.2.1**).

Because of having a continuing liability under the lease, the assignor should take an indemnity from the assignee for future breaches of covenant, although this is implied by the Law of Property Act 1925, s. 77, in unregistered title if the assignment is for value, and by the Land Registration Act 1925, s. 24, in registered title (whether for value or not): see **6.5.1.1**. Standard Condition 4.5.3 provides for such an indemnity. In *Middlegate Properties Ltd* v *Bilbao* (1972) 24 P & CR 329 it was held that an assignee's indemnity covenant could apply to continuing breaches of covenant, such as a repairing covenant, before assignment and should not be construed as applying only to breaches after assignment. The assignee's indemnity should therefore be limited to breaches of covenant occurring while the assignee is the tenant.

The normal pre-completion searches need to be made before completion of the assignment, and after completion any stamp duty paid and the transfer registered, assuming the title is registered. If the leasehold title is not yet registered, it will be registrable if there is more than 21 years of the term left.

2.3 The Grant of a Sublease

Many of the considerations which apply to the grant of a lease will apply also to the grant of a sublease, and the tenant's solicitor should be prepared to negotiate any unfavourable terms. The enquiries and searches to be made on behalf of the sublessee will be much the same.

A sublessee is not entitled to call for deduction of the freehold title (Law of Property Act 1925, s. 44) but may require production of the head lease out of which the sublease is to be granted, and of any assignments going back for 15 years. Standard Condition 8.2.4 (that the seller will deduce title to the purchaser so as to enable him to register a lease of over 21 years with title absolute) applies to a sublease in the same way as it applies to a lease, however, so that if the lessor is not able to deduce title to the freehold, this condition should be excluded. It will not apply, of course, unless a contract is used which incorporates the Standard Conditions, and a sublease is usually granted, in the same way as a lease, without any prior contract.

The sublessee should ask to see the receipt for the last insurance premium and instalment of rent paid under the head lease, and should require an assurance that the covenants under the head lease have been performed. The head lessor's consent will usually be necessary for a sublease and Condition 8.3.2 (as to obtaining consent) and 8.3.4 (as to the right of either party to rescind if consent is not forthcoming) apply.

It is very important that the covenants in the sublease correspond with those in the head lease. Otherwise the sublessor may be sued by the head lessor for a breach of covenant in the head lease but not have any recourse against the sublessee. The sublessee should take a covenant from the sublessor to pay the rent due under the head lease and to observe and perform the covenants in the head lease. An example of such a covenant would be:

> **To pay the rents reserved by the lease under which the landlord holds the demised premises and to perform and observe the tenant's covenants therein contained but only insofar as the superior lessor shall require the same to be performed and observed and except insofar as the same are to be performed and observed by the tenant under this lease.**

2.4 The Assignment of a Sublease

The same considerations apply on the assignment of a sublease as on the assignment of a head lease. The Law of Property Act 1925, s. 45(3), provides, however, that the purchaser shall assume that all covenants have been performed and rent paid under the sublease and any superior lease on production of the last receipt for rent due.

2.5 Occupation prior to the Completion of a Lease, Sublease or Assignment

Although a tenant may be anxious to move into premises, to take advantage of pre-Christmas trade, for example, this may prejudice the tenant's negotiating position and ultimately may not be in the tenant's best interests. However, it might be possible to occupy the premises as a tenant at will or a licensee. A tenancy at will may be created expressly (*Manfield and Sons Ltd* v *Botchin* [1970] 2 QB 612) and will be outside the protection of Part II of the Landlord and Tenant Act 1954: see **1.2.3**. A licensee will not have any interest in the land, and a purchaser who takes possession before completion is within one of the categories of occupation which Lord Templeman specifically mentioned in *Street* v *Mountford* [1985] AC 809 as not presumed to be a tenant. Condition 5(2) of the Standard Conditions of Sale expressly provides that a purchaser who occupies premises before completion does so as a licensee and not a tenant.

A tenant who does take possession before completion would be very unwise to spend money on improvements. Quite apart from the risk that the transaction may not proceed to completion for some reason, any such improvements would not rank for compensation under the Landlord and Tenant Act 1927 and may not be within the disregard in any rent review clause (see **7.8.2** and **9.4.4.3**(c)(vi)).

2.6 Planning Considerations

Since the Town and Country Planning Act 1947, a system for the management and control of land use has operated. It has been the responsibility of local government authorities to manage land in the best economic and social interests of their communities. Since then, various other allied responsibilities, such as the preservation of conservation areas, listed buildings and tree preservation orders, have been included in land administration. There has been a growing recognition of the scarcity value of land in urban areas and the requirement for careful planning for the needs of a community. More recently, environmental issues have warranted consideration, sometimes emanating from the European Community.

2.6.1 THE DEVELOPMENT PLAN

The 1947 Act required local planning authorities to prepare a development plan for their areas. This requirement is now contained in Part II of the Town and Country Planning Act 1990 as amended by the Planning and Compensation Act 1991.

The current provisions require a non-metropolitan county council to produce a structure plan for the whole county designating areas generally for types of user such as education, recreation or housing. The plan must include a written statement on general policies for the development and use of land.

Additionally, a local plan must be prepared by non-metropolitan local planning authorities (other than metropolitan councils) which must indicate in more detail proposed land use consistent with the overall structure plan.

A metropolitan council must prepare a unitary plan, which includes both the elements of the structure plan outlining general policy and the more specific details of the local plan.

A minerals local plan and waste local plan should also be prepared by each county council or metropolitan council.

2.6.2 DEFINITION OF DEVELOPMENT

With some exceptions, there is now a general requirement to obtain planning permission for any development.

Section 55(1) of the 1990 Act states that '"development" means the carrying out of building, engineering, mining or other operations in, on, over or under land, or the making of any material change in the use of any buildings or other land'. The definition therefore encompasses two types of activity — one being operations carried out on the land and the other relating to a change in the user of the land.

2.6.3 PLANNING PERMISSION FOR DEVELOPMENT

Section 70(2) of the 1990 Act requires a local planning authority to have regard to the development plan and to 'any other material considerations' in determining planning applications.

Section 54A of the 1990 Act (inserted by the Planning and Compensation Act 1991, s. 26) requires the authority to determine any planning applications in accordance with the development plan 'unless material considerations indicate otherwise'. The development plan will also be relevant for the modification or discontinuance of any planning permissions. The effect of s. 54A is that there is a presumption in favour of granting planning consent for a development which is consistent with the development plan, but a presumption against consent for a development which is inconsistent with the plan.

The Secretary of State for the Environment has produced a number of Planning Policy Guidance Notes (known as PPGs) and circulars to assist authorities in determining planning applications and PPG1 (revised in 1992) states that 'An applicant who proposes a development which is clearly in conflict with the development plan would need to produce convincing reasons to demonstrate why the plan should not prevail'.

The 'material considerations' referred to in s. 70(2) have been widely interpreted to include any consideration relating to the use and development of land. In *R* v *Westminster City Council, ex parte Monahan* [1988] JPL 107 the Court of Appeal accepted that the financing of a proposed development was a material consideration in granting planning permission for another development nearby. In that case, a development in Covent Garden which involved the demolition of buildings, some of them listed, was permitted in order to finance an extension to the Royal Opera House.

The courts take the view that the determination of planning applications is essentially the job of the local planning authorities, and they will not upset a decision made by an authority unless, on the *Wednesbury* principle (established in the case of *Associated Provincial Picture Houses Ltd* v *Wednesbury Corporation* [1948] 1 KB 223), the decision is so unreasonable that no reasonable authority could ever have come to it.

In *Bendles Motors Ltd* v *Bristol Corporation* [1963] 1 WLR 247 Lord Parker CJ expressed personal reservations about the decision of the Minister that a small egg-vending machine placed on the forecourt of a garage amounted to a change of use which required planning permission, but nevertheless said 'This court can only interfere if satisfied that it is a conclusion that he could not, properly directing himself as to the law, have reached'.

2.6.4 PLANNING ENFORCEMENT

A local authority may issue an enforcement notice in respect of a development without planning permission, or for a breach of condition attached to a planning consent. PPG 18 (1991) provides that such notices should only be issued if the authority considers it to be necessary in the interests of planning. Failure to comply with such a notice is a criminal offence. In the event of an appeal against an enforcement notice, a stop notice may be used to suspend the operation of either kind of development, but compensation is payable for this if the appeal is successful.

In addition, there are two further notices which may be served: the planning contravention notice where the local planning authority believes there has been a breach of planning control, and the breach of condition notice where a condition has not been observed.

2.6.5 PLANNING AGREEMENTS OR OBLIGATIONS

Under the Town and Country Planning Act 1990, s. 106, it is possible for a local planning authority and a developer to enter into a planning agreement which does not fall within the normal planning procedure. Agreements under the section have been made in the past whereby a developer conveyed open-space land to the authority in return for planning permission to develop other land. Such agreements have been criticised as effectively allowing developers to buy planning consent, but s. 106A and s. 106B (s. 12 of the 1991 Act amending s. 106 of the 1990 Act) widens the scope of the original s. 106. The new s. 106 allows a developer to enter into a planning obligation, either by agreement or by unilateral undertaking. The obligation may require the developer to use the land in a specified way, or may specify operations or activities to be carried out on the land to be developed. Payments to the authority may be required for matters not connected with the development, or, apparently even planning objectives.

In *Wimpey Homes Holdings Ltd* v *Secretary of State for the Environment* (1993) Wimpey unilaterally undertook to transfer open-space land to the authority and to make a payment for its maintenance. It was held that the money payment was within s. 106 as amended, but the transfer of title to other land was not as it did not impose any restriction on the land which was the subject of the application. Whilst money payments unconnected with the site to be developed are therefore within the new s. 106, it would appear that the transfer of open-space land in lieu is not.

Although the planning obligation supersedes the planning agreement under the old s. 106 of the 1990 Act, any agreements made under the old section are still valid.

2.6.6 ENVIRONMENTAL CONSIDERATIONS

The European Community's Directive on Environmental Assessment (85/337/EEC) requires that the environmental effects of certain developments should be considered before consent is granted. The Directive was introduced into the planning procedure by the Town and Country Planning (Assessment of Environmental Effects) Regulations 1988 (SI 1988/1199).

The Regulations divide potentially environmentally damaging developments into two categories listed in sch. 1 and sch. 2. Schedule 1 includes large projects, such as aerodromes and land-fill sites, where the environmental impact must be assessed as part of the planning procedure. Schedule 2 projects require only an environmental assessment where the nature, size or location of the project make it likely that it will have a significant effect on the environment. A circular issued by the Department of the Environment (Environmental Assessment: Implementation of the EC Directive 15/88 WO 23/88) gives guidance on whether sch. 2 projects should be environmentally assessed. There should be assessment if the project has more than merely local significance, is in a sensitive or vulnerable location, or is unusually complex and could have potentially adverse effects. Schedule 2 comprises a long list of projects under generic headings such as agriculture, energy, food, rubber industry, processing of metals, glass-making, extractive industry, chemical industry, textile, leather and wood and paper industries, knackers' yards and industrial estate development.

Where a project falls to be environmentally assessed, the applicant for planning permission must produce an environmental statement to the local planning authority. Certain bodies, such as the Nature Conservancy Council, the Countryside Commission, and in some cases HM Inspectorate of Pollution, must be notified of the proposed development and consulted about it. The planning application must then include a statement describing the development and assessing its likely impact on 'human beings, flora, fauna, soil, water, air, climate, the landscape, the interaction between any of the foregoing, material assets and the cultural heritage'.

If it is not clear whether a development falls within sch. 2 or not, an applicant can apply to the local planning authority to determine whether an environmental statement is necessary. The authority has three weeks in which to make a decision. If a planning application is submitted without a statement where the authority thinks a statement should be submitted, it must notify the applicant of this requirement within three weeks. The Secretary of State has a general power to require an environmental statement on any appeals to him.

Where an environmental statement is required, the planning authority has 16 weeks to consider the application instead of the usual eight weeks.

2.6.7 CONTAMINATED LAND

A more controversial environmental provision is the Environmental Protection Act 1990, s. 143, which requires local authorities to keep a register of contaminated land. One problem is that

91207533

whether or not some substances should be included in the 'contaminated' list has not yet been decided.

The proposed register has met with considerable opposition from those involved in the property professions and has so far not been implemented. A market survey of developers of, investors in, and occupiers of land was reported in the *Estates Gazette* (23 October 1993, p. 274).

There was general concern among vendors selling land which might be classified as contaminated as they felt that this would be covered by the standard form of preliminary enquiries, although of course the usual cryptic reply to such enquiries ('not so far as the vendor is aware') might presumably avoid liability. About 40 per cent of landlords who responded to the survey were aware that they had land which might be designated as contaminated, and were considering what amendments might be necessary to future leases to cover a tenant's contamination. Tenants, on the whole, were not concerned, although, as the survey suggests, this attitude could be misplaced given the present extensive continuing liabilities of tenants on leasehold covenants.

It is doubtful if clearing contaminated land would fall within the scope of the usual repairing covenant. It would seem more likely to fall within the ambit of a covenant not to do anything which would cause a nuisance or annoyance to the landlord or to neighbouring landowners. This might presumably cover not only contamination to the leased land but also to neighbouring land from the flow of air, water or soil.

2.6.8 THE TOWN AND COUNTRY PLANNING GENERAL DEVELOPMENT ORDER 1988

This order (SI 1988/1813 known as the GDO) as amended sets out various developments which may be carried out without consent. These include (*inter alia*) minor operations such as the erection of gates and fences of a certain height, the construction of an access to a highway (not being a trunk or classified road) in connection with a development, the provision of temporary buildings or structures and a change of use to another use within the same use class, and sometimes between the classes, under the Town and Country Planning (Use Classes) Order 1987 (SI 1987/764).

2.6.9 SIMPLIFIED PLANNING ZONES

Under ss. 82 to 87 of the Town and Country Planning Act 1990 a local planning authority may designate an area as a simplified planning zone (SPZ). The authority may then make a scheme, operative for 10 years, applicable to the whole or part of the zone, and specifying types of development for which planning consent is not necessary within the area of the scheme. The scheme may be a general one under which there is general consent to development, or a specific one giving consent to only certain types of development. The Secretary of State has indicated that such zones might be used for the development of large tracts of land, such as old railway sidings. They could be used to give consent to new industrial parks or the redevelopment of an old industrial estate.

2.6.10 CERTIFICATES OF LAWFULNESS OF AN EXISTING USE OR DEVELOPMENT

For a long time there has been something similar to a limitation period for proceedings for infringements of planning law. After a certain time, both operational and user development were to be regarded as 'established use' which then became immune from proceedings for infringement.

Section 10 of the Planning and Compensation Act 1991 (inserting new ss. 191 to 194 into the 1990 Act) has extended and amended the procedure whereby an owner could apply for a certificate of established use.

Any person may now apply to a local planning authority for a certificate of lawfulness of an existing operational development or use, or a certificate of lawfulness of a *proposed* operational development or use.

In both cases, the onus of proof is on the applicant to furnish sufficient evidence of the grounds for such certificate. If the evidence presented is satisfactory, the planning authority must issue the certificate and it does not have any discretion in the matter.

Section 4 of the 1991 Act (new s. 171B(3) of the 1990 Act) sets out the time-limits after which a development is to become lawful. It confirms that the time for operational development is four years after the *substantial* completion of the work. It is also four years where there is a change of user to a single private dwellinghouse. The period for development by change of user other than this is 10 years, as is the period for breach of a condition attached to a planning consent.

A certificate of lawfulness of a proposed use or development will be appropriate where the activity would not constitute development (such as a change from an established use to one in the same class), or would be a permitted development under a GDO, or there is an existing planning permission relating to it.

A solicitor acting for a client where there may be some doubt about the lawful use of premises should take advantage of the certification procedure and not merely rely upon a statement from a planning officer. In *Western Fish Products Ltd* v *Penwith District Council* [1981] 2 All ER 204, developers acted upon assurances from a planning officer about the established use of a site. The Court of Appeal held that the assurances were not binding on the authority, and Megaw LJ said 'An estoppel cannot be raised to prevent the exercise of a statutory discretion or to prevent or excuse the performance of a statutory duty'.

2.7 Conditions Attached to Planning Permissions

A planning permission may be granted with conditions attached. Any such conditions must be fair and reasonable, relate to the permitted development, and be imposed for planning purposes and not for any ulterior motive. Conditions which do not comply with these requirements may be quashed.

A solicitor acting for a prospective tenant should ensure that any such conditions do not impede the tenant's proposed user of the premises. In *GP & P Ltd* v *Bulcraig and Davies* [1988] 1 EGLR 138, solicitors acting for prospective lessees on the grant of a lease failed to discover that the planning permission relating to the property to be leased restricted part to use as offices for the printing trade only. This made it impossible to dispose of the lease, which was eventually surrendered to the landlord. The solicitors were held liable in negligence to the lessees and were ordered to pay substantial damages.

In practice, a local planning authority will often attach conditions, such as landscaping, to a planning consent in order to reach a compromise between the applicant and those opposing the application. Conditions for the restoration of land after mineral workings or relating to land-fill sites are usual.

The 1991 Act has made it possible for an authority to serve a breach of condition notice on someone who fails to comply with any condition. It is a criminal offence to fail to comply with a notice within the time specified, which must not be less than 28 days.

2.7.1 DEVELOPMENT INVOLVING BUILDING ETC. OPERATIONS

The Town and Country Planning Act 1990, s. 55(1A), defines building operations as including demolition, rebuilding, and structural alterations or additions to buildings. The word 'includes' used in the section indicates that the definition is illustrative rather then exhaustive. 'Building' includes also structures and erections. Section 55(2) exempts from the definition alterations affecting the internal, but not the external, appearance of a building, although such alterations may of course require approval under the Building Regulations 1991 (SI 1991/2768) if they are structural alterations. An underground extension does, however, require planning consent.

To obtain planning consent, the applicant (who need not necessarily be the owner of the land) should first apply for an outline planning consent. This avoids the applicant incurring the expense involved in producing detailed plans for a development which may not receive approval at all. If the outline consent is granted, it will be subject to reserved matters, and detailed plans must be submitted for approval by the local planning authority in respect of these matters.

The development must be commenced within five years of the outline permission, or within two years of the final approval of the reserved matters, whichever is later.

2.7.2 DEVELOPMENT INVOLVING ANY MATERIAL CHANGE OF USE

This second head of development must be read subject to the Town and Country Planning (Use Classes) Order 1987. This Order deregulates the development process by exempting certain changes of user from the requirement to obtain planning permission.

The Town and Country Planning Act 1990, s. 55(2)(f), therefore states that it shall not amount to development where buildings or other land, or part of them, used for a purpose in any class are to be used for another purpose in the same class. Even a change of user from one class to another class will not necessarily be development unless it amounts to a 'material change in the use'. It has already been mentioned in **2.6.3** that, on the application of the *Wednesbury* principle, the courts regard themselves as having only a very limited jurisdiction to intervene in planning decisions.

It was sometimes the practice, when granting planning permission for a change of use under the 1972 order (which preceded the 1987 order) to make it subject to a condition that it would not apply to any other user in the class. The Secretary of State's Circular 13/87, para.12, makes it clear that such a practice under the new order would be considered unreasonable.

The Town and Country Planning General Development Order 1988 (SI 1988/1813) provides additionally that certain specified changes of user from one use class to another are 'permitted development'. Examples of these are A2 (financial services to the public) to A1 (shop), and B2 (general industrial use) to B1 (business use).

A change of use within a class will be lawful only if the original use has been implemented. A tenant of a new building for which planning consent has been granted for one class use might need to apply again for planning consent (*Kwik Save Discount Group Ltd* v *Secretary of State for Wales* (1980) 42 P & CR 166).

2.7.3 THE USE CLASSES

In addition to deregulation, the 1987 order sought to recognise changes in business user. For example, the rapidly developing 'high-tech' industries have more in common with office user than with other manufacturing industries. The increase in numbers of hot-food take-away businesses, which could be a nuisance in residential areas, made it desirable to put this in a separate class from shops, so that consent is necessary to a change of use from, say, a greengrocer's shop to a fish and chip shop. Consent is also necessary to change from use as a shop to an office offering financial services to the public, so that planning authorities have some control over the erosion of retail shops in town centres.

Class A1 covers various retail shops and A2 financial, professional and other services for the public appropriate for a shopping area. A3 covers the consumption of food and drink on the premises and hot food off the premises.

Class B1 covers office use not within class A2 and research and development of products or processes. This includes light industrial purposes with no adverse effects in a residential area. B2 is general industrial use and B4 to 7 industrial uses giving rise to pollution. These last classes are currently under review, as many of the uses therein are outdated and are likely to be controlled anyway under the Environmental Protection Act 1990. Class B8 is storage and distribution, but retail warehouses are within A1, however much floor space is used for storage.

Class C is residential use, including C1 (hotels and hostels), C2 (residential institutions where care or treatment is provided and residential educational facilities) and C3 (dwellinghouses).

Class D1 is non-residential social and community uses, such as museums and libraries. Class D2 is assembly and leisure centres, such as cinemas and sports centres.

In addition to the classes, there are certain uses which are *sui generis*. These include a theatre, amusement arcade, launderette, the sale or display of motor vehicles and the sale of fuel for motor vehicles, a taxi or car-hire business, a scrapyard or knacker's yard, and work registrable under the Alkali etc. Works Regulation Act 1906. Additionally, uses involving hazardous substances in notifiable quantities could make a use within B1 a *sui generis* use.

2.7.4 ABANDONMENT OF USE

Where a use has been abandoned, planning permission is necessary to resume it. It will depend upon the circumstances in each case whether there has in fact been an abandonment of the use or not. The actual act of abandonment itself, however, is not a material change of use.

In *Trustees of the Castell-y-Mynach Estate* v *Secretary of State for Wales* [1985] JPL 40, a case involving the resumption of a residential use of a derelict house, the Divisional Court accepted a submission that factors which could be taken into account in deciding whether or not there had been an abandonment were the physical state of the premises, the period of non-user, any intervening use and the owner's intentions.

2.7.5 SUB-DIVISION OF PREMISES

A subdivision of a larger unit into smaller units within the same class will not amount to development. Subdivision of a unit with a user outside the Use Classes Order might be development however. It may also be necessary, in this context, to consider the principal user and any ancillary user.

2.7.6 POSSIBLE DRAFTING IMPLICATIONS OF THE USE CLASSES ORDER

The most substantial change of user permissible without consent, not being a material change of use, is the change from A2 (offices for financial services) to B1 (general offices), which can then be changed to use for light industrial purposes. A landlord who wishes to prevent this should consider a user clause prohibiting a change from one use class to another.

From a tenant's point of view, a B1 light industrial use could conceivably be used to argue that office user would be permitted with a resulting adverse effect on a rent review clause. So for use within this class, a user clause should specify exactly which use is permitted and not simply refer to the class.

The new order is not comprehensive any more than the 1972 Order was, so that the problem which arose in *Wolf* v *Enfield London Borough Council* [1987] 1 EGLR 119 could arise again. The user clause in the lease permitted 'use for any purpose within class III' of the 1972 Order. It was held that the user as a non-teaching service unit for Middlesex Polytechnic was not within the class. Rent had to be assessed by reference to class III use only which resulted in a lower rent.

It is possible that, in time, if change of use within the classes becomes habitual, it might be regarded as unreasonable for a landlord to refuse consent to a change of user under a qualified covenant against this. Possibly a refusal of consent to assign on these grounds might also be deemed unreasonable in the same way.

Given the wider uses within certain classes, it would seem preferable to state explicitly in the lease what user is permitted rather than to rely upon the shorthand reference to user within certain use classes.

A clause requiring the tenant to furnish full information about occupation and user of premises might well assist the landlord in establishing exactly which use class has been applicable to demised premises.

2.7.7 INTERPRETATION OF REFERENCE IN USER CLAUSE TO USE CLASS

A typical interpretation clause in a lease might be:

> **Any reference to a statute (whether specifically named or not) shall include any amendment or re-enactment of such statute for the time being in force and all instruments, orders, notices, regulations, directions, by-laws, permissions and plans for the time being made, issued or given thereunder or deriving validity therefrom.**

The 1972 and 1987 Use Classes Orders are so different that it is arguable that a reference in a lease to the 1972 order cannot be interpreted now in terms of the 1987 order. In *Brett* v *Brett Essex Golf Club Ltd* [1986] 1 EGLR 154 it was held that, although it might be reasonable to interpret any reference to a statute as that statute is amended, each clause must be construed in its context. In that case, a reference to the Landlord and Tenant Act 1954, s. 34, was construed as a reference to the section in its original form before it was amended by the Law of Property Act 1969. Presumably it would be open to a court to construe a reference to a use class similarly.

THREE

THE LEASE: PARTIES, PARCELS, RIGHTS AND RESERVATIONS: TENANTS' FIXTURES

Most leases of commercial property will be lengthy documents as they have to cover many areas of agreement between the parties.

To abbreviate the lease as much as possible and to avoid argument, the lease will usually define certain terms such as 'the demised premises' and 'service charge'. In a long and complex lease of, say, a unit in a shopping precinct, there may be two or three pages of definitions which precede the commencement of the lease. A less complicated lease will usually contain definitions at the beginning of the lease.

In order to make the lease as comprehensible as possible and to keep the provisions relating to a particular aspect together, the draftsman will use schedules to the lease. Rights granted to the tenant and reservations excepted to the landlord will almost certainly be set out in schedules. Additionally, separate schedules may deal with matters such as rent review, insurance, service charges and regulations for the management of a shopping precinct. It is possible that the actual body of the lease, including the parties, the term, the rent and the parcels, will be no more than two or three pages, and will leave all other matters, including the tenant's and the landlord's covenants, to be set out in schedules. Obviously the extent to which schedules are used is a matter for the individual preference of the draftsman, but they may assist in making the document easier to read, and quicker to refer to on some particular point.

3.1 The Parties to a Lease

3.1.1 DEFINITION OF THE PARTIES

The lease will start, as any other deed, by setting out the parties. There will usually be an interpretation clause somewhere in the lease which will provide that:

In this lease, unless the context indicates otherwise, the masculine shall include the feminine, the singular shall include the plural, and words denoting a person shall include a corporation or other entity.

A lease will usually define the parties by stating that the terms 'landlord' and 'tenant' shall, where the context so admits, include their successors and assigns. This will be particularly important for the passing of the benefit of personal covenants; and, in *Griffith* v *Pelton* [1958] Ch 205, the benefit of an option to purchase the reversion on a lease passed to an assignee of the tenant where the lease stated:

The lessee' which expression shall include her executors, administrators and assigns where the context so admits.

In *Queensway Marketing Ltd* v *Associated Restaurants Ltd* (1984) 271 EG 1106, affirmed [1988] 2 EGLR 49, a subtenant successfully sued its immediate landlord for a breach of a covenant for quiet enjoyment in the sublease caused by the actions of the head lessor. The lease contained a covenant for quiet enjoyment by: **'the landlord or any person or persons lawfully claiming through, under, or in trust for the landlord'** and further defined landlord as including: **'the successors in title of the landlord'** and also **'the superior lessors'**. It was held that the express covenant in the sublease extended to the actions of a superior lessor.

3.1.2 DIFFERENT LEGAL ENTITIES AS LANDLORD

If a landlord who is an individual dies, the reversion will vest in the landord's personal representatives, who will then vest it in the person entitled under the deceased's will or on intestacy. The personal representatives and the person entitled will have the same rights and obligations as an assignee of the reversion (see **6.2** and **6.3**).

If two or more persons are joint landlords, then the most desirable situation from the tenant's point of view is that they should covenant jointly and severally, but the Law of Property Act 1925, s. 81, will have this effect unless a contrary intention is expressed.

If the landlord is a company, then a company search will disclose its financial position, and if it has the power to grant a lease.

3.1.3 DIFFERENT LEGAL ENTITIES AS TENANT

3.1.3.1 Individual

On the death of a tenant who is an individual, the term will pass to his or her personal representatives who will vest it in the person entitled under the tenant's will or on intestacy. On the bankruptcy of an individual tenant the term will pass to the trustee in bankruptcy. Neither of these devolutions will involve a breach of a covenant against assignment. A trustee in bankruptcy may disclaim the lease (see **chapter 14**) or may assign it. Any assignment is, however, subject to any covenant against assigning without consent which there may be in the lease.

3.1.3.2 Co-owners

If two or more persons are joint tenants, then covenants should be made by them jointly and severally so that the landlord may sue all or any of them, although the legal title cannot be vested in more than four co-owners (Law of Property Act 1925, s. 34).

3.1.3.3 Partners

The most usual situation where there are co-owner tenants is where partners take a lease. Although the Partnership Act 1890, s. 9, provides that all partners are liable for the partnership debts, it is desirable to include any partners in whom the legal estate is not vested as parties to the lease as guarantors. From the landlord's point of view, it saves having to prove in any action the existence of the partnership and that the premises are partnership property, and liability can be clearly stated to be both joint and several. From the tenants' point of view, if one of the partners in whom the legal estate is vested dies, the landlord would find it difficult to object to an assignment vesting the lease in a partner who had previously been accepted as a guarantor. It is preferable to be liable as a tenant than as a guarantor, as acceptance of rent from a tenant in breach of covenant may waive the right to forfeit; but payment by a guarantor will be regarded as payment of a contractual obligation and not of rent, and will not therefore waive any right of forfeiture (*London and County (A and D) Ltd* v *Wilfred Sportsman Ltd* [1971] Ch 764).

From the tenants' point of view, there are disadvantages in having the lease in the name of one partner only. In the event of death, the property will devolve through personal representatives instead of passing automatically to the surviving partners by the right of survivorship. Also the provisions in the Landlord and Tenant Act 1954, s. 41A, as to the service of notices with regard to a new tenancy, will not apply.

A provision for relaxation of any covenant requiring consent to an assignment in the case of assignment to a partner is desirable from the tenants' point of view to allow for changes in the partnership. The landlord may be reluctant to agree to this, however, as it could be used as a means of evading the consent covenant altogether, as two assignments could effectively change the ownership completely. Difficulties with regard to obtaining consent to assign may possibly be avoided anyway by one partner allowing the partnership to use the premises, or to share the premises with him or her. Such an arrangement would still be a breach of a covenant against parting with possession of the whole or any part of the premises — a very usual addition to a covenant against assigning or subletting. It will not be a breach of a covenant against assignment if one partner remains in possession after dissolution of a partnership unless there is an assignment to that partner alone.

Where a partnership has been dissolved, the court can, if necessary, compel joint tenant trustees of the legal estate to join with a surviving partner to serve a counter-notice for a new lease under the Landlord and Tenant Act 1954 (*Harris* v *Black* (1983) 46 P & CR 366). In that case, however, the two partners had quarrelled and were occupying separate parts of the premises, and in these circumstances the court declined to compel the unwilling partner to take on the commitments of a new lease which he did not want.

3.1.3.4 Company

If the tenant is a company, an effective assignment may be achieved by a sufficient disposition of the company shares to pass control. If the landlord wishes to maintain control, there should be a provision in the lease that disposition of a certain proportion of the company's shares shall be deemed to be an assignment. The appointment of a liquidator will not amount to an assignment without consent, although any assignment by the liquidator is subject to any requirement to obtain consent. A usual safeguard for the landlord is to provide that in the event of liquidation of the company the landlord shall have a right of re-entry (see **14.1**).

3.1.4 GUARANTOR'S COVENANTS AND LIABILITIES

3.1.4.1 Form of covenant advantageous to the landlord

If the landlord is uncertain about the financial standing of the tenant, or the tenant is a limited company, the landlord may require a guarantor for the tenant's liabilities under the lease. The guarantor will be a party to the lease and will enter into a covenant with the landlord.

A landlord may also seek to include a covenant in the lease that on assignment to a company, guarantees for rent will be given by at least two directors. An example of this is where a tenant's (fully) qualified covenant not to assign contains the following proviso:

> **Provided that if an intended assignee shall be a limited company then upon the landlord's request at least two (or more if the landlord shall reasonably require) of the directors of such intended assignee shall join in the deed of assignment as sureties for such company in order jointly and severally to covenant with the landlord as sureties that such company will observe and perform the covenants of the lease (including the covenant to pay rent) and to indemnify the landlord against all losses, damages, costs and expenses arising by reason of any default by the company.**

The tenant should try to resist any such requirement as it may well impede assignment. A surety for an assignee company will be primarily liable for the payment of rent in the event of liquidation, and will therefore be liable to repay to the original tenant any rent which the original tenant has had to pay on being sued by the landlord under privity of contract (*Becton Dickinson UK Ltd* v *Zwebner* [1989] QB 208).

A surety of an assignee tenant in default is thus potentially at great risk:

(a) If the landlord sues and recovers, for instance, rent arrears from the original tenant, the original tenant can in turn recover from the surety of the assignee in default (*Becton Dickinson UK Ltd* v *Zwebner*).

(b) If the landlord sues and recovers from the original tenant's surety, that surety can sue the surety of the assignee in default (*Selous Street Properties Ltd* v *Oronel Fabrics Ltd* (1984) 270 EG 643).

A surety has, however, some rights:

(a) A surety has a right of recovery from the tenant whose obligation has been guaranteed.

(b) A surety who has paid the rent or other sum due under the lease may also have a right to be subrogated to the landlord's rights against the tenant (see McLoughlin, *Commercial Leases and Insolvency* (London: Butterworths, 1993), p. 133).

3.1.4.2 Form of covenant advantageous to the guarantor

A surety should try to ensure that the covenant limits liability to the period during which the term is vested in the tenant whose liability is being guaranteed. In *Johnsey Estates* v *Webb* [1990] 1 EGLR 80 the guarantor's covenant was limited for 'so long as the term hereby granted is vested in the tenant', and the guarantor was held not liable for the subsequent default of an assignee. If the landlord is not prepared to accept this limitation on the surety's liability, then an alternative might be to limit the guarantee until such time as a substitute can be found. In practical terms, however, it might be very difficult to find a substitute.

If the lease contains a covenant requiring the landlord's consent to assign, it is arguable at least that if the landlord has approved an assignee whom the guarantor has had no opportunity of approving the landlord should then bear the burden of any loss due to the default of that assignee. The same argument will not however be effective to limit a tenant's continuing liability for rent under privity of contract (see **6.1.1**).

The guarantor should take a covenant from the landlord to serve copies of all notices upon him and to give him notice of any breach of covenant. A provision in the lease entitling the guarantor to take an assignment of the term and to act in the name of the tenant in obtaining relief against forfeiture might assist a guarantor to recoup some of his losses in the event of the tenant's default.

3.1.4.3 Position of solicitor acting for tenant and guarantor

A solicitor who is acting for a tenant company should consider whether he or she can act also for a guarantor of the company. If the guarantor is a director of the company, or involved in the business in some way, then there would not seem to be any problem as no conflict of interest would arise. If the guarantor is not connected with the company then there may be a conflict of interest between the guarantor and the company, and the guarantor should be advised to seek independent legal advice. The same situation could potentially arise with any surety. Even where there is no conflict of interest, the solicitor should ensure that he or she advises both clients personally and does not rely upon the tenant to inform the guarantor of obligations under the guarantee. A letter, or written memorandum of the interview, should be kept on the file to avoid any doubt about this in the future.

3.1.4.4 Guarantor's obligations and their discharge

It should be borne in mind that the general rule as regards sureties is that their liability cannot be unilaterally increased, so that any release of the tenant's liability, or variation in the terms of the guarantee, may release the guarantor. In *Selous Street Properties Ltd* v *Oronel Fabrics Ltd* (1984) 270 EG 643, an assignee defaulted on payment of rent. The rent had been increased under a rent review clause. This, in itself, would not have been sufficient to release the original tenant's guarantor, but the increase in rent took account of alterations which the landlord had allowed, contrary to a prohibition against alterations in the lease. It was held that, although this did not release the original tenant, it would have been sufficient to discharge its guarantor, except that the guarantee clause expressly provided that he should not be released by any variations in the lease.

The moral of this case from a landlord's point of view is that the lease should expressly provide that the surety shall not be released by any act or forbearance, or variation of the lease, but only by an express release from the landlord. A suitable clause to achieve this would be one by which the tenant covenants to obtain a covenant from the surety with the landlord:

> **That no variation of the terms of this lease (including any reviews of the rent payable hereunder) or any assignment of this lease nor any neglect, delay or forbearance of the landlord in attempting to obtain payment of the rents or the amounts required to be paid by the tenant or in enforcing the performance or observance of any of the tenant's obligations under this lease shall release, determine or in any way lessen or affect the liability of the guarantor as principal debtor under this lease or otherwise prejudice or affect the right of the landlord to recover from the guarantor to the full extent of this guarantee.**

Even in the absence of such a provision, however, the compromise of a court action may not amount to a forbearance which will release the surety. Thus, in *Collin Estates Ltd* v *Buckley* [1992] 2 EGLR 78, various disputes between the landlord and tenant were compromised by the tenant's agreement to pay £10,000 under a consent order. The tenant became insolvent and it was held that the compromise payment, being a sum in settlement of claims for rent and breach of other covenants, was payable by the surety.

If the landlord wishes to retain an action for recovery of rent from the surety in addition to forfeiture proceedings, then the lease should also state that refusal of rent from the tenant where a right of re-entry has arisen will not release the surety. An appropriate means of achieving this is a tenant's covenant to procure a covenant from the surety with the landlord:

> **That a refusal by the landlord to accept rent tendered by or on behalf of the tenant at a time when the landlord is (or would after the service of a notice under the Law of Property Act 1925, section 146, have been) entitled to re-enter the demised premises shall not release, determine, discharge or in any way lessen or affect the liability of the guarantor.**

The landlord will not be prejudiced at all in forfeiture proceedings by accepting a payment for rent from the guarantor, as it is not regarded as rent but a payment under a contractual obligation of guarantee (*London and County (A and D) Ltd* v *Wilfred Sportsman Ltd* [1971] Ch 764; and see **4.8**).

A surety's liability on disclaimer of the lease on bankruptcy or liquidation of the original tenant and of an assignee is dealt with at **14.8.3.2**. It should be noted, however, that in order to avoid the loss incurred by the landlord in *Murphy* v *Sawyer-Hoare* [1993] 27 EG 127, the surety for an assignee should undertake a primary liability for the covenants in the lease, and the undertaking should be to take a new lease to run from the date of the disclaimer. A suitable provision dealing with both disclaimer and surrender would be a covenant by the tenant to procure a covenant by the surety with the landlord:

> **That in the event of this lease being disclaimed or surrendered by a liquidator or trustee in bankruptcy, the guarantor shall, if so requested by the landlord (which request shall be made in writing and in the case of a surrender within three months thereof and in the case of a disclaimer within three months of the landlord's receiving notice thereof),**

accept from, execute and deliver to the landlord a counterpart of a new lease of the demised premises for a term commencing on the date of the disclaimer or surrender and continuing for the then unexpired residue of the term of this lease and such lease shall be subject to the same covenants, conditions and provisos (including those relating to the payment of rent and re-entry) as are contained in this lease and the costs of the landlord in connection with the grant of such new lease (including the reasonable costs and expenses of the landlord's solicitors) shall be paid by the guarantor.

Such a clause could conceivably also be of some benefit to the surety as it could allow him the opportunity to recoup some of his losses, as with an assignment of the lease.

It was held in *Coronation Street Industrial Properties Ltd* v *Ingall Industries plc* [1989] 1 WLR 304 that such a covenant by a guarantor is one which touches and concerns the land, and the benefit of it therefore passes to an assignee of the landlord's. Lord Templeman made a cricketing analogy in that case where he said, 'A surety for a tenant is a quasi-tenant who volunteers to be a substitute or twelfth man for the tenant's team and is subject to the same rules and regulations as the player he replaces'. This case was an application of the slightly earlier decision of the House of Lords in *P. and A. Swift Investments* v *Combined English Stores Group plc* [1989] AC 643, where it was held that a surety's covenants touch and concern the land, so that the benefit of the covenants and the surety's corresponding liability pass to an assignee of the reversion without the necessity for any separate assignment of them.

The surety is liable, however, only during the contractual term. He will not be liable during any extension of the tenancy under the Landlord and Tenant Act 1954 (*Junction Estates Ltd* v *Cope* (1974) 27 P & CR 482), unless his covenant expressly provides that his liability shall continue during any statutory continuation of the term. Similarly, he will not be liable under a new lease granted under the Landlord and Tenant Act 1954.

The landlord should also include a provision in the lease for the tenant to inform him of the death or bankruptcy of the surety and to provide a substitute in these circumstances. Thus the tenant might covenant:

In the event of the guarantor (or, if more than one, any one or more of the guarantors) dying or becoming insolvent, the tenant shall forthwith in writing notify the landlord of such event and shall, if the landlord shall so request, deliver to the landlord within three months of such notification a deed containing covenants by another acceptable guarantor being covenants identical to those entered into by the guarantor who has died or become insolvent.

A lease may provide for the liability of the existing sureties to be ended if the tenant gives notice to the landlord and substitute sureties are provided. It is important that the landlord ensures that such a clause is drafted so that the liability of existing sureties is not terminated merely by the tenant's notice (cf. *L.E. Grovewood Ltd* v *Lundy Properties Ltd* (15 October 1993, ChD).

3.1.5 SERVICE OF NOTICES ON PARTIES TO A LEASE

The Law of Property Act 1925, s. 196, provides that any notice required to be served upon (*inter alia*) a landlord or tenant or other person, shall be deemed to have been served if it is left at the person's last known place of abode or business, or sent by registered post (or recorded delivery by amendment to the section) to his place of abode or business and is not returned by the Post Office. The notice will be sufficient if it designates the person as lessee or lessor even if it does not actually name him. This is a very useful section which most leases will incorporate by reference, and a usual clause effecting this would be:

The provisions of section 196 of the Law of Property Act 1925, as amended by the Recorded Delivery Service Act 1962, shall apply to any notice required or given under this lease.

3.2 The Demise

The operative part of the lease will state that, in consideration of the rent reserved, the demised premises are granted to the tenant for a term. If much of the agreement between the parties is to be consigned to schedules, this part of the lease may be very short and could read thus:

In consideration of the rents hereinafter reserved and the covenants on the part of the tenant hereinafter contained the landlord DEMISES unto the tenant the demised premises (already defined) TO HOLD the same unto the tenant for a term of [length of term] years commencing on [date term is to commence] TOGETHER WITH the benefit of the rights contained in the first schedule hereto but EXCEPT AND RESERVING to the landlord the rights reserved in the second schedule hereto YIELDING AND PAYING therefor the rent set out in the third schedule hereto.

There would then be covenants by the tenant and by the landlord, which might also be put into schedules, and possibly declarations and provisos.

3.2.1 THE PARCELS CLAUSE

The demised premises, which may appear briefly in the definitions under the lease, will be set out more fully in the 'parcels' clause. As previously mentioned, this may be in the body of the lease itself or in a schedule. It should be set out in sufficient detail and clarity to identify the premises, and may or may not refer to a plan. A plan is not necessary unless the property is part of a title registered at HM Land Registry when it will be necessary to submit a plan with the transfer of part to obtain registration of a separate title.

If the demised premises are a single self-contained building, then reference to the land contained in the Land Registry title number, or the previous deed of conveyance, will probably be sufficient. If it is a unit in a larger building or development, or even a shared building, then a plan will be almost essential to define not only the demised premises, but also such common rights as access, parking and dustbin areas. Any plan included in the lease should be signed by both parties, and in the case of a company, by two directors or a director and the secretary.

In any event, if a plan is used, it should be made clear in the parcels clause if it is merely for identification ('the property shown edged red on the plan attached for the purpose of identification only') or whether the plan is an accurate scale drawing of the property ('the property edged red and more particularly delineated on the plan attached hereto'). In the event of any disparity between the wording of the parcels clause and the plan, the parcels clause takes precedence over the plan if the former wording is used, but the plan takes precedence if the latter is used.

3.2.2 THE EXTENT OF THE DEMISE OF A UNIT IN A BUILDING

It will be particularly important to decide, and to define clearly, what is included in the demised premises, where the demise is of part of a building, as it will affect such matters as liability to repair, access and possible liability for trespass. There are different ways of arranging for the repair of structural and other parts of the building, and the parcels clause will have to be drafted carefully to reflect the intended arrangement.

The first possibility is that the landlord will retain all structural and load-bearing parts of the building, including any main walls of this description within the demised premises, and undertake to repair these. The landlord will recoup the cost of repair as part of the service charge payable by all the tenants (see **chapter 11**). Such an arrangement may be achieved by a careful definition of the 'demised premises' and 'the building' as follows:

The demised premises means the internal surfaces of all walls (both internal and external), floors and ceilings bounding or within the said premises and the windows and

door-frames and doors thereof and the glass in such window frames but excluding all load-bearing structural walls and any walls separating the demised premises from any other part of the building or any other premises and excluding all sewers, pipes, ducts [etc.] within the demised premises other than those which solely serve the premises.

The building means the building known as [address] including the boundary walls and fences thereof, the yards and forecourts and corridors and the roof and roof area and other areas not included in the demise of any premises and the foundations thereof and all load-bearing structural walls.

The second possible arrangement is that all external walls of the building are included in the demise, but vertical and horizontal walls adjoining other demised premises are party-walls with cross-rights of support. The two owners are then jointly liable for the maintenance of the party-walls. The following clause would reflect such an arrangement:

There is included in this demise the entirety of all external boundary walls but a moiety only severed vertically of walls between the demised premises and other parts of the building and a moiety only severed horizontally of floors and ceilings between the demised premises and other parts of the building and all such dividing walls, floors and ceilings shall be deemed to be party-walls.

Obviously, whichever mode of division is adopted should be maintained throughout the building and reflected in all the leases.

In the absence of any express provision to the contrary, it was said in *Graystone Property Investments Ltd* v *Margulies* (1983) 47 P & CR 472 that it is 'almost invariable conveyancing practice' that the horizontal part of any unit is between the floor space and the underside of the floor above. This may be very important for the installation of services requiring pipes and cables. In *Graystone*, the parcels clause described the property as being 'formed on the first floor of the block'. There were some false ceilings and the tenant wanted to use the space above them to form a mezzanine floor. The landlord objected, arguing that this space was not part of the demise. The court was strongly influenced by the fact that the false ceilings were only in some rooms and not throughout. They accepted the general rule in *Sturge* v *Hackett* [1962] 1 WLR 1257 that in the absence of any definite indication in the wording, external walls will belong to the demised premises. To have included in the demise the space between the walls up to ceiling level only (including the false ceilings) would have resulted in the landlord retaining a number of irregularly shaped voids. It was therefore held that the word 'formed' was not sufficient to displace the usual practice of a demise up to the underside of the floor above.

If the demise of top-floor premises includes the roof then the tenant will be free to develop the roof space, which will be deemed to belong to the roof (*Haines* v *Florensa* [1990] 1 EGLR 73). If there is a possibility that the landlord will want to add further units to the building one day then the roof should be excluded from the demise and expressly reserved to the landlord.

3.2.3 EXPRESS GRANT OF EASEMENTS AND RIGHTS APPURTENANT TO THE DEMISED PREMISES

Following on from the description of the demised premises in the parcels clause will be a description of any easements or rights to be included in the demise and any exceptions and reservations. Both of these are likely to be found in separate schedules to the lease so as to keep the main part of the lease uncluttered. If the demise is of a self-contained building, these are not likely to be extensive or complicated, but the demise of a unit in a building will probably involve extensive rights and reservations. The tenant should be granted easements ensuring access, the supply of services through other parts of the building, and a right to enter on to other demised premises to carry out repairs. An example of such a schedule granting rights to the tenant might be:

The right at all times during the term for the tenant, its servants, licensees and invitees in common with others authorised by the landlord:

(a) to pass and repass over the common parts of the building;
(b) after reasonable prior written notice by appointment during normal business hours (except in an emergency) to enter upon any part of the building not hereby demised for the purpose of carrying out any repairs, renewals, maintenance or authorised alterations to the demised premises or any part thereof, the tenant causing as little damage as possible and remedying any damage so caused;
(c) to free passage and running of gas, electricity, water and soil and other services to and from the demised premises through and along the conduits forming part of the building but not included in the demised premises and the right to make connections thereto;
(d) to support and protection for the demised premises from the remainder of the building.

The schedule of reservations should include reciprocal rights reserved to the landlord and other tenants of the building.

It is probably wiser to list the rights which are intended to pass with the property rather than to add general words such as 'together with the appurtenances thereto belonging', as this may have the effect of conferring rights which were never intended to pass. In *William Hill (Southern) Ltd* v *Cabras Ltd* (1987) 54 P & CR 42, the lease demised the premises '**together with appurtenances thereto**'. This was held to pass the right to display two signs over the door at ground-floor level, which did not belong to the tenant. The lease also contained a general clause against the grant of easements, but this was held to be insufficient to allow the grantor to derogate from his grant by detracting from the specific grant of appurtenances.

3.2.3.1 Access

Rights of access granted should consider annoyance to other tenants and possible security risks, and it may therefore be appropriate to limit them to certain hours. Unloading, particularly, may cause inconvenience to other tenants, and some restrictions on this may be desirable. In the development of a large site or shopping precinct, such matters may be dealt with in regulations drawn up for the management of the centre which the tenant covenants to observe. It may be advisable to limit rights of access to '**on foot and with or without motor vehicles**'.

This wording was sufficient in *White* v *Richards* [1993] RTR 318 to exclude juggernauts from a narrow unmetalled roadway.

It should be remembered that the owner of a servient tenement over which others enjoy an easement is not liable for its upkeep (*Holden* v *White* [1982] QB 679) so that provision should be made in the lease for contribution by the tenant to the upkeep of any access (if this is not to be done by the landlord and the cost recovered as part of the service charge). The following covenant by the tenant would cover this situation:

to contribute a fair proportion according to use of the cost of repairing and maintaining the access ways, yards and gardens coloured blue on the plan attached hereto.

Although there will generally be no implied obligation on the landlord to maintain any access way, there may be an implied obligation to take reasonable care to maintain an access which is essential for enjoyment of the demised premises (*Liverpool City Council* v *Irwin* [1977] AC 239).

It may be necessary to consider whether a right of access to a fire escape needs to be reserved or granted. Care should be taken to see that this is granted or reserved as an easement and not as a licence (see *IDC Group Ltd* v *Clark* [1992] 2 EGLR 184 below).

A new lease granted under the Landlord and Tenant Act 1954 will include a right of way if this was appurtenant to the holding under the old lease (*Nevill Long and Co. (Boards) Ltd* v *Firmenich and Co.* (1983) 47 P & CR 59 where a right of way appurtenant to the holding was held to be included in the new lease). It will not be appurtenant to the holding if the right of way was granted to the tenant under an entirely separate lease of the right of way itself however (*Land Reclamation Co. Ltd* v *Basildon District Council* [1979] 1 WLR 767, where a right of way over a road was granted for a seven-year term quite separately from the lease of the holding, and was not therefore appurtenant to it).

3.2.3.2 Services

The tenant should be granted an easement to use all services passing through other parts of the building or estate, subject to a similar reservation to the landlord and other tenants of services passing through the demised premises. This should include not only services presently installed, but any future services to be installed within 80 years (the limit for the grant of a future interest in land under the Perpetuities and Accumulations Act 1964, s. 1).

3.2.3.3 Sanitary facilities

The tenant may also require the use of sanitary facilities. It was recognised in *Miller* v *Emcer Products Ltd* [1956] Ch 304 that the use of a lavatory could be a valid easement. Even if the use of sanitary facilities is only granted to the tenant as a licence, it may amount to a derogation from the landlord's grant to revoke the licence during the currency of the lease (*Creedon* v *Collins* (1964) 191 EG 123).

3.2.3.4 Repairs

The tenant may require a right of entry to adjoining demised premises in order to carry out repairs to the demised premises themselves. Such a right should be granted subject to the tenant giving reasonable notice of its exercise, and will usually be restricted to reasonable hours in the daytime except for emergency work. The right usually includes the right to enter with workmen and is granted on condition that any damage caused to the premises entered is made good. A corresponding reciprocal reservation over the demised premises in favour of the landlord and adjoining tenants should also be made. See the schedule of rights set out above for an example of this.

3.2.3.5 Parking

Parking facilities may be covered by the inclusion in the demised premises of parking places in a central car park in the building or grounds. The case of *Copeland* v *Greenhalf* [1952] Ch 488 suggests that the right to park a car in a particular place could satisfy the requirements for an easement, and this has been confirmed by the Court of Appeal in *London and Blenheim Estates Ltd* v *Ladbroke Retail Parks Ltd* [1994] 1 WLR 31. An alternative to individual parking spaces being included in the demise would therefore be for the landlord to retain the car park and to grant easements over certain spaces to the tenants. Alternatively, the tenant may be granted a licence to park in a common parking area, although presumably here some limitations on the number and types of vehicles would have to be included. Following the principle of *White* v *Richards*, presumably the wording of an easement of parking expressed to be for cars might not cover vans or lorries, and the tenant should consider whether car parking is sufficient.

3.2.3.6 Signs

Tenant

The tenant will almost certainly want to put up a plate or advertising signs, and possibly directions to premises on an industrial estate. There is unlikely to be any problem with regard to this if the sign is attached to the demised premises, although it will have to comply with the Town and Country Planning (Control of Advertisements) Regulations 1989 (SI 1989/670) and the tenant must comply with any covenants in the lease (see **Chapters 7 and 8** for alterations and user covenants which could affect the right to put up signs, in addition to any covenant specifically dealing with it). If the sign is to be erected on a building or land not included in the demise, however, the tenant will require an easement for this, such as:

the right at all times to display and maintain in the entrance foyer or other entrance door a suitable sign of a size and kind first approved in writing by the landlord showing the tenant's trading name.

The tenant should reserve the right to vary the sign. If the sign is to be affixed to the tenant's demised premises then the landlord may take a covenant from the tenant that the tenant will first obtain the landlord's approval to the type and size of the sign.

3.2.3.7 Easement or licence?

Many, if not all, of the rights mentioned here could have been granted to the tenant by a licence. It is important to remember the difference between a licence and an easement. A licence is an agreement between two parties (the landlord and the tenant in this context) which is usually revocable and will only bind third parties in certain circumstances. An easement is an incorporeal hereditament — an interest in land which subsists through different ownerships — and, if legal or, if equitable, protected by registration or as an overriding interest in registered land, binds third parties. All easements derive from a grant, whether express, implied or presumed grant. If there is no grant but merely a licence, then an easement will not have been created. This was the ruling in *IDC Group Ltd* v *Clark* [1992] 2 EGLR 184, which concerned a right of passage through a connecting door in a party-wall to use a fire escape. Although granted in a deed and therefore capable of being a legal easement, it was held in essence to be a licence as this was how it described itself. The subsequent owner of the premises could not therefore claim damages against the successor in title of the adjoining premises when the connecting doorway was blocked up.

3.2.4 EASEMENTS IMPLIEDLY GRANTED WITH THE DEMISED PREMISES

As well as easements expressly granted in the lease, easements may be impliedly granted in certain circumstances, and the landlord should be particularly wary of this when granting a lease of part of premises. It is advisable to include a clause negativing the inadvertent grant of easements in this way. The following clause would have this effect:

Nothing contained in this lease shall impliedly confer upon or grant to the tenant any easement, right or privilege other than those expressly granted.

As well as easements of necessity such as access (*Liverpool City Council* v *Irwin* [1977] AC 239), the law may imply such easements as are deemed to be intended to give business efficacy to an agreement. These will generally be rights of support to a building, but may include other rights which satisfy the requirements for an easement. Thus, in *Wong* v *Beaumont Property Trust Ltd* [1965] 1 QB 173, the tenant of restaurant premises in a basement was required by health regulations to have adequate ventilation. This necessarily entailed a ventilation shaft in the wall of the landlord's premises, and it was held that the tenant acquired an easement for this as it was necessary to give business efficacy to the lease of the premises, which could not be used as a restaurant without it.

The Court of Appeal decision in *Nickerson* v *Barraclough* [1981] Ch 426 suggests that an express exclusion clause can also exclude easements of necessity.

Easements may also be impliedly granted to a tenant under the rule in *Wheeldon* v *Burrows* (1879) 12 ChD 31 if they were enjoyed by the demised property immediately prior to the demise and were continuous, apparent and reasonably necessary for the enjoyment of the demised premises. The rule applies to an agreement for a lease as well as to a lease by deed (*Borman* v *Griffith* [1930] 1 Ch 493).

Probably most dangerous for a landlord, Law of Property Act 1925, s. 62, operates to pass with a conveyance of land all rights appurtenant to and enjoyed with it at the time of the conveyance. The section was intended to be a time-saving conveyancing section, but can in fact result in rights previously enjoyed only by licence becoming fully fledged easements. Thus in *Wright* v *Macadam* [1949] 2 KB 744 a weekly tenant used a shed for storing coal. The landlord granted her a one year lease in writing. It was held that s. 62 operated to give the tenant an easement of storage. The lease was a legal lease within s. 54(2) and therefore a 'conveyance' within the definition in s. 205(1)(ii). The section does not apply to a contract for a lease, which is not a 'conveyance' within the section. It will only apply if the demised premises and the servient tenement were separately occupied immediately prior to the lease, and will not apply if it is expressly excluded. If it can be shown that there was a common intention or agreement to exclude the section, then it may be possible to obtain rectification of a lease after execution to exclude it.

3.2.5 EXCEPTIONS AND RESERVATIONS FROM THE DEMISED PREMISES

Exceptions and reservations will also be included in the parcels clause of the lease. Many of these will be the reciprocal rights which have been granted to the tenant and have been referred to in **3.2.3**. It is important, however, that they should be included, as the general principle that a grantor may not derogate from his grant will preclude any implied reservation except for easements of necessity, which may be limited to rights of access, and possibly intended easements.

In addition to the reciprocal rights referred to above, the landlord may wish to reserve the right to enter and view the state of repair of the premises or any landlord's fixtures (although where the landlord has covenanted to repair, this right will be implied) or to erect a notice advertising the premises during the last six months of the tenancy. A precedent for the former right of entry is to be found in **10.2.5** and the latter may be achieved by a covenant by the tenant:

> **For a period of six months immediately preceding the determination of this lease to permit a notice-board to be exhibited on some conspicuous part of the demised premises intimating that the same are to be let or sold.**

If the lease is a sublease, the right should be reserved to the head lessor to enter in order to comply with any of the covenants in the head lease. The following clause would achieve this:

> **Any rights given to the landlord of entry upon the demised premises for the purpose of inspecting or executing any works to, on or from the demised premises shall be deemed also to be given to every superior landlord and to agents, workers and others authorised by the landlord and any superior landlord.**

If there is a possibility that the landlord will want to develop either the demised premises or adjoining premises at some time in the future, then the acquisition of any easement of light should be expressly negatived. Under the Prescription Act 1832, a tenant may acquire an easement of light against his landlord by 20 years' user; and he will do so if the right to build is not expressly reserved to the landlord. The right to erect scaffolding should be expressly reserved too, as this may otherwise be a trespass to the demised premises. It may in any event be an actionable nuisance, or an interruption of the landlord's express or implied covenant for quiet enjoyment (*Owen* v *Gadd* [1956] 2 QB 99).

It would seem from *Haines* v *Florensa* [1990] 1 EGLR 73 that a landlord who has included the roof in the demise of a top-floor unit will not be able to build on any additional floors. If the landlord has this in mind as a possibility then the roof and roof space should be excluded from any specific demises and the right to build up or convert the roof space specifically reserved.

3.3 Fixtures on the Demised Premises

Fixtures are chattels which lose their identity as chattels and become part of the premises. It is not always easy to decide whether any particular object is or is not a fixture, but there are two tests which may be applied to assist in determining this.

First, is the object physically attached to the premises or to the land? If so, then prima facie it will be a fixture. This is particularly so if it cannot be removed without substantially damaging the premises. This test is not conclusive however, and if attached, it is then necessary to ask, secondly, for what purpose the object was attached. Was it attached to improve the building, or was it attached merely for the better enjoyment of the chattel? In *Leigh* v *Taylor* [1902] AC 157 tapestries were fixed to a wall, but it was held that they did not become fixtures as they were attached in order to enjoy them, and not to improve the building. A contrary conclusion was reached in *D'Eyncourt* v *Gregory* (1866) LR 3 Eq 382 where garden ornaments and statues forming part of the landscaping of a garden were held to be fixtures, although not attached at all, as they were an essential feature of the garden.

It has always been recognised that it could be unfair to deprive a tenant of expensive fixtures which he may have attached to the demised premises, and which have therefore become part of the property. For this reason, a tenant may remove certain tenant's fixtures, including trade fixtures, at the end of a lease. Trade fixtures are objects which the tenant has attached to the premises for the purposes of his trade or business, and the term has been very liberally construed by the courts in favour of a tenant. They have been held to include plant and machinery and shop fittings, extractor fans (*Mancetter Developments Ltd* v *Garmanson Ltd* [1986] QB 1212) and petrol pumps (*Smith* v *City Petroleum Co. Ltd* [1940] 1 All ER 260 — even though these were bolted to the petrol tanks below, as they were capable of being severed from the tanks without damage).

The tenant must make good any damage caused by the removal of the fixtures and will be liable for the tort of waste for failure to do so (*Mancetter Developments Ltd* v *Garmanson Ltd*, discussed fully in **7.1.3**).

The tenant may remove fixtures at any time before the termination of the tenancy, and within a reasonable time after its termination. This is the position if the lease provides expressly that the tenant may remove them at the *end* of the tenancy, or if the notice required to terminate the tenancy is very short, as in the case of a tenancy at will, or a weekly tenancy (*Smith* v *City Petroleum Co. Ltd*).

The provision to allow the tenant to remove tenant's fixtures is usually inserted by way of exception in the part of the lease which requires the tenant to yield up the premises at the end of the term. It would appear in a tenant's covenant as follows:

> **To yield up the demised premises at the expiration or sooner determination of the term together with all additions and landlord's fixtures but excepting all tenant's fixtures.**

In *New Zealand Government Property Corporation* v *HM and S Ltd* [1982] QB 1145 the tenants of Her Majesty's Theatre in the Haymarket had installed seating and other fixtures during the currency of a 72-year lease which terminated on 30 September 1970. The tenants remained in occupation at the end of the tenancy and applied for a new tenancy under the Landlord and Tenant Act 1954, which was granted in 1973 to run for 21 years from 1 October 1970. In 1977 it was necessary to determine a new rent under a rent review clause in the new tenancy, and a dispute ensued over whether the tenants' fixtures should be taken into account for this purpose. If the tenants had lost the right to remove the fixtures, so that they had become landlord's fixtures, then it was proper that they should be taken into account as part of the demised premises in determining the open market rent. If, however, they remained tenants' fixtures, then they should be disregarded.

It was held that a tenant has a right to remove fixtures at any time during which he remains in possession of the demised premises, including the period of a new lease under the Landlord and Tenant Act 1954. The fixtures therefore remained tenants' fixtures and fell to be disregarded for the purposes of a rent review. Lord Denning MR also expressed the opinion that the 'improvements' to be taken into account in fixing a rent on a new tenancy under the Act were improvements by the tenant to the landlord's fixtures and not to the tenant's fixtures.

FOUR

VAT AFFECTING COMMERCIAL PROPERTY

The impact of VAT on commercial property is complex, and this chapter deals only with the basic principles. The normal rule is that the grant of an interest in land is, for purposes of VAT, exempt (Value Added Tax Act 1983, sch. 6, group 1). The grant of an interest in land includes both a conveyance of a freehold estate and the grant of a lease.

4.1 Freehold Conveyance of Commercial Premises

If V Ltd sells and conveys freehold business premises to P Ltd for £10 million, no VAT is levied on the V-P conveyance (i.e. there is no output tax); but, the supply being exempt, V cannot recover any VAT which it has itself incurred — for instance, on having the building refurbished (i.e. V cannot recover any input tax).

A conveyance of the freehold of a new or uncompleted commercial building is, however, not subject to the normal rule (Value Added Tax Act 1983, sch. 6, group 1). For this purpose, a building is new if it was completed less than three years before the grant (ibid., note 4). A building is completed when an architect issues a certificate of practical completion or when it is first fully occupied, whichever happens first (ibid., note (2)). If, therefore, V Ltd has built or redeveloped the premises conveyed within this period, the conveyance is subject to VAT at the standard rate. If P Ltd itself reconveys the freehold within the three-year period after completion, that transaction will also be subject to VAT at the standard rate.

4.2 Grant of Lease

If L grants T1 a 25-year lease of business premises at a premium of £500,000 and at an initial annual rent (subject to five-yearly reviews) of £200,000, the normal rule applies. This means that the grant is an exempt supply, so L does not charge VAT on any premium or rent received; but neither can L recover any input tax incurred (e.g. on refurbishment).

4.3 Assignment of Lease

The grant of an interest in land includes an assignment (Value Added Tax Act 1983, sch. 6, group 1, note (1)). If, therefore, T1 assigns the lease to T2, the normal rule is that the assignment is an exempt supply. No VAT is payable on any premium for the assignment, but T1 cannot recover any input tax which it incurred.

4.4 Surrender of Lease

4.4.1 PREMIUM PAID BY TENANT TO LANDLORD

Before 1989, the surrender of a lease was an exempt supply. The Finance Act 1989, however, restricted the exemptions specified in the Value Added Tax Act 1983, sch. 6, group 1, so that it no longer applies to a surrender. The normal rule does not, therefore apply to a surrender, so that any consideration paid by the tenant is liable to standard-rate VAT. The tenant cannot avoid liability to VAT by purporting to 'assign' the lease to the landlord, since such a disposition comprises a surrender and is taxed as such.

4.4.1.1 Surrender where new lease is granted

A tenant may surrender the lease in exchange for the grant of a new lease from the same landlord. If the consideration payable by the tenant under the new lease is less than it would otherwise be because the tenant is surrendering an existing lease, the difference is treated as consideration for the surrender and is standard-rated. Such consideration could comprise a monetary sum, a reduced rent or rent-free period under the new lease, or the landlord's agreeing not to charge a premium in circumstances where a premium would normally expected to be charged. If, however, the consideration payable by the tenant under the new lease is not so reduced, the transaction is simply treated as the cessation of one lease and the commencement of another, so that no VAT is charged. See further C & E Notice 742B, para.12(d).

4.4.2 COUNTER-PREMIUM PAID BY LANDLORD TO TENANT

In *Lubbock Fine & Co.* v *Commissioners of Customs and Excise* [1993] EGCS 219, the Court of Justice for the EC held that the removal of surrenders from the exemption was contrary to art. 13B of the Sixth EEC Directive, so that consideration paid by a landlord to the tenant (i.e. a counter-premium) upon the latter's surrender of the lease was not liable to VAT. This decision could lead to challenges to the legality of the removal from the exemption of premiums paid by tenants to landlords. It is, however, understood that Customs and Excise treat the decision as applicable only to counter-premiums, and continue to treat payments by tenants as subject to VAT.

4.5 Landowner's Election to Waive Exemption

A landowner is given the option to convert a conveyance or lease into a taxable supply (Value Added Tax Act 1983, sch. 6A, paras 2 to 4). If the grantor exercises the option, the consideration for the conveyance of a freehold bears standard-rate VAT. Where the grant is of a lease, any premium and all rents thereafter payable under the lease are liable to standard-rate VAT. The advantage for the grantor of opting for a taxable supply is that (provided it is registered for VAT) it is then entitled to deduct its input tax from the output tax payable on the grant. The grantor may wish to exercise the option where it has incurred a large amount of input tax, e.g. on refurbishing or constructing the premises.

Once exercised, the exercise of the option is irrevocable. If the grantor has not previously made an exempt supply in respect of the premises concerned, the grantor may exercise the option as of right. In the case of the grant of a lease, this will generally be possible before the lease is granted. If, however, the landlord wishes to exercise the option after the lease has been granted and any premium or rents have been received as exempt supplies, the consent of the Commissioners for Customs and Excise must be obtained. The landlord will have to satisfy them that it will make a fair and reasonable attribution between the exempt supply and the future standard-rated supply.

From 1 January 1992, input tax incurred by the landlord before the exercise of the option is recoverable. If the landlord wishes to recover such earlier input tax, it must, when seeking the approval of Customs and Excise to opt to be taxed, show that it will apportion such input tax fairly and reasonably between the exempt supplies and future supplies at the standard rate.

If the option is exercised, the tenant will thereafter be obliged to pay standard-rate VAT on the rent. The landlord may exercise the option without consulting the tenant or obtaining its consent. If the tenant is itself registered for VAT, it can deduct VAT payable on the premium, rent or other monetary sums, from any output tax it incurs. If, however, the tenant is itself exempt from VAT (e.g. if it is a bank, an insurance company, a charity, a school, or a private health care association), it will be unable to recover such VAT (although non-recoverable VAT is deductible as a business expense for purposes of corporation tax or income tax). The landlord, for its part, should bear in mind that the option relates to all future taxable supplies in respect, not of the lease, but of the buildings or land. An option to tax may therefore depress the level of rent obtainable under a later lease.

4.5.1 SAFEGUARDING TENANT FROM VAT LIABILITY

4.5.1.1 Where option already exercised at grant of lease

If the option to make a lease subject to VAT has already been exercised at the time the lease is granted, the landlord will have to account for VAT on the rent. Unless, however, the lease states otherwise, the amount stated to be payable as rent will be taken to be inclusive of VAT. The landlord could, of course, merely take this into account when agreeing the amount of rent payable; but this is not desirable for the landlord, given that the rate of VAT may later be increased. The landlord should therefore ensure that the stated amount is expressed to be exclusive of VAT, and that the tenant covenants to pay the rent and other sums reserved by the lease.

4.5.1.2 Where option not exercised at grant of lease

The position in regard to VAT is slightly different if the option is exercised after the lease is granted. In this event, the landlord is permitted to add VAT to the rent charged to the tenant unless the lease expressly forbids it (Value Added Tax Act 1983, s. 42). In order to protect itself against the landlord later exercising the option to tax, the tenant (particularly an exempt tenant, such as a bank) should insist that the lease contains a covenant by the landlord with the tenant either not to exercise the option, or, in the event of the option being exercised, not to add VAT to the rent. An example of the first type is a covenant by the landlord:

> **Not to exercise its option to waive the exemption to value added tax on the demised premises.**

Because it is as yet unclear whether the burden of such a covenant will bind the landlord's assignee, Lewison suggests that the tenant should seek a covenant from the landlord to obtain a direct covenant with such assignee (Lewison, *Drafting Business Leases* (Longman, 1993), p. 71).

An example of the second type is a covenant by the landlord:

> **That in the event that the landlord should at any time exercise its option to waive the exemption to value added tax on the demised premises it will not add such tax to the rent hereby reserved.**

If the tenant cannot persuade the landlord to covenant in either of these ways, it should try to ensure that any VAT that may become payable is expressly reserved as rent. The reason for this is that, since 1991, the Stamp Duty Office has levied stamp duty on VAT not charged as rent. Therefore, except in very long leases (i.e., leases for a term of 100 years or more — which is longer than most commercial leases), there is a stamp duty saving if the VAT is reserved as rent. See further: Marsh, 'Stamp duty on VAT on rent' [1991] 42 EG 94. This can be achieved by an additional reservation (after the reservation of the basic annual rent) into the operative part of the lease, thus:

and also YIELDING AND PAYING by way of additional rent any value added tax (at the rate for the time being in force) as shall be chargeable thereon

The tenant's covenant to pay rent should also include (*inter alia*) 'all sums reserved as rent'. It should be noted that the not uncommon practice of stating that any payments of VAT 'shall be recoverable as rent in arrear' is not effective to reserve VAT as rent. For further discussion of the problem of VAT on rents, see Lewison, *Drafting Business Leases*, (Longman, 1993), pp. 70–2, 140–1.

4.6 Service Charges

A service charge payable in respect of the general maintenance of the structure of the premises and grounds, or for the services of, for instance, a caretaker, is regarded as part of the consideration for the grant, If therefore the landlord has opted for a taxable supply, the service charge is also subject to VAT at the standard rate. It should be noted that it is irrelevant for this purpose whether the lease itself provides for the service charge to be recoverable as rent or not.

Any services — such as heating or lighting — provided by a third party directly to the tenant's office or business are not treated as part of the consideration for the grant of the right to occupy. VAT is therefore charged at the appropriate rate: see further C & E Notice 742B and VAT leaflet 701/19, *Fuel and Power*.

See further **11.1.5**.

4.7 Rent-free Periods

If the lease imposes a full repairing covenant on the tenant and also grants the tenant a rent-free period, VAT is payable by the tenant on the basis that it is providing a taxable supply (building services) to the landlord. The value of the supply is the amount of rent forgone. This was held to be the position in *Ridgeons Bulk Ltd* v *Commissioners of Customs and Excise* [1992] VATTR 169, where the lease provided for the first three years of the term to be rent-free. The VAT tribunal held that, although the lease did not itself state that the rent-free period was consideration for the performance by the tenant of its repairing obligations, it was nevertheless entitled to look at extrinsic evidence that this was in fact intended. In that case, such evidence was found in a letter from a director of the landlord company to its solicitors.

The decision is of great importance, since it means that in practice most tenants who have covenanted to repair will be subject to VAT in respect of rent-free periods. There is therefore the possibility that the grant of a rent-free period in consideration for effecting repairs represents a taxable supply both by the tenant (as held in *Ridgeons Bulk* itself) and also by the landlord (in respect of the building services received in lieu of rent, where the option to convert has been exercised). In each case the measure of the supply will be the rent forgone. It cannot be correct that the same transaction represents a taxable supply by both parties, and the decision seems unsound. See further the comments at (1992) 34 Taxes 905.

4.8 Guarantors

If a third party guarantees to the landlord the tenant's obligations under a lease and the tenant defaults in the payment of rent, are payments made to the landlord by the guarantor payments of rent liable to VAT (where the landlord has exercised the option to tax)? The Commissioners of Customs and Excise treat such payments as if they were payments of rent so that, if the landlord has opted for tax, VAT is payable. This view is, however, challengeable. Thus in *London and County (A and D) Ltd* v *Wilfred Sportsman Ltd* [1971] Ch 764, the Court of Appeal held that the payment by a guarantor did not discharge the tenant from his contractual obligation under the lease. The reason, stated by Russell LJ, is that the guarantor's payment is not a payment of rent, but payment made under a guarantee in satisfaction of the guarantor's own contractual obligations. On this basis, a guarantor's payment should not be taxable.

4.9 Release of Tenant from Covenant

If the landlord releases a tenant from a covenant in a lease (such as a covenant to repair) in consideration for a payment by the tenant, this is a taxable supply by the landlord to the tenant and is therefore standard-rated.

FIVE

RESTRICTIONS ON THE LESSEE'S RIGHT OF DISPOSITION

At common law, a lessee has complete freedom to dispose of the term in any way he wishes, e.g. by assignment, sublease, mortgage, or parting with possession. In the context of leases of commercial property, the only restrictions upon this freedom of disposition are those which may be contained in the lease itself.

5.1 Types of Restriction

5.1.1 COVENANT

The lease may contain a covenant by the tenant not to assign, sublet etc. This is the most common type of restriction on disposal.

5.1.2 CONDITION OR LIMITATION

The lease may be expressed to be subject to a condition subsequent, i.e. upon the tenant's not assigning, subletting or parting with possession, or attempting to do any of these things.

Alternatively, the lease may be expressed to be determinable, e.g. it may provide that it is to continue 'for so long as' or 'while' the tenant does not (or does not attempt to) assign, sublet or part with possession.

5.2 Extent of Restriction

A covenant restricting disposition can take one of three forms: absolute, qualified or fully qualified:

(a) An *absolute* covenant against assignment is one in which the tenant simply covenants not to assign.

(b) A *qualified* covenant against assignment is one in which the tenant covenants not to assign without the landlord's consent.

(c) A *fully qualified* covenant against assignment is one in which the tenant covenants not to assign without the landlord's consent, such consent not to be unreasonably withheld.

An absolute covenant by the tenant against disposition might take the following form:

Not to assign, transfer, charge underlet or part with or share possession or occupation of all or any part or parts of the demised premises.

Occasionally, the landlord might also wish to prevent the tenant declaring itself a trustee of the demised premises. An absolute covenant designed to achieve this might be:

Not to hold all or any part of parts of the demised premises on trust.

5.3 Construction of Restrictions on Disposition

A restriction on disposition is construed against the person seeking to rely upon it, i.e. against the lessor. Thus a general restriction upon assignment will be construed to comprise only assignments in which the lessee is a willing assignee. It would not, therefore, include an assignment by way of compulsory purchase, or the taking of the lease by the tenant's judgment creditor in execution, or the vesting of the lease in the lessee's trustee in bankruptcy or in his or her personal representatives upon death. If, therefore, the lessor wishes to restrict assignments in such cases, the wording of the covenant would have to be widened in the appropriate manner.

The usual form of wording of a covenant restricting disposition includes a prohibition on parting with possession. An ouster of the tenant by an adverse possessor is not an assignment, neither is it a willing act on the part of the tenant. It would, however, be a parting with possession (see **6.8.1.1**).

5.4 Effect of Disposition in Breach of a Restriction

A lease does not come to an end merely because there is a disposition by the tenant which breaches either a condition or a limitation, or a covenant which provides for the lease to terminate upon its breach. The landlord must take steps to forfeit the lease, and before this can be done he must serve a notice under the Law of Property Act 1925, s. 146: see **13.4**.

An assignment of the lease in breach of a covenant or condition is effective to vest the term in the assignee, albeit subject to the landlord's right to proceed to terminate the lease in accordance with the statutory requirements (*Old Grovebury Manor Farm Ltd* v *W. Seymour Plant Sales and Hire Ltd (No. 2)* [1979] 1 WLR 1397). The notice under s. 146 should therefore be served on the assignee: see **13.4.2**.

5.5 The Running of Disposition Covenants

A covenant not to assign without the lessor's consent 'touches and concerns' the land (*Williams* v *Earle* (1868) LR 3 QB 739). The same principle would seem to apply where the covenant is absolute, and also to other types of disposition covenants, i.e. covenants against subletting or parting with possession.

5.6 Qualified Covenants against Disposition

In some instances, statute intervenes to turn a qualified covenant into a fully qualified covenant, i.e. it implies into the covenant an additional qualification that the lessor's consent is not to be unreasonably refused. The following statutory provisions apply only to covenants that are in terms already qualified. None of them applies where the covenant against disposition is absolute.

5.6.1 LAW OF PROPERTY ACT 1925: CONSENT TO MORTGAGE

Where a licence is required to subdemise by way of legal mortgage, such licence is not to be unreasonably refused (Law of Property Act 1925, s. 86(1)). Further, where a licence to assign is required on a sale by a mortgagee, such licence is not to be unreasonably refused (s. 89(1)).

5.6.2 LANDLORD AND TENANT ACT 1927: GENERAL APPLICATION

Because of its generality, the most important statutory provision is the Landlord and Tenant Act 1927, s. 19(1)(a). This applies to leases that contain a covenant, condition or agreement against assigning, underletting, charging or parting with possession of the demised premises (or part thereof) *without licence or consent.* Such covenant etc. is, notwithstanding any express provision to the contrary, deemed to be subject to a proviso to the effect that such licence or consent is not to be unreasonably withheld.

As mentioned above, this provision applies only to qualified covenants, not to covenants that are absolute. Furthermore, it applies only to covenants against disposition. For the impact of the Act on covenants restrictive of improvements, see **Chapter 7**; and for its impact on user covenants, see **Chapter 8**.

5.6.2.1 Parties cannot define what is reasonable

The parties to the lease cannot weaken the impact of s. 19(1)(a) by trying to specify in the lease the circumstances in which a refusal is to be regarded as reasonable. It is therefore important that the lessor does not attempt in the lease to define what comprises a reasonable refusal to consent.

Thus in *Balfour* v *Kensington Gardens Mansions Ltd* (1932) 49 TLR 29, a lease of a flat contained a qualified covenant by the tenant against subletting. The covenant was, however, subject to a proviso that the landlord could require, as a condition of consent, that the proposed sublessee enter into a direct covenant with the lessor to perform and observe the covenants in the head lease. It was further provided that 'non-compliance with such condition shall be deemed a reasonable ground for refusing such consent'. The court held that the final proviso was void and therefore to be disregarded in deciding what was reasonable. On the facts the court held the landlord's refusal unreasonable: first, because the sublessee would already be bound to pay the rent under the sublease to his immediate landlord; and, secondly, since there had been a fall in the rents since the lease had been granted, no sublessee could be expected to covenant to pay the lessor a rent higher than that reserved in the sublease.

A similar approach was adopted in *Re Smith's Lease* [1951] 1 All ER 346, where a fully qualified covenant against disposal was expressed to be subject to the proviso that a refusal of consent should not be deemed unreasonable merely because the lessor at the time of refusal also offered to accept a surrender; and, in the event of such an offer being made, the lessee was to surrender the tenancy. The proviso was held ineffective (and the refusal was held unreasonable).

Some older leases provide that:

> **The landlord shall not unreasonably refuse consent in respect of a respectable and responsible person.**

'Respectable' in this context appears to refer to a person's general reputation; whereas 'responsible' relates to a person's financial ability to pay the rent and observe and perform the other covenants in the lease. It has been suggested that such a qualification also falls foul of s. 19(1)(a): see Crabb, *Leases: Covenants and Consents* (London: Sweet & Maxwell, 1991), p. 36. In *Moat* v *Martin* [1950] 1 KB 175, however, a clause in terms similar to this, but with the word 'unreasonably' omitted, was upheld on the basis that the section did not invalidate a provision whereby the landlord conceded more than the statute required of him. The clause meant that the landlord could not object to any proposed assignee who was respectable and responsible, even though the landlord might, but for the proviso, have reasonably objected on other grounds.

5.6.2.2 Condition precedent as a way around s. 19(1)(a)

Although the parties cannot themselves agree what is a reasonable refusal to consent, they are nevertheless free to agree that the tenant's right to dispose of the lease is not to arise unless and until he first complies with a specified procedure. Such a covenant was upheld in *Adler* v *Upper Grosvenor Street Investment Ltd* [1957] 1 WLR 227. The covenant began in the usual form of a qualified covenant not to assign; but this was subject to a proviso that if the tenant should wish to assign he had first to offer voluntarily to surrender the lease, and the landlord could accept such offer within 21 days. Such a clause was held valid on the basis that the subsection bites only when the lessee has a right to assign (albeit qualified by consent); whereas under an *Adler*-type clause such a right did not arise until the tenant had first made an offer to surrender and such offer had not been accepted by the landlord. The validity of such a clause was affirmed in *Bocardo SA* v *S & M Hotels Ltd* [1980] 1 WLR 17.

The use of the condition precedent as a means of avoiding the Landlord and Tenant Act 1927, s. 19(1)(a), sometimes arose (as in the *Adler* case itself) in the context of offer-to-surrender clauses. However, the impact of the Landlord and Tenant Act 1954, s. 38(1), as interpreted in *Allnatt London Properties Ltd* v *Newton* [1981] 2 All ER 290, affirmed [1984] 1 All ER 423, has reduced the value of offer-to-surrender clauses in commercial leases: this is fully discussed at **12.4.4**.

5.6.3 LANDLORD AND TENANT ACT 1927: BUILDING LEASES

It is clearly important for the tenant of a building lease not to be restricted in its ability to assign or sublet, since this is a means by which the tenant is enabled to recoup on its investment: see Yates and Hawkins, *Landlord and Tenant Law*, 2nd ed. (London: Sweet & Maxwell, 1986), p. 301. To ensure that such tenants are free to dispose, there is special statutory provision in the shape of the Landlord and Tenant Act 1927, s. 19(1)(b). This paragraph, which applies only to building leases of at least 40 years, subjects a qualified disposition covenant, condition or agreement to the proviso that no consent is required for an assignment, underletting, charging or parting with possession effected more than seven years before the end of the term, provided that written notice is given to the lessor within six months after the transaction is effected. For the purpose of para. (b), a building lease is a lease made in consideration for the erection, substantial improvement, addition or alteration of buildings.

Paragraph (b) does not apply if the landlord is a government department, or local, public or other statutory authority. Thus, for instance, local authorities involved in building schemes in the inner cities may retain control over them: see Yates and Hawkins, ibid.

A provision in a lease may make the landlord's consent conditional upon the obtaining by the tenant of both a guarantor of the obligations of the assignee and also a direct covenant from the assignee to observe and perform the covenants in the lease. Such provision is not invalidated by s. 19(1)(b) (*Vaux Group plc* v *Lilley* [1991] 1 EGLR 60).

5.6.4 DEMAND BY LESSOR OF PAYMENT FOR CONSENT TO DISPOSITION

5.6.4.1 Expenses of giving licence

The Landlord and Tenant Act 1927, s. 19(1)(a), expressly states that the implied proviso does not preclude the right of the landlord to require payment of a reasonable sum in respect of any legal or other expenses incurred in connection with the licence or consent. This means that a demand for such a payment is not to be taken as an unreasonable refusal to consent to the disposition. It is generally advisable, however, to provide for this in the lease expressly. A covenant by the tenant to pay the landlord's costs of consenting to the disposition may well be one of several covenants entered into by the tenant relating to the landlord's costs (including, for instance, the costs of a s. 146 notice). A covenant (or the part of a covenant) relevant for present purposes is as follows:

To pay and indemnify the landlord against all reasonable costs, charges, fees, disbursements and expenses properly incurred by the landlord, including (but not restricted to) those payable to solicitors in relation to any application for consent to [assign, sublet, part with possession, etc.] whether or not such consent is granted

(except in the circumstances where the landlord is obliged not to withhold consent unreasonably and the withholding of such consent is held to be unreasonable) and whether or not the application for consent is withdrawn.

5.6.4.2 Demand for other payments

If the landlord demands some other form of payment as a condition of giving its consent to assign, underlet etc., there are two possible effects. Such demand:

(a) may constitute an unreasonable refusal to consent under the Landlord and Tenant Act 1927, s. 19(1)(a);
(b) may be contrary to the Law of Property Act 1925, s. 144.

The Law of Property Act 1925, s. 144, applies to all leases containing a covenant, condition or agreement against assigning, underletting, or parting with possession, or disposing of the land or property leased without licence or consent. It deems such restriction to be subject to a proviso that no fine or other sum of money in the nature of a fine shall be payable for such consent; but this does not preclude the right to require payment of a reasonable sum in respect of legal or other expenses incurred in relation to such licence or consent.

For the following reasons, the section is of limited practical effect:

(a) It states that the lease may contain an express provision to the contrary, so it is easily avoided.
(b) Like the Landlord and Tenant Act 1927, s. 19(1)(a), it does not apply to absolute covenants against assignment etc.
(c) It does not refer, and has been held not to be applicable, to dispositions of part of the premises only.
(d) It merely inserts the proviso into the lease: it does not make the demand itself unlawful. This means that, provided the demand is not otherwise unlawful (e.g. unless it is made fraudulently, or under duress or undue influence) if the tenant pays the sum demanded, it cannot be recovered (*Andrew* v *Bridgman* [1908] 1 KB 596).

The only substantial effect of s. 144 therefore is that, if the landlord demands a fine that is not provided for in the lease itself, the tenant is relieved of the need to obtain the lessor's consent to assign or otherwise dispose of the property. The lessee can simply go ahead and assign etc. without consent (*Andrew* v *Bridgman*). It also means that, before the fine has been paid, the tenant can withdraw from any agreement to pay it.

It would appear that the section points to a sum of money that is to go irrevocably into the pocket of the lessor (*Re Cosh's Contract* [1897] 1 Ch 9). This includes a demand for a higher rent (*Jenkins* v *Price* [1907] 2 Ch 229 at p. 234) but not a demand that a prospective assignee enter into a direct covenant with the lessor (*Waite* v *Jennings* [1906] 2 KB 11). Where there has been a serious breach of a repairing covenant, a demand as a condition of consent to assign that a prospective assignee deposit a sum of money as security against the cost of the repairs is probably not a demand for a fine within s. 144 (cf. *Orlando Investments Ltd* v *Grosvenor Estate Belgravia* (1989) 59 P & CR 21 where the issue was not raised). If, however, the lessor demands that the prospective assignee pay him a specified sum to enable the lessor to effect the repairs, such demand might well be caught by the section. Apart from s. 144, however, these demands must still satisfy the reasonableness test of the Landlord and Tenant Act 1927, s. 19(1)(a): see **5.6.2** and **5.8.2**.

5.7 The Landlord and Tenant Act 1988

This statute was passed as a result of two Law Commission Reports which concluded that the law did not adequately protect tenants who wished to dispose of their lease and also led to unacceptable delays in conveyancing (Law Com. Nos. 141 (1985) and 161 (1987)). Specific problems were:

(a) In most cases, a tenant had no action in damages against a landlord who had refused consent to assign unreasonably.

(b) The landlord might not come to a decision or communicate it to the tenant very speedily.

(c) The landlord did not have to give reasons for refusal, thus making it difficult for the tenant to know if the refusal was unreasonable or not.

(d) The burden of proof was on the tenant, i.e. it was for the tenant to establish that the refusal was unreasonable, not for the landlord to prove that it was reasonable.

Although, as has been seen, an assignment or other disposition made without consent is effective to vest the legal estate in the assignee or disponee (**5.4**), few prospective purchasers would be willing to risk going ahead where consent had not been obtained.

The position is now changed as a result of the Landlord and Tenant Act 1988, which clearly has the potential to generate considerable litigation. The reason that it has as yet produced relatively little case law is the recession: when property is difficult to let, landlords would rather permit an assignment than risk the insolvency of an existing tenant.

5.7.1 SCOPE

The Act applies to tenancies whenever made which contain (whether expressly or by statutory implication) a *fully qualified* covenant against assignment, underletting, charging or parting with possession. It therefore applies to qualified covenants that are made fully qualified by the Landlord and Tenant Act 1927, s. 19(1)(a); but it does not apply to absolute covenants prohibiting disposition.

5.7.2 APPLICATION BY TENANT AND LANDLORD'S NOTICE

If the tenant serves upon the landlord a written application for consent to the transaction, the landlord owes the tenant a duty within a reasonable time to give consent, unless it is reasonable not to give it (Landlord and Tenant Act 1988, s. 1(3)). Giving consent subject to an unreasonable condition does not satisfy this duty (s. 1(4)). The landlord must also serve a written notice of decision on the tenant. Where consent is withheld, such notice must specify the reasons for withholding it. Where consent is given subject to conditions, the notice must specify the conditions (s. 1(3)).

The reasonableness or unreasonableness of a landlord's withholding of consent is to be judged solely by reference to the circumstances existing and known to the landlord at the time of making the decision. Furthermore, evidence of matters occurring or emerging subsequently is not admissible for the purpose of supporting reasons already advanced. Thus in *CIN Properties Ltd* v *Gill* [1993] 38 EG 152, the landlord refused consent to assign in November 1989. The court held inadmissible as part of the landlord's evidence the accounts of the tenant's proposed assignee company for the year ending September 1990.

In the pre-1988 Act case of *Bromley Park Garden Estates Ltd* v *Moss* [1982] 1 WLR 1019, the majority of the Court of Appeal took the view that, in considering whether a refusal was reasonable, the court was entitled to consider reasons other than those which the landlord had specified to the tenant when refusing consent, provided that such reasons had influenced the landlord at the time of deciding to withhold consent. Following the Act, however, it would seem that the only reasons that the court will consider are those specified in the landlord's written notice; and it would seem that the Act makes provision for only one such notice.

5.7.2 1 Reasonable time

The Act does not specify what is meant by a reasonable time but it would appear that anything more than a few weeks will be regarded as unreasonable (*Midland Bank plc* v *Chart Enterprises Inc.* [1990] 2 EGLR 59 (on the facts, 10 weeks' delay was held unreasonable).

5.7.3 BURDEN OF PROOF REVERSED

It is now for the landlord to show that a refusal was reasonable, that any conditions attached to a consent were reasonable, and that notice of the landlord's decision was served within a reasonable time (s. 1(6)).

5.7.4 TORTIOUS CLAIM FOR BREACH OF STATUTORY DUTY

A landlord who is in breach of obligations under the Landlord and Tenant Act 1988 is liable to the tenant in damages for breach of statutory duty (s. 1(4)). If, for instance, the tenant were to lose a sale to an assignee because of an unreasonable refusal, the tenant could sue the landlord for damages for the lost sale. Again, if, as a result of a delayed consent, a tenant has to sell to an assignee at a reduced price, the tenant can sue the landlord for the difference in price. Such action is additional to any other course of action the tenant may have, e.g. assigning to a willing assignee without consent, or applying to the court for a declaration that consent has been unreasonably withheld.

5.8 What Constitutes a Reasonable Withholding of Consent?

The Landlord and Tenant Act 1988 is of no assistance in ascertaining when a withholding of consent is reasonable. All it states is that, for the purposes of the Act, 'it is reasonable for a person not to give consent to a proposed transaction only in a case where, if he withheld consent and the tenant completed the transaction, the tenant would be in breach of covenant' (s. 1(5)). This, however, is clearly circular. As a result, the existing case law on what is reasonable or unreasonable continues to apply.

5.8.1 GENERAL APPROACHES

The case law is, alas, not entirely consistent. Four different approaches have been advanced.

5.8.1.1 Circumstances of the case

First, it has been suggested that reasonableness depends simply on the circumstances of each case, and that the authorities lay down, not rules of law, but mere propositions of good sense (*Bickel* v *Duke of Westminster* [1977] QB 517, CA).

5.8.1.2 Personality or proposed user of assignee

Secondly, the view that held sway for many years was that an objection to a disposition is reasonable only if it concerns either the personality of the proposed assignee, or his proposed user of the property (*Re Gibbs and Houlder Brothers and Co. Ltd's Lease* [1925] Ch 575, CA), per Warrington LJ. In that case the landlord refused consent on the ground that the proposed assignee was an existing tenant of adjoining property that the landlord would find difficult to relet. The refusal was held unreasonable.

5.8.1.3 Matter of contract

Thirdly, in recent years there is a growing acceptance of a contractual approach, i.e. that what is reasonable depends upon what was within the reasonable contemplation of the parties at the time the lease was made. Put another way, a ground is unreasonable if it does not affect the subject-matter of the contract that forms the relationship between the landlord and the tenant (*Re Gibbs and Houlder Brothers and Co. Ltd's Lease* [1925] Ch 575 per Sargant LJ). If the landlord withholds consent on such a ground, the landlord is seeking to obtain for himself an advantage that the lease did not confer on him, i.e. a collateral advantage.

In *Bromley Park Garden Estates Ltd* v *Moss* [1982] 1 WLR 1019, a restaurant and the flat above had been leased to different persons on separate leases. The flat was let subject to a qualified covenant against assignment. A few months before the lease of the flat expired, the tenant sought to assign; but the landlords refused, eventually arguing that this was in the interests of good estate management, i.e. that they would obtain a higher rent if the flat were let together with the restaurant. In substance, the landlords' argument was based upon the personality of the proposed assignee, but the court held the refusal unreasonable because the interests of estate management were wholly outside the intention to be imputed to the parties at the time the lease was granted.

The court may be able to find that the bargain between the parties goes beyond what is expressly stipulated in the lease, i.e. that particular terms are to be implied into the lease, or that the parties made a collateral agreement. There was no evidence of this in the *Bromley Park* case, but a collateral contract may explain *Premier Confectionery (London) Co. Ltd* v *London Commercial Sale Rooms Ltd* [1933] Ch 904: see **8.4.1** (although such a collateral contract, if made after 26 September 1989, might now be void under the Law of Property (Miscellaneous Provisions) Act 1989, s. 2).

In order to preclude the implication of additional terms or collateral contracts, the lease may provide that the terms contained in the lease embody its entire terms. A suitable form of wording is a statement that:

> This lease sets out the entire agreement between the parties.

5.8.1.4 Propositions in the *International Drilling* case

Fourthly, in *International Drilling Fluids Ltd* v *Louisville Investments (Uxbridge) Ltd* [1986] Ch 513, Balcombe LJ summarised the relevant law in a series of propositions, the essence of which is as follows:

(a) The purpose of a qualified covenant against assignment is to protect the landlord from having his premises used in an undesirable way or by an undesirable tenant or assignee.

(b) Thus the landlord is not entitled to refuse consent on grounds other than those which relate to the relationship of landlord and tenant in regard to the subject-matter of the lease.

(c) It is not necessary for the landlord to prove that the conclusions that led him to refuse consent were justified if they were conclusions that might have been reached by a reasonable man in the circumstances. (It was recently confirmed that this is still the law: it remains unnecessary for the landlord to justify as a matter of fact the matters upon which he relies (*Air India* v *Balabel* [1993] 30 EG 90, CA; also *Beale* v *Worth* [1993] EGCS 135, CA).)

(d) It may be reasonable to refuse consent on the ground of the purpose for which the proposed assignee intends to use the premises, even if that purpose is not expressly forbidden in the lease (*Bates* v *Donaldson* [1896] 2 QB 241). For a detailed discussion of this, see **8.4.1**.

(e) While the landlord need usually consider only his own relevant interests in deciding whether to refuse consent, there may be cases where a refusal of consent will cause disproportionate harm to the tenant compared with the resulting benefit to the landlord. In such cases, refusal may be unreasonable. See further **8.4.1**.

(f) Subject to the foregoing, the reasonableness of a refusal is in each case a question of fact, dependent upon all the circumstances.

Although these propositions were set out in the context of a qualified covenant against assignment, they would appear to be equally relevant to qualified covenants restrictive of other types of disposition.

5.8.2 CONSENT SUBJECT TO CONDITIONS

5.8.2.1 Where the lease is silent

The imposition of a condition is unreasonable if it seeks to obtain for the lessor a collateral advantage, i.e. one not contemplated in the lease. Thus the demand that an assignee of a sublease enter into a covenant not to use the premises for a specified purpose was held an unreasonable refusal to consent where the sublease permitted such user (*Premier Rinks Ltd* v *Amalgamated Cinematograph Theatres Ltd* [1912] WN 157).

By contrast, consent conditional upon the assignee providing security for the completion of repairs was held not to constitute an unreasonable withholding of consent in *Orlando Investments Ltd* v *Grosvenor Estate Belgravia* (1989) 59 P & CR 21. There were serious and long-standing breaches of a repairing covenant in the lease, and the landlord was entitled to have the covenant complied with. The demand was not, therefore, a collateral advantage.

5.8.2.2 Where the lease provides

Whether a landlord can satisfy the reasonableness test by specifying in the lease what conditions may be imposed has not been clearly resolved. According to the contract-based approach (**5.8.1.3**), consent that is made subject to a condition is never an unreasonable refusal to consent if the condition is provided for in the lease. This view is, however, difficult to square with *Balfour* v *Kensington Gardens Mansions Ltd* (1932) 49 TLR 29 (see **5.6.2.1**), where a consent to sublet subject to conditions was held unreasonable even though such conditions were specified in the lease. Such approach, however, might now be considered outmoded. In practice, many commercial leases provide that the lessor is to be entitled to demand that an assignee enter into a direct covenant to observe and perform the covenants in the lease and to provide a guarantor. Alternatively, a future court might treat the *Balfour* case as limited to consent to sublet and to its special facts: as was stated in the case itself, no subtenant could be expected to covenant to pay the rent provided for in the head lease when this was higher than that payable under the sublease.

5.8.3 SOME SPECIFIC INSTANCES OF REASONABLE OR UNREASONABLE WITHHOLDING OF CONSENT

5.8.3.1 Disponee's proposed user

This is a common instance of withholding of consent and is dealt with at **8.4.1**.

5.8.3.2 Standing, status or personality of disponee

It is reasonable to refuse consent to assign to an assignee who is unlikely to be able to comply with the financial obligations imposed by the lease, i.e. the payment of rent and service or other charges (*Air India* v *Balabel* [1993] 30 EG 90). A landlord may request references and a sight of the assignee's accounts (*British Bakeries (Midlands) Ltd* v *Michael Testler and Co. Ltd* [1986] 1 EGLR 64; *Ponderosa International Development Inc.* v *Pengap Securities (Bristol) Ltd* [1986] 1 EGLR 66).

In *Oil Property Investment Ltd* v *Olympia and York Canary Wharf Ltd* [1993] EGCS 129, the lease, which contained a fully qualified covenant against assignment, conferred on Enterprise Petroleum Ltd (EPL) — the original tenant — and upon that company only, the right to determine the lease at the end of the 10th year of the term (i.e. on 8 March 1995). EPL assigned to Olympia in 1987, which in 1992 wished to assign back to EPL. The landlord had no objection to EPL *per se*. It nevertheless refused to grant consent on the ground that, if EPL determined the lease, it was likely (in view of the slump in the commercial property market) that the premises would not be let for a year or more, that the rent would be reduced by more than half, and that the value of its reversion would fall. It was clear that a reasonable landlord could come to the same conclusions, and the court held that the injunction that the landlord had obtained against an assignment to EPL was to continue until after 8 March 1995.

In *Re Cooper's Lease* (1968) 19 P & CR 541, a tenant with no security of tenure himself wished, three years before the expiry of his lease, to sublet to an oculist. The landlord, fearing that the oculist would have security of tenure under the Landlord and Tenant Act 1954, Part II, was unwilling to consent to the subletting unless there was an application to the court for such protection to be excluded. The refusal to consent was held reasonable.

In *West Layton Ltd* v *Ford* [1979] QB 593, a landlord was held to be reasonable in refusing consent to sublet to a person who would thereby obtain security of tenure. The lease, made in 1971, was of a butcher's shop, with a flat above. The lease contained a covenant by the tenant not to sublet the flat except on a service tenancy to an employee or on a fully furnished tenancy. In 1971, occupiers of fully furnished tenancies did not have security of tenure under the Rent Acts, but they obtained such protection in 1974. The tenant sought consent to sublet to a furnished tenant in 1977. The court, looking to the intention rather than to the letter of the covenant, found that its purpose was to preserve the letting's commercial character, i.e. to ensure that the shop and the flat could be relet as a single unit. The landlord was therefore held reasonable to refuse consent.

A landlord who, as in *West Layton Ltd* v *Ford*, is letting property which has mixed business and residential occupation, might therefore be well advised to insist that there is a covenant against subletting part, and that such covenant is absolute. Alternatively, the landlord might be prepared to permit subletting of the residential part on terms which ensure that the residential subtenant does not acquire security of tenure. This might be achieved by a proviso to a restriction on subletting in the following form:

> **Provided that if the tenant wishes to sublet the residential part of the demised premises on an assured shorthold tenancy the tenant shall be permitted to create such a sublease only if the tenant obtains in advance of such subletting the lessor's consent in writing, such consent not to be unreasonably withheld.**

It has been held unreasonable to refuse consent to sublet to a foreign diplomat merely on the ground that diplomatic immunity would prevent the landlord from obtaining possession were the head lease to be determined (*Parker* v *Boggon* [1947] KB 346, where moral pressure was considered sufficient). It has been suggested, however, that refusal to consent to an *assignment* to such a person would probably be reasonable, because an assignment creates privity of estate (Crabb, *Leases: Covenants and Consents* (London: Sweet & Maxwell, 1991), pp. 94–5).

Refusal by a landlord to consent on the ground of the disponee's gender or race may contravene the Sex Discrimination Act 1975, s. 31, or the Race Relations Act 1976, s. 24. There is a saving in each case if the premises are small (as there defined), are occupied by the person refusing consent or a close relative (as there defined) who shares part of the accommodation with other residents who are not members of his or her household.

5.8.3.3 Existing breaches of covenant

If existing breaches of covenant are serious, they may justify a withholding of consent (*Goldstein* v *Sanders* [1915] 1 Ch 594) or the imposition of conditions (*Orlando Investments Ltd* v *Grosvenor Estate Belgravia* (1989) 59 P & CR 21. Trivial breaches, however, do not justify a refusal to consent (*Farr* v *Ginnings* (1924) 44 TLR 249, where the landlord's attempt to use them to persuade the tenant to surrender was treated as an attempt to secure a collateral advantage; also *Beale* v *Worth* [1993] EGCS 135, CA).

5.9 Conditions Relating to Disposition Commonly Found in Commercial Leases

In addition to other matters dealt with above, a lease which does not absolutely prohibit disposition will probably contain additional covenants by the tenant designed to protect the landlord's interest.

5.9.1 ASSIGNMENT

5.9.1.1 Lessee's covenant to obtain direct covenant by assignee with lessor

This is a common obligation in a commercial lease: see further **6.4.1**. A suitable form of words (which takes account of *Estates Gazette Ltd* v *Benjamin Restaurants Ltd* [1993] 4 All ER 367, discussed **6.4.1**) might be a covenant by the tenant:

Before any permitted assignment, to procure that the intended assignee enters into direct covenants with the landlord to pay the rents hereby reserved and to observe and perform the tenant's covenants contained in this lease during the remainder of the term of this lease.

5.9.1.2 **Lessee's covenant to obtain surety for assignee**

In order to provide additional security, the landlord may well require one or more sureties for an assignee. The obligations of such a surety are essentially the same as those of a surety for the original tenant. Thus, an assignee's surety will generally provide:

(a) a guarantee of the assignee's obligations under the lease;
(b) a primary obligation to take a new lease in the event of disclaimer by the trustee in bankruptcy or liquidator of the tenant for the time being.

The position of sureties is considered in more detail at **3.1.4, 14.2.2.6** and **14.8.3.2**.

The form of covenant by the tenant may be very elaborate; but a basic form of wording might be as follows:

To obtain, at the landlord's request, an acceptable guarantor for any prospective assignee, which person shall execute and deliver to the landlord a deed containing covenants by such guarantor (or, if more than one such guarantor, joint and several covenants from such guarantors) with the landlord in the following form:

(a) that the tenant or the guarantor will during the remainder of the term of the lease observe and perform all the covenants on the part of the tenant herein contained; and
(b) that if a liquidator or trustee in bankruptcy shall disclaim or surrender this lease the guarantor shall, upon three months' written notice given to him by the landlord, execute and deliver to the landlord (at the cost of the guarantor) a new lease of the demised premises (which lease shall have been submitted to him by the landlord) for a term commencing on the date of disclaimer and continuing for the then unexpired residue of the term of this lease, and such new lease shall be at the same rent and shall contain the same covenants, terms and conditions as are contained herein.

5.9.2 SUB-LETTING

The landlord will often require a tenant to covenant in the lease that, before subletting, the tenant will obtain the landlord's consent to certain matters and ensure that the sublease contains specified terms and covenants.

5.9.2.1 **Lessee's covenant to obtain direct covenant by sub-lessee with the head lessor**

The tenant may covenant that, before applying for consent to sublease, the tenant will submit a licence to sublet to the landlord, such licence to contain a covenant by the subtenant with the head landlord to observe and perform all the covenants and conditions in the head lease (other than those relating to rent). This ensures privity of covenant between the head landlord and the subtenant, and enables the landlord to proceed for breach of covenant, if necessary, directly against the subtenant. A form of covenant by the tenant is:

Before any permitted underletting, to procure that the undertenant enters into a direct covenant with the landlord to observe and perform all the tenant's covenants and other provisions contained in this lease (other than those relating to the payment of rent).

A landlord who wishes to prevent a subtenant creating a sublease (i.e. a sub-underlease) may insist that such covenant includes a direct covenant with the landlord not to sublet.

5.9.2.2 Lessee's covenant to grant sublease at a rack-rent without a premium

The tenant may covenant that the sublease is not to be granted at a premium or a fine, and that the rent payable under the sublease is to be a rack-rent and, in any event, is not to be less than the rent at that time payable under the head lease. Such a covenant is clearly designed to ensure that, if the lease of the head tenant were to terminate before the sublease, the head landlord would thereafter gain maximum financial benefit from the subletting. Were the tenant to grant the sublease at a premium or a fine, the rent under the sublease would, as a consequence, clearly be less than a rack-rent. A suitable precedent might be a covenant by the tenant:

Not to underlet the whole of the demised premises in consideration of a fine or at a premium or at a rent less than whichever shall be the higher of the rent payable under this lease and the open market rental value of the demised premises at the time of such underletting.

5.9.2.3 Lessee's covenant to ensure that any sublease contains proviso for re-entry

Like any well-drawn lease, the sublease will invariably contain a proviso for re-entry — it is, after all, in the tenant's (i.e. the sublessor's) own interests. In the event that the subtenant should become an immediate tenant of the landlord at some time, however, the landlord has an interest in ensuring that the sublease does contain such a proviso. So the tenant may covenant:

to procure that every permitted underlease contains a proviso for re-entry on breach of any covenant by the undertenant.

5.9.2.4 Lessee's covenant regarding rent review in sublease

The lessee may be required to covenant that any sublease is to contain provisions for rent review in terms parallel to those contained in the head lease, and that the dates specified for rent review in the sublease are to be identical to those specified for rent review in the head lease. But for this, there might be a rent review in the head lease which increases the rent under the head lease without there being a similar review of rent in the sublease. This would increase the chance that the head tenant might not be able to pay the rent under the head lease. This can be provided for by the addition of the following words to the foregoing covenant:

and to provide in any such underletting for the rent thereunder reserved to be reviewed at the same time or times and upon the same basis as is herein provided for the review of the rent hereby reserved.

This will not in itself be sufficient, however, to give the landlord any voice in the setting of the rent in the sublease at review. The landlord might therefore wish to add words such as the following:

but not to agree any reviewed rent with the undertenant nor any rent payable on a renewal thereof without the prior written consent of the landlord (such consent not to be unreasonably withheld).

The landlord might, of course, prefer to retain even greater control over the rent review procedure under the sublease, e.g. if the sublease is to give the sublessor the power to select either an expert or arbitrator at review, the landlord might wish to make his own written consent necessary before the sublessor can make such decision, and to ensure that he is entitled to make his own representations to such independent person.

5.9.2.5 Lessee's covenant not to surrender or vary the terms of the sublease

The lessee may covenant that any sublease granted is not to be surrendered or its terms varied without the landlord's consent. A suitable covenant is:

Not to vary the terms or to accept a surrender of any permitted underlease without the landlord's prior written consent (such consent not to be unreasonably withheld).

5.9.2.6 Lessee's covenant to have sublease excluded from Part II of the Landlord and Tenant Act 1954

Occasionally, the landlord requires a covenant by the tenant to have any sublease excluded from the protection of Part II of the Landlord and Tenant Act 1954: see **15.1.5**. Such a clause might be drafted thus:

Before the grant of any underlease, to obtain an order of the court under section 38(4) of the Landlord and Tenant Act 1954 authorising an agreement excluding in relation to such intended underlease the provisions of sections 24 to 28 of that Act.

SIX

THE RUNNING OF THE BENEFITS AND BURDENS OF LEASEHOLD COVENANTS

It is vital to know to what extent covenants in the lease are enforceable by, or binding upon, the original parties to the lease and their successors in title.

In the examples in this chapter, L1 refers to the original landlord, L2 the original landlord's immediate assignee, and L3 the assignee from L2. Similarly, T1 refers to the original tenant, T2 to the original tenant's immediate assignee, and so on.

6.1 Enforceability between Original Parties

As between the original parties to the lease, there exists both privity of contract and privity of estate. The doctrine of privity of contract means that all the covenants in the lease, regardless of whether they relate to the land leased, are enforceable by and against each of the original parties to the lease. Thus L1 can sue T1 on all the tenant's covenants in the lease; and T1 can sue L1 on all the landlord's covenants in the lease.

6.1.1 CONTINUING LIABILITY DURING TERM AFTER ASSIGNMENT

After either of the original parties has assigned its estate to a third party, the privity of estate which exists between the original parties comes to an end. Unless the lease provides otherwise, however, each of the original parties to the lease remains liable on the covenants in the lease under the doctrine of privity of contract throughout the remainder of the contractually agreed term.

Thus, after T1 has assigned the lease to T2, T1 will remain liable to L1 for breaches of the tenant's covenants in the lease which occur even after the assignment, i.e. even after T1 is unable to comply with the covenants in the lease. Similarly, even after L1 has assigned the reversion to L2, L1 will remain liable to T1 on the landlord's covenants in the lease. In practice such continuing liability is of greater concern to the tenant. There are two reasons for this. First, most of the obligations in a typical commercial lease are tenant's obligations: see Law Com. No.174 (1988), para. 2.1. Secondly, in practice, the covenant which is most likely to be enforced against an original party after assignment is the original tenant's covenant to pay rent.

This is why a lease invariably contains, not merely a provision specifying the rent to be paid, but also a covenant by the tenant to pay the rent. In the absence of such a covenant, the obligation to pay the rent would be enforceable by the landlord for the time being against the tenant for the time being; but, being merely a term of the estate, would not be enforceable by L1 against T1 after T1 has assigned to T2. A covenant by T1 to pay the rent, however, means that, under general principles, T1 remains liable on the covenant even after assignment to T2.

This principle means that, if T2 (or a later assignee, T3 for instance) defaults in the payment of the rent, L1 can proceed to recover it against T1. T1 cannot require L1 to sue the defaulting tenant first. The reason is that, as between T1 and L1, T1's liability remains a primary one: T1 cannot argue that, after assignment, he is merely a surety for the performance by the defaulting tenant (*Baynton* v *Morgan* (1888) 22 QBD 74).

Having been sued and forced to pay, T1 may be able to recover the payment from T2 or (if a subsequent assignee) the tenant in default. This is considered more fully below, at **6.5**. He may also be able to recover from the defaulting tenant's surety (*Becton Dickinson UK Ltd* v *Zwebner* [1989] QB 208), and see **3.1.4.1**. In practice, however, L1 will generally proceed initially against the defaulting tenant and any surety which that tenant may have provided. L1 will therefore usually seek to recover from T1 only where the tenant for the time being is insolvent and either did not provide a surety, or provided one who cannot now pay. In these circumstances, T1 may be left with a liability which cannot be recovered.

The Law Commission has criticised the principle of a tenant's continuing liability and has put forward recommendations which would severely curtail it: see Law Com. No.174 (1988). The government has indicated its intention to legislate broadly on the lines of the Law Commission's proposals, but no Bill was proposed in the Queen's Speech of November 1993.

6.1.1.1 Attempts to restrict continuing liability

Where possible, the tenant should seek to limit its liability on the covenants in the lease to the period during which it remains the tenant under the lease. A suitable form of wording might be a proviso to the tenant's covenants such as one in the following form. In this and in the following precedents, clause *x* prohibits assignment without the landlord's consent, and clause *y* requires the tenant to procure that the assignee (and any surety for the assignee) enters into direct covenants with the lessor:

Provided that the liability of [the name of the original tenant] under the tenant's covenants contained herein shall cease in respect of breaches which occur after an assignment by him of this lease if:

(a) at the date of such assignment [the name of the original tenant] shall not be in breach of any of the tenant's covenants contained herein; and
(b) such assignment comprises the whole of the property demised by this lease and is made in accordance with clauses *x* and *y* hereof.

A tenant who cannot obtain such immediate cessation of liability upon assignment might seek to include a clause which limits its liability only in respect of breaches which occur during its own time as tenant and during the time as tenant of its immediate assignee. This provides some limited safeguard for T1 since T1 can at least select the prospective assignee, and therefore check such person's creditworthiness. Such a limitation might be expressed thus:

Provided that the liability of [the name of the original tenant] under the tenant's covenants contained herein shall cease in respect of breaches which occur after an assignment (the relevant assignment) of this lease by his immediate assignee (the relevant assignee) but only if:

(a) at the date of the relevant assignment neither [the name of the original tenant] nor the relevant assignee shall be in breach of any of the tenant's covenants contained herein; and
(b) both the assignment to the relevant assignee and the relevant assignment comprise the whole of the property demised by this lease and are made in accordance with clauses *x* and *y* hereof.

Failing this, where the lease contains a qualified covenant against assignment without the landlord's consent, T1 might seek to include a clause in the lease under which L1 covenants with T1 to take reasonable care in choosing a subsequent assignee, i.e. not the immediate assignee from T1, whom T1 can himself select. A breach of such a covenant by L1 would free T1 from liability for subsequent breaches. An express covenant, however, is required: the court will not be willing to imply any such term into the lease (*Norwich Union Life Insurance Society* v *Low Profile Fashions Ltd* [1992] 1 EGLR 86).

An original tenant, T1, who cannot negotiate a restriction of liability may suffer hardship because the terms of the contract between T1 and L1 are treated as subject to variation between L1 and T1's assignee. T1 is treated as putting T2 into the position of being able to vary the terms agreed. Thus T1 has been held liable to pay a higher rent agreed after the assignment between T2 (or T3 etc.) and L1 (*Centrovincial Estates plc* v *Bulk Storage Ltd* (1983) 46 P & CR 393). Similarly, T1 remains liable even if the landlord and the assignee agree to vary the terms of the lease by substituting a different method of rent review from that specified in the lease (*GUS Property Management Ltd* v *Texas Homecare Ltd* [1993] 27 EG 130). It would, however, appear that if the variation agreed is so substantial as to change the fundamental nature of the lease, T1 might be discharged from liability on the basis that a new lease has arisen which causes the old lease to be surrendered by operation of law: see **12.4.2**.

A tenant who cannot obtain any other reduction in liability might therefore seek to include a term in the lease limiting its continuing liability to pay the rent to the amount of rent payable at the time of the assignment. A suitable precedent might be the following proviso:

Provided that after an authorised assignment of this lease the liability of [the name of the original tenant] under the tenant's covenants herein contained to pay rent that falls due after such assignment shall not exceed such amounts as would have fallen due had the rent after such authorised assignment continued to be payable at the rate payable at the date of such authorised assignment.

In this clause 'authorised assigment' means an assignment by [the name of the original tenant] that:

(a) is made at a date when [the name of the original tenant] shall not be in breach of any of the tenant's covenants contained herein; and
(b) comprises the whole of the property demised by this lease and is made in accordance with clauses *x* and *y* hereof.

6.1.1.2 Continuing liability during extension of the lease under the Landlord and Tenant Act 1954, Part II

As explained at **15.2.1**, when the contractual term of a fixed-term tenancy subject to the Landlord and Tenant Act 1954, Part II, expires, s. 24(1) of that Act prolongs the tenant's estate subject to a statutory variation as to the mode of determination. The 'tenancy' continued under the subsection, however, is the tenancy only of the person who is the tenant at that time. If that tenant is not T1 but an assignee then T1 is not thereby made liable to L1 for breaches of covenant committed by the assignee during the period of holding over. Any continued liability through privity of contract will arise only where the original parties agree that it should continue after the expiry of the contractual term (*City of London Corporation* v *Fell* [1993] 3 WLR 1164, HL).

Therefore, a landlord who wishes to continue the liability of T1 during such period must stipulate for this expressly in the lease. A simple method of extending the tenant's liability in this way is by extending the definition of 'term' as follows:

The expression 'the said term' shall where the context admits include not only the term hereby granted but also the period of any holding over or any extension thereof whether by statute or at common law.

This form of wording will suffice to make the original tenant liable for the contractual rent during the period of holding over by an assignee; and this will probably include liability to pay any higher rent settled under a rent review clause. It is not, however, sufficient to make the original tenant liable for the difference between the contractually agreed rent and any higher rent provided for in an interim rent order (as to which see **15.2.3**) (*Herbert Duncan Ltd* v *Cluttons* [1993] 1 EGLR 93 at 95–96, CA). A landlord who wishes to make the original tenant liable to pay any increase resulting from such an order will therefore need to ensure that the lease also contains a covenant by the tenant on the following lines:

> **The tenant hereby covenants to pay (without deduction or set-off) any additional rent which may become payable under the lease during any period of holding over by virtue of any interim rent order made under the Landlord and Tenant Act 1954 or any re-enactment or statutory modification thereof.**

The tenant should resist the inclusion of such a clause vigorously.

6.1.2 RESTRICTED ABILITY TO SUE AFTER ASSIGNMENT

Although liability therefore continues after assignment, the assignor loses, after assignment, the right to sue on those covenants which 'touch and concern' the land leased. For the meaning of 'touch and concern', see **6.2.1.1**.

In the case of the assignment of the reversion, this principle is laid down by the Law of Property Act 1925, s. 141(1) (*Arlesford Trading Co. Ltd* v *Servansingh* [1971] 1 WLR 1080). See further **6.2.1.2**. This subsection refers to covenants which have reference to the subject-matter of the lease; but this has the same meaning as 'touch and concern'. In the case of the assignment of the lease, the principle was laid down in *Spencer's Case* (1583) 5 Co Rep 16a, under which there passes to the assignee the benefit of those tenant's covenants which 'touch and concern' the land.

6.2 Enforceability between One Original Party and the Assignee of the Other

The issues here are whether L2 (or a subsequent assignee of the reversion) can sue or be sued by T1; and whether T2 (or a subsequent assignee of the lease) can sue or be sued by L1. It will be assumed, here that there is no separate express covenant between the original party and the assignee: the impact of such a covenant is discussed at **6.4.1**.

6.2.1 CAN L2 SUE T1?

The assignment of the reversion by L1 to L2 does not create privity of contract between L2 and T1 (*Re King* [1963] Ch 459). It does, however, create privity of estate. The Law of Property Act 1925, s. 141, annexes to the reversionary estate, upon its assignment by the lessor, the benefit of every lessee's covenant 'having reference to the subject-matter' of the lease.

6.2.1.1 Covenants within section 141

The requirement that the covenant have reference to the subject-matter of the lease has been held to be a mere reformulation of the older terminology, which required the covenant to 'touch and concern' the demised premises. This means that there does not pass to L2 the benefit of all the covenants contained in the lease. There will pass to L2 only the benefit of those covenants which affect the parties in their capacities as lessor and lessee. Thus the benefit of covenants of a purely personal nature will not pass.

The distinction between those covenants which run with the land and those which do not (personal covenants) has been criticised as purely arbitrary and, for the most part, quite illogical (*Grant* v

Edmondson [1931] 1 Ch 1 at p. 31). In practice, however, most covenants (including all the most important covenants commonly found in leases) satisfy the 'touching and concerning' test. These include covenants by the lessee:

(a) to pay the rent;
(b) to repair;
(c) not to assign without the lessor's consent (see **5.5**);
(d) to restrict user;
(e) to restrict sales of goods to those produced by the lessor only.

Examples of personal covenants, the benefit of which does not pass to L2 by virtue of an assignment of the reversion include the performance of personal services by the lessee. A personal covenant therefore remains enforceable by L1 against T1 even after L1 has assigned the reversion to L2.

6.2.1.2 The rights which pass under section 141

Section 141(1) states that the benefit of *every* covenant in the lease having reference to the subject-matter thereof passes with the reversionary estate to the assignee. This clearly includes the right to sue for breaches of covenant which occur after the assignment of the reversion. It has, however, been held that the subsection also passes to the assignee the right to sue for breaches of covenant which occurred before the assignment (*Re King* [1963] Ch 459). What this means is that, if rent is in arrears at the time L1 assigns the reversion to L2, the right to sue for those arrears passes to L2. L1 therefore loses the right to sue for them, even though the rent in arrear accrued due during L1's own time as landlord (*London and County (A and D) Ltd* v *Wilfred Sportsman Ltd* [1971] Ch 764). This might appear harsh on L1; but it should be borne in mind that, if rent is in arrear, L1 can use this in order to try to obtain a higher price for the assignment to L2.

In respect of 'touching and concerning covenants', the subsection also operates to prevent L1, after assignment to L2, from suing T1 under the doctrine of privity of contract. The right to sue on such covenants also passes to L2 (*Arlesford Trading Co. Ltd* v *Servansingh* [1971] 1 WLR 1080). In that case, T1 committed breaches of covenant (non-payment of rent) and then (while L1 was still the landlord) assigned the lease to T2. L1 then assigned the reversion to L2. It was held that s. 141(1) enabled L2 to sue T1 in respect of those breaches. This shows the far-reaching effect of the subsection, because at no time was there either privity of contract or of estate between L2 and T1.

In the *Arlesford Trading Co. Ltd* case, T1 had himself committed the breaches. Would T1 have been liable to L2, however, had the breaches been committed by T2? Clearly, T1 would be liable to L1 for breaches committed by T2 during L1's time as landlord. But what if the breaches occur when the landlord is L2? The facts would then be as follows: T1 assigns the lease to T2; L1 then assigns to L2; T2 then breaches a covenant. Can L2 sue T1? There is no direct authority, but the answer is probably no. The reason is that, when L1 assigns the reversion to L2, he loses (under s. 141) the right to sue T1 on touching and concerning covenants. It is therefore difficult to see how s. 141(1) could pass to L2 a right against T1 which L1 does not himself possess.

6.2.2 CAN T1 SUE L2?

This is governed by the Law of Property Act 1925, s. 142(1), which states that the obligation under a lessor's covenant having reference to the subject-matter of the lease passes with the reversionary estate to bind the assignee, and it may be enforced by the person in whom the term is from time to time vested.

6.2.2.1 Covenants within s. 142

The expression 'having reference to the subject-matter of the lease' has the same meaning as in s. 141(1), i.e. it imports a 'touching and concerning' requirement. Lessors' covenants that touch and concern, and therefore fall within s. 142(1), include covenants:

(a) to repair or insure the demised premises;
(b) to give the tenant quiet enjoyment;
(c) to renew the lease (see further **6.9.1**).

Lessors' covenants which do not touch and concern include covenants:

(a) to sell the reversion to the lessee at the option of the lessee (see **6.9.2**);
(b) to give the lessee a right of pre-emption on the sale of the reversion (see **6.9.2**);
(c) to repay a security deposit (*Hua Chiao Commercial Bank Ltd* v *Chiaphua Industries Ltd* [1987] AC 99).

The decision in the *Chiaphua* case means that, at the end of the lease, the tenant cannot recover the deposit from L1's assignee; but only from L1 itself. The risk for the tenant here is that L1 may by then be insolvent or (in the case of an individual) have died and his estate have been wound up, or (in the case of a company) have gone into liquidation.

6.2.2.2 The rights which pass under section 142(1)

Section 142(1) does not in terms annex to the term the benefit of the lessor's covenants. This means that, even after assignment of the lease to T2, T1 retains the right to sue L2 for breaches of the lessor's covenants which occurred while T1 was tenant (*City and Metropolitan Properties Ltd* v *Greycroft Ltd* [1987] 1 WLR 1085).

6.2.2.3 The extent of L2's liability

Section 142(1) imposes the liability of 'touching and concerning' covenants upon L2, so that L2 is liable in respect of breaches which occur during its own time as landlord. The subsection does not, however, operate to render L2 liable for breaches which occurred before the assignment of the reversion to it (*Duncliffe* v *Caerfelin Properties Ltd* [1989] 2 EGLR 38).

6.2.3 CAN L1 SUE T2?

L1 can sue T2 on 'touching and concerning' covenants. This is the rule of common law laid down in *Spencer's Case* (1583) 5 Co Rep 16a.

6.2.4 CAN T2 SUE L1?

Similarly, T2 can sue L1 on 'touching and concerning' covenants. This was also established in *Spencer's Case* (1583) 5 Co Rep 16a. T2 will not, however, acquire the right to sue L1 for breaches which occurred *before* the assignment to T2 (*City and Metropolitan Properties Ltd* v *Greycroft Ltd* [1987] 1 WLR 1085). (Note that this is in marked contrast to the rights which L2 acquires against T1 under s. 141(1): see **6.2.1.2**).

6.3 Enforceability between the Assignees of each Original Party

It will again be assumed for present purposes that there is no separate express covenant between the assignees. The effect of such a covenant is considered at **6.4**.

6.3.1 CAN L2 SUE T2?

Although there is no privity of contract between L2 and T2, there is (while they are landlord and tenant) privity of estate. L2 acquires the right to sue for breach of the tenant's covenants by virtue of the Law of Property Act 1925, s. 141(1). The liability of the tenant's covenants passes to T2 at common law. Therefore L2 can sue T2, whether T2 commits the breach before or after the assignment of the reversion to L2. T2 will not, however, be liable for breaches which occurred before the assignment of the lease to him.

6.3.2 CAN T2 SUE L2?

Although there is no privity of contract between L2 and T2, there is (while they are landlord and tenant) privity of estate. T2 can sue on 'touching and concerning' covenants under *Spencer's case* (1583) 5 Co Rep 16a; and L2 is liable for breach of such covenants under the Law of Property Act 1925, s. 142(1). Therefore T2 can sue L2, but only in respect of breaches committed after the assignment of the lease to T2: cf. *City and Metropolitan Properties Ltd* v *Greycroft Ltd* [1987] 1 WLR 1085. Furthermore, L2 will not become liable for breaches which occurred before the assignment of the reversion to him (*Duncliffe* v *Caerfelin Properties Ltd* [1989] 2 EGLR 38).

6.4 Action for Damages against Intermediate Assignee

Under the foregoing principles, an *intermediate* assignee of the lease (T2) is not liable for breaches committed by a subsequent assignee (T3). The reason is that, after assignment of the lease, there is no longer privity of estate between the intermediate assignee and the landlord. Furthermore, since the intermediate assignee was not an original party to the lease, it is not liable under the doctrine of privity of contract.

6.4.1 SEPARATE COVENANT WITH INTERMEDIATE ASSIGNEE

A landlord might, however, seek to include a clause in the lease which includes a qualified covenant against assignment and provides as a condition of such consent that the prospective assignee enter into a direct covenant with the landlord to observe and perform all the covenants in the lease during the remainder of the term. An intermediate assignee who has entered into such a covenant will therefore be liable for breaches committed even after it has assigned the lease. Such a clause is frequently seen in commercial leases: see the precedent at **5.9.1.1**.

The landlord must, however, take care in drafting the clause.

First, express words are necessary to make an assignee liable for breaches which occur after the assignee has parted with the term. Thus an assignee who covenants 'to pay the rent reserved in the lease' but does not covenant to pay it 'during the remainder of the term', will not be liable for rent which accrues due after it has assigned (*Estates Gazette Ltd* v *Benjamin Restaurants Ltd* [1993] 4 All ER 367).

Secondly, in the case of a qualified covenant against assignment, the consent must not be unreasonably withheld (Landlord and Tenant Act 1927, s. 19(1)(a)). The parties cannot weaken the impact of s. 19(1)(a) by specifying the circumstances in which refusal is to be regarded as reasonable (*Balfour* v *Kensington Gardens Mansions Ltd* (1932) 49 TLR 29). At least in the case of consent to assign (as opposed to consent to subletting), however, the court would probably accept that consent conditional upon the assignee entering into a direct covenant is reasonable if it is provided for in the original lease. See further **5.8.2.2**.

Alternatively, the landlord could draft a clause which would make the obtaining of a direct covenant from a prospective assignee a condition precedent to the tenant's right to assign. The idea has been held valid in the context of offer-to-surrender clauses (*Adler* v *Upper Grosvenor Street Investment Ltd* [1957] 1 WLR 227, and see **12.4.4**). Section 19(1)(a) is sidestepped because it bites only when the tenant has a right to assign; whereas, by making the right to assign subject to a condition precedent, the tenant's right to assign does not arise unless and until the specified procedure is complied with. This is the method usually adopted in practice: see, e.g. the precedent at **5.9.1.1**.

If the landlord has not made any provision in the lease to obtain a direct covenant from an assignee, the demand for such a covenant would be subject to s. 19(1)(a) scrutiny. It would probably be treated as an unreasonable refusal on the ground that it is a demand for a collateral advantage. It should be remembered that the Landlord and Tenant Act 1988 has strengthened the position of the tenant: it is now for the landlord to show that the refusal was reasonable (s. 1(6)), and the tenant may have a tortious claim for damages for breach of statutory duty (s. 4): see **5.7**.

6.5 Rights as between Original Tenant and Subsequent Assignees of Lease

If there is a breach of a tenant's covenant after T1 has assigned the lease, the landlord (as has been explained) may have a choice of actions. First, it can bring an action against the tenant for the time being (i.e. the tenant who has committed the breach). Secondly, if the landlord is the original party to the lease, i.e. L1, it can bring an action for damages for the breach against the original tenant, T1. Thirdly, the landlord may have a right of action against an intermediate assignee, if such intermediate assignee entered into a separate covenant with the landlord to observe and perform all the covenants in the lease. Fourthly, the landlord may have an action against a guarantor provided by a tenant who is liable for the breach.

Assume therefore that L1 remains the landlord throughout. At some time in the past, T1 assigned the lease to T2, and T2 in turn later assigned to T3. T3 has now breached a covenant in the lease. If L1 sues T1 for the breach, T2 may have two alternative courses of action. First, T1 might recover an indemnity from T2, and T2 might in turn recover from T3. In these circumstances, T1 can recover from T2 only if T2 entered into an indemnity covenant with T1. Secondly, T1 might be able to recover directly from T3 without involving T2. This second course of action depends upon restitutionary principles exemplified in the rule in *Moule* v *Garrett* (1872) LR 7 Ex 101. If, alternatively, L1 sues T2, the issue is merely whether T2 can recover from T3. Again, this is possible, either under an indemnity covenant between T2 and T3, or under the rule in *Moule* v *Garrett*. Indemnity covenants will be considered first.

6.5.1 INDEMNITY COVENANTS

It is necessary to distinguish between implied and express indemnity covenants.

6.5.1.1 Implied (or statutory)

In an assignment for valuable consideration of the entire land comprised in a lease, there is implied a covenant by the assignee with the conveying parties (Law of Property Act 1925, s. 77(1)(C)). This is a covenant that the assignees, or persons deriving title under them, will duly pay the rent due and observe and perform all the covenants and conditions in the lease, and that they will keep the conveying parties indemnified against all proceedings, costs, claims and expenses on account of their omission to pay the rent or any breach of the said covenants and conditions (Law of Property Act 1925, sch. 2, Part IX). Where there is an assignment of part, a parallel covenant is implied, which imposes corresponding obligations in relation to the apportioned rent and the covenants and conditions which relate to the land assigned (Law of Property Act 1925, s. 77(1)(D) and sch.2, Part X). Similar covenants are implied in assignments of leases with registered title (Land Registration Act 1925, s. 24). See also **2.2.2**.

In *RPH Ltd* v *Mirror Group (Holdings) Ltd* [1993] 1 EGLR 74 it was T4 who had defaulted in the payment of the rent. Both T4 and T2 were insolvent companies in administration. L sought to recover the rent from the original tenant, T1. T1 brought an action claiming that T2 should be compelled either to sue T3 to require it to pay the rent to L, or else assign to T1 its right of action against T3 under the statutory indemnity covenant implied by the Land Registration Act 1925, s. 24. T1 failed because the indemnity covenant was an asset in the administration of T2. The administrators of T2 could, if they wished, assign the benefit of the covenant to T1 (no doubt for a consideration); but they could not be compelled to do so (nor could they be compelled to sue T3) because there was no direct legal nexus between the indemnity covenants given by T3 and T2.

6.5.1.2 Express indemnity covenant

Because of the principle that T1 continues to be liable on the covenants in the lease for the whole of the term, even for breaches committed after assignment, T1 will generally seek an express indemnity covenant from its immediate assignee, T2. When T2 assigns, it will in turn naturally seek an indemnity covenant from T3, and so on. This means that there can be a chain of indemnity covenants. There is, therefore, as between the original tenant and successive assignees, an order of priority. If obliged to pay, the original tenant can recover from later assignees, who can in turn recover from assignees further down the line (*Selous Street Properties Ltd* v *Oronel Fabrics Ltd* (1984) 270 EG 643 and 743). A break in the chain, caused (for instance) by the insolvency of an intermediate assignee, can therefore leave the immediately preceding assignee with a liability which cannot be recovered, unless recourse can be had to the rule in *Moule* v *Garrett*.

6.5.2 RULE IN *MOULE* v *GARRETT*

Although, as has been seen, as between L1 and T1, T1 cannot argue it is merely a surety for the assignee responsible for the default, as between T1 and such assignee, the latter is primarily liable. The restitutionary principle underlying the rule is that where the plaintiff has been compelled to pay to a creditor a sum for which the defendant is primarily liable, the plaintiff can recover such sum from the defendant. In *Moule* v *Garrett* (1872) LR 7 Ex 101 itself, T1 had assigned to T2, and T2 had later assigned to T3. T3 defaulted in the payment of the rent to L1, who compelled payment from T1. T1 brought an action directly against T3, who, not being T1's immediate assignee, had given no indemnity covenant, express or implied to T1. The court nevertheless relied on the foregoing principle to give judgment for T1.

Although the court in *Moule* v *Garrett* considered the principle to be based upon an implied contract, the more modern view is to treat the rule in *Moule* v *Garrett* as a rule of law. The importance of the difference is that the parties cannot agree to exclude a rule of law. Thus in *Re Healing Research Trustee Co. Ltd* [1991] BCLC 716, T2 defaulted in the payment of the rent, and L1 called upon T1 to pay. T2 contended that, since the assignment of the lease to it contained a clause excluding the statutory indemnity covenant in the Law of Property Act 1925, sch. 2, Part IX, the rule in *Moule* v *Garrett* was also ousted. The court rejected this argument, evidently holding that the rule is one of law. This means that an assignee of a lease cannot, even by express exclusion of the statutory indemnity covenants, exclude liability under *Moule* v *Garrett* to indemnify an earlier assignee who has been (or is being) compelled to pay.

In *Moule* v *Garrett* itself, recovery was made from the assignee in default. Could T1 use the same principle to recover from an intermediate assignee, i.e. from a party which has not itself committed the breach? No such argument was presented in *RPH Ltd* v *Mirror Group (Holdings) Ltd* [1993] 1 EGLR 74. It might be contended that T1 ought to have been able to recover from T3 on the ground that, as between T1 and T3, the latter was primarily liable since it had itself assigned to the defaulting assignee, T4. If, however, unjust enrichment is the basis for the rule in *Moule* v *Garrett*, then the rule cannot apply because it is difficult to see how the intermediate assignee, T3, is unjustly enriched.

6.6 Position of Sureties

This is discussed at **3.1.4**.

6.7 Enforceability of Covenants in Subleases

If the tenant (T) sublets the property to a subtenant (S), there is neither privity of contract nor privity of estate between the head landlord (L) and S. Therefore, L cannot enforce against S any of the covenants in the head lease. There are, nevertheless, four ways in which L might be able to ensure compliance by S with the covenants in the head lease.

6.7.1 ACTION AGAINST T

First, L may be able to ensure compliance indirectly. Because T remains liable on the covenants in the head lease after subletting (T does, after all, remain the tenant), T will invariably extract from S a covenant in the sublease that S will observe and perform all the covenants in the head lease. This means that, although L cannot itself sue on such covenants in the sublease, it can proceed against T for breach of the covenant in the head lease; and T will in turn sue S on the sublease.

6.7.2 ACTION ON A DIRECT COVENANT WITH S

Secondly, the head lease may contain a covenant by T not to sublet without L's consent, such consent being conditional upon T's securing from S a direct covenant with L to observe and perform all the covenants and conditions in the head lease during the remainder of the term of the head lease. If a landlord can secure a direct covenant from S in these terms, it can bring a direct action against S for breach of the covenants in the head lease. A landlord should therefore ensure that the lease contains a covenant in a suitable form: see precedent at **5.9.2.1**. Reference should be made, *mutatis mutandis*, to **6.4.1**.

6.7.3 FORFEITURE OF HEAD LEASE

Thirdly, if there is a breach of the covenants in the head lease, L may be able (assuming there is a proviso for re-entry for breach) to forfeit the head lease. If the head lease is forfeit, any sublease falls with it; although S (as well as T) may be able to claim relief from forfeiture: see **13.4.5.4**. The point, therefore, is that the possibility of forfeiture ensures that S takes an interest in seeing that the covenants in the head lease (which are invariably reproduced in the sublease) are complied with.

6.7.4 ENFORCEMENT OF RESTRICTIVE COVENANTS

Fourthly, under the doctrine of *Tulk* v *Moxhay* (1848) 2 Ph 774, L may be able to enforce against S (by means of an injunction), covenants in the head lease which are of a negative or restrictive nature.

Restrictive covenants in a lease cannot be registered as land charges (Land Charges Act 1972, s. 2(5)). Under the doctrine of *Tulk* v *Moxhay*, therefore, the burden of a restrictive covenant in a head lease (whether made before 1926 or after 1925) binds all sublessees except a bona fide purchaser for value of the legal estate without notice.

A prospective sublessee is not, under an open contract, entitled to inspect the head lease. A sublessee will nevertheless be treated as having constructive notice of restrictive covenants in the head lease, and will therefore be bound by them (*Hill* v *Harris* [1965] 2 QB 601). It is therefore vital for a solicitor acting for a prospective sublessee to insist upon inspecting the head lease. Failure to do so could render the solicitor liable to an action in negligence should the sublessee suffer resulting loss. (A solicitor acting for an intending sublessee must additionally ensure that covenants affecting the *freehold* title are also discovered.)

6.8 Enforceability of Leasehold Covenants against Adverse Possessors

After 12 years' adverse possession, the title of the owner of the estate adversely possessed is barred (Limitation Act 1980, s. 15). If a person has 12 years' adverse possession against land which is leased, only the title of the lessee is barred, not the title of the reversioner.

6.8.1 LAND WITH UNREGISTERED TITLE

In land with unregistered title, subject to one qualification, L cannot enforce against the adverse possessor (A) the covenants in the lease, nor sue A for the rent which the lease reserves. The reason is that, in unregistered land, the Limitation Act 1980 does not operate as a Parliamentary conveyance, i.e. the estate of A is not the former estate of T (*Tichborne* v *Weir* (1892) 67 LT 735 in which it was held that L is unable to sue A for breach of a repairing covenant in T's lease). There is therefore no privity of estate between L and A, and neither is there privity of contract. A has an independent estate whose length is co-terminous with that of T's, which has been barred. Since therefore A is not L's lessee, no action of forfeiture can be brought against A, and it might appear that L must wait until the expiration of the term of T's (barred) lease before being able to claim possession against A.

In practice, however, L's position may be stronger that this.

6.8.1.1 Action against T to forfeit lease for breach of covenant

First, L's lease with T may contain both a covenant by T (whether absolute or qualified) not to part with possession and a right of re-entry for breach of covenant. In such circumstances, A's adverse possession is a breach of covenant by T, which enables L to bring an action to forfeit the lease. Such a right, being that of L rather than that of T, is not barred by the Limitation Act 1980. In an action by L against T to forfeit the lease, A (not having privity of estate with L) cannot claim relief from forfeiture (*Tickner* v *Buzzacott* [1965] Ch 426). This indicates the importance to a landlord of extracting from the prospective tenant a covenant against parting with possession: see **5.3**. Neither a covenant against assignment, nor a covenant against subletting, would be breached by an act of adverse possession.

6.8.1.2 Surrender by T

Secondly, the House of Lords has held that, even after the Limitation Act 1980 has barred T's title, T still retains the power to surrender the lease to L, thus enabling L to obtain possession against A (*Fairweather* v *St Marylebone Property Co. Ltd* [1963] AC 510. Collusion between L and T can therefore have the desired result for L.

6.8.1.3 Enforcement of restrictive covenants against S

Thirdly, restrictive covenants in the L-T lease (which are not registrable) will be binding on A because A cannot establish the defence of bona fide purchaser for value of a legal estate in the land without notice: the reason is that A acquires title, not by purchase, but by operation of law (*Re Nisbet and Potts' Contract* [1905] 1 Ch 391).

6.8.2 LAND WITH REGISTERED TITLE

In land with registered title, the Land Registration Act 1925 provides that, after adverse possession for 12 years, T's title is held in trust for A. Thus, at the end of that period, the Land Registry will transfer T's title to A on A's application. Between the expiry of the period of 12 years' adverse possession and the transfer of T's estate to A, T holds the estate upon trust for A (Land Registration Act 1925, s. 75(1)). Thus, in land with registered title, the combined effect of the Limitation Act 1980 and the Land Registration Act 1925 is indeed to pass to A, upon its application, the same estate in the land as was formerly vested in T (*Spectrum Investment Co.* v *Holmes* [1981] 1 WLR 221).

Upon registration, A is therefore placed into the position of assignee of T's lease, so that L and T are entitled to enforce against each other the covenants in the lease. L would, of course, still be entitled to bring an action for forfeiture for breach of a covenant against parting with possession; but it would appear that A, having privity of estate with L, could claim relief from forfeiture. Furthermore, T would not, in the case of registered land, have an estate which he could surrender in order to enable L to claim possession.

Until the title is transferred to the adverse possessor, his rights under the Limitation Act 1980 (whether acquired or in course of being acquired) are protected as an overriding interest (Land Registration Act 1925, s. 70(1)(f) and (g)).

6.9 Particular Rights

6.9.1 LESSEE'S RIGHT TO RENEW THE LEASE

A right conferred on a lessee to renew the lease at the end of the term has been held to touch and concern the land, and therefore to run with the lease (to benefit T1's assignees) and with the reversion (to burden L1's assignees) (*Richardson* v *Sydenham* (1703) 2 Vern 447).

However, in *Beesly* v *Hallwood Estates Ltd* [1960] 1 WLR 549, at p. 557, it was held that an option to renew the lease is an estate contract for the purposes of (what is now) the Land Charges Act 1972. Therefore, although an option to renew the lease does touch and concern the land, such a right will not bind a purchaser for money or money's worth of a legal estate (which L2 will generally be) unless protected by registration as a land charge, class C(iv). This decision has been subsequently affirmed in *Taylors Fashions Ltd* v *Liverpool Victoria Trustees Co. Ltd* [1982] QB 133 (where, however, equitable estoppel applied) and in *Phillips* v *Mobil Oil Co. Ltd* [1989] 1 WLR 888.

In registered land, the position is different, because, if the tenant is in actual occupation, its option to renew the lease will be binding on L2 as an overriding interest under the Land Registration Act 1925, s. 70(1)(g) (*Webb* v *Pollmount Ltd* [1966] Ch 584).

6.9.2 LESSEE'S OPTION TO PURCHASE OR RIGHT OF PRE-EMPTION

The lease may confer upon T the right to purchase the reversion (i.e. the interest of L), or (in the case of a right of pre-emption) the right to purchase the reversion if L wishes to sell or otherwise dispose of the reversion.

Such rights do not touch and concern the land, because the rights affect the parties, not in their capacities as landlord and tenant, but only as vendor and purchaser. They do not therefore run with the land or with the reversion (*Woodall* v *Clifton* [1905] 2 Ch 257 (option); *Charles Frodsham and Co. Ltd* v *Morris* (1974) 229 EG 961 at p. 962 (pre-emption). This means that, unless the lease restricts the right to the period T1 is tenant, T1 is entitled to exercise the option against L1 even after T1 has assigned to T2. If, however, L1 has itself assigned the reversion to L2, T1 can sue L1 only for damages for breach of covenant.

6.9.3 ASSIGNMENT OF PERSONAL RIGHTS

6.9.3.1 The benefit

Although the benefit of an option to purchase or right of pre-emption cannot pass to T1's assignee by annexation, it may pass to T2 in some other way. Each of these rights is a chose in action which can (unless in terms restricted) be assigned to a third party and exercised by it. Such a right may therefore be assigned to T2, either contemporaneously with the lease, or even subsequently.

Whilst an assignment is best effected expressly, the courts seem willing to find that an assignment of such rights has been effected impliedly. In *Griffith* v *Pelton* [1958] Ch 205, the option to purchase the reversion was conferred upon 'the lessee', which term was defined in the lease to include the tenant's executors, administrators and assigns. The Court of Appeal held that this showed that the original parties intended that the option should be exercisable by T1's assignees as well; and, furthermore, that a mere assignment of the term was to operate as an assignment of the benefit of the option. Since most leases define the term 'lessee' to include (*inter alia*) an assignee, this principle is of potentially wide application. See also *Re Button's Lease* [1964] Ch 263.

6.9.3.2 The burden

It was suggested in *Griffith* v *Pelton* [1958] Ch 205 that, by a parallel process, the burden of such a covenant could pass to L2. However, even if this is correct, an option to purchase the reversion or a right of pre-emption would need (at least in the case of land with unregistered title) to be protected by registration.

SEVEN

COVENANTS AGAINST ALTERATIONS

The landlord will want to retain some control over the physical layout of the demised premises, and to this end, most leases contain a covenant by the tenant not to make alterations, either in an absolute form or in a qualified form (not to do so without the landlord's consent). Before considering these covenants in more detail, however, it should be noted that there are other factors which may affect a tenant's freedom to make alterations to the premises, and it is proposed to consider these first.

7.1 Obligations Implied into Leases which may Prevent Alterations

7.1.1 WASTE

There is an implied obligation on all tenants not to commit waste, and the lease will sometimes contain an express covenant by the tenant.

7.1.2 DIFFERENT TYPES OF WASTE

The law has recognised different types of waste. Voluntary waste involves positive acts which change and damage the premises, so diminishing the value of the reversion. Equitable waste is an extreme form of this where the acts are committed maliciously. There will also be an implied covenant against ameliorating waste; but as this consists of acts which improve the premises, the landlord is unlikely to have any remedy in damages or by way of an injunction. An example of ameliorating waste where an injunction was refused is *Doherty* v *Allman* (1878) 3 App Cas 709, where a tenant with a 999-year lease converted a barracks into cottages by the erection of easily removable partitions.

7.1.3 TORTIOUS LIABILITY FOR WASTE

In most cases, the implied liability for waste and the implied contractual obligation to use the premises in a tenant-like manner (see **7.1.4**) will be coextensive. An act of waste gives rise to a tortious liability, however, which may be relevant where there is no contractual relationship between the landlord and the person committing waste. In *Mancetter Developments Ltd* v *Garmanson Ltd* [1986] QB 1212 the defendant company purchased fixtures from the tenant of factory premises and occupied the premises, either as licensee or tenant. The second defendant, a director who controlled the company, ordered the removal of extractor fans and pipes installed by the tenant, as a result of which large holes were made in the walls. By a majority, the Court of Appeal found the making of the holes in removing trade fixtures to be waste, and Dillon LJ considered that this was also a breach of an implied contractual obligation to make good any damage caused by removing tenant's fixtures. The defendant company went into liquidation, so that any implied contractual obligation against it was of no assistance to the landlord. The landlord was able to recover damages for waste from the second defendant, however, as he was a director who had given instructions to carry out the acts which amounted to waste and so were a tort.

7.1.4 IMPLIED COVENANT TO USE THE PREMISES IN A TENANT-LIKE MANNER

An additional obligation implied into all tenancies (unless expressly excluded) is the implied contractual obligation of a tenant to use and deliver up the premises in a tenant-like manner. In *Marsden* v *Edward Heyes Ltd* [1927] 2 KB 1 this obligation was implied into an oral yearly tenancy, and was held to have been broken where the tenant of a dwellinghouse and shop removed a wall, staircase and fireplace in order to convert the premises into an enlarged shop.

There is a discussion of waste and the implied obligation to use premises in a tenant-like manner in **10.1.2**.

7.2 Covenants in the Lease which may Affect the Tenant's Right to Alter the Demised Premises

It is possible that some other covenant contained in the lease may prevent the tenant from carrying out alterations. For example, a covenant not to cause a nuisance or annoyance to neighbouring occupiers could be infringed by an alteration which interfered with a neighbouring property's right of light or access (see clause in **8.3**).

7.2.1 INTERFERENCE WITH EASEMENTS

There may be a covenant not to do anything which will interfere with the landlord's access to light or other easements. Alterations involving additions to the demised premises could involve a breach of this covenant. Interference with an easement will of course amount to a nuisance for which an action for damages and an injunction may lie in any event.

In *Heard* v *Stuart* (1907) 24 TLR 11, the tenant (a tailor) sublet for billposting the wall of a house which faced the main entrance to a church. As well as being held to be a breach of the covenant not to make any alterations to the premises' external appearance, this was held to be a breach of other covenants in the lease: namely, a covenant not to do anything which would be an annoyance to the neighbourhood, and (evidence being given that the wall was part of the demised premises) of a covenant to keep in repair. Joyce J thought that there might also have been a breach of a covenant to use the premises only for the business of a tailor and of a covenant not to assign or part with the possession of any part of the premises.

7.2.2 USER COVENANTS

Another likely covenant to be infringed by an alteration is a covenant as to user (discussed in **chapter 8**). In the absence of any covenant as to user, however, alterations carried out to enable the premises to be used differently will not necessarily amount to a breach of a repairing covenant or to waste (*Hyman* v *Rose* [1912] AC 623. In that case, alterations were made to enable the tenant to use a chapel as a cinema, and the changed user, which was not inconsistent with the lease, was held by Lord Loreburn LC to be the 'governing factor'. The lease did not contain a covenant against the alterations; but the principle of the case might conceivably be relevant in considering whether a landlord has unreasonably refused consent to alterations (see **7.6**).

7.2.3 COVENANT NOT TO COMMIT WASTE

As well as the implied obligation not to commit waste, there may be an express covenant in the lease. An example of this would be a covenant by the tenant:

Not to commit or permit or suffer any waste, spoil or destruction in or upon the demised premises or any part thereof.

The lease under consideration in *F. W. Woolworth and Co. Ltd* v *Lambert* [1937] 1 Ch 37 contained conflicting covenants. There was a covenant not to commit waste and a covenant not to make alterations without the landlord's consent. Romer LJ was of the opinion that the covenant not to commit waste, which precluded the acts for which consent was sought, must be read subject to the covenant allowing alterations with the landlord's consent.

7.2.4 RESTRICTIVE COVENANTS

In addition to covenants contained in the lease, there may also be restrictive covenants on the freehold title which affect a lessee or sublessee (see **8.1.1** and **8.1.3**). It may, however, be possible to obtain an order for modification or discharge of these (see **8.1.2**).

7.3 Statutory Requirements which Override Covenants against Alterations

Statutes may provide that certain premises must comply with health or safety regulations. A lease will often contain a covenant by the tenant to comply with any statutory requirements, such as the following covenant:

To comply with all obligations imposed by and do or cause to be done and executed all such works as under or by virtue of any Act of Parliament or regulations made thereunder for the time being in force shall be properly directed or necessary to be done or executed upon or in respect of the demised premises or any part thereof by the lessee, tenant or occupier and at all times to keep the lessor indemnified against all claims, demands and liability in respect thereof.

In the absence of such a covenant, the statute may provide for the court to vary or set aside any clause in a lease which prohibits necessary alterations. The following statutory provisions allow for this.

7.3.1 FACTORIES ACT 1961, SECTION 169

This section provides that where the owner or occupier of a building, of which the whole or part is let as a factory, is unable to carry out structural or other alterations required to comply with the Act because of the terms of the agreement under which it is let, he may apply to the county court. The county court may set aside or modify the terms of the agreement after hearing evidence. Section 170 allows the court to apportion the expenses of the alterations between the parties, and to determine the lease if either party requests this.

7.3.2 OFFICES, SHOPS AND RAILWAY PREMISES ACT 1963, SECTION 73

This section allows a person, who is required by a notice served under the Act to carry out structural or other alterations, but who is prevented from doing so by the terms of a lease or an agreement, to apply to the county court to modify or set aside the terms. The court has power, in doing so, to apportion the expense between the landlord and the tenant and to make adjustments in the rent if it sees fit.

7.3.3 FIRE PRECAUTIONS ACT 1971, SECTION 28

A person who is prevented from carrying out structural or other alterations to comply with the requirements of this section may apply to the county court for an order to set aside or modify any terms of a lease or agreement to enable him to do so. As before, the court may apportion the expense or adjust the rent.

7.3.4 TELECOMMUNICATIONS ACT 1984, SECTION 96

This section provides that any alterations to a leased building in connection with the provision of a telecommunications system shall be subject to the lessor's consent, such consent not to be unreasonably withheld. The question of unreasonableness is to be decided bearing in mind all the circumstances, and on the premise that a person should not unreasonably be denied access to a telecommunications system.

The section applies to a lease of a year or more, and to an agreement for a lease, taking effect after the section came into force, although there is provision for the Secretary of State to apply it retrospectively.

7.4 Trespass to other Premises

7.4.1 THE EXTENT OF THE DEMISED PREMISES

A further preliminary matter which should not be overlooked with regard to alterations covenants is the extent of the demised premises. Will the tenant's alterations constitute a trespass to adjoining property which is not part of the demised premises? Are the walls and roof of the premises included in the demise, or do they belong to the landlord or someone else? In *Haines* v *Florensa* [1990] 1 EGLR 73 the Court of Appeal held that the tenant of a top-floor flat, whose demise expressly included the roof and roof space, could extend the roof space by raising the height of the roof as the air space above it belonged to him. This alteration was an improvement to which the landlord's consent could not be unreasonably withheld (see **7.6**).

If the demised premises are part only of a building belonging to the landlord, it is quite probable that the walls and roof are not included in the demise and therefore belong to the landlord or even another tenant (see **3.2.2**). In leases of a unit in a building, structural and common parts of the building usually belong to the landlord.

The tenant is not entitled to make any alterations which involve a trespass. In *Frederick Berry Ltd* v *Royal Bank of Scotland* [1949] 1 KB 619 it was held that the tenant of a third floor who had covenanted not to exhibit signs had no right to put up a name-plate at the main entrance of a building on a wall which was not part of the demised premises. If he required this facility, it should have been expressly granted to him as an easement (see **3.2.3**).

7.4.2 TRESPASS OR NUISANCE IN THE COURSE OF CARRYING OUT ALTERATIONS

The actual process of carrying out alterations may also involve a trespass or a nuisance if it interferes with an easement. This could arise, for instance, where the alterations cannot be carried out without erecting scaffolding covering other parts of the building. In *Owen* v *Gadd* [1956] 2 QB 99 the erection of scaffolding over the door and window of a shop to carry out repairs to premises above was a nuisance, and also a breach of the implied covenant for quiet enjoyment.

From the tenant's point of view, it is obviously advisable to cover such situations by expressly including in the lease easements of access for the purpose of carrying out such alterations. The leases of units in a building will often contain a covenant by the tenant to allow the landlord and other tenants access for the purpose of carrying out repairs and alterations (see clause in **10.2.5**).

The Access to Neighbouring Land Act 1992 allows the court to make an order for access on to neighbouring premises in certain circumstances for preservation work. The court may also make an order for access for alterations or improvements which the preservation work 'incidentally involves' if the court deems it to be fair and reasonable to do so. For non-residential premises, a reasonable consideration may be required for this.

7.5 The Form of a Covenant against Alterations

Just like any other agreement, a covenant against alterations may be infinitely variable in its form. Should a dispute arise, it is the actual covenant contained in the lease which the court will have to interpret. Although the covenants are often drafted using precedents used before, there may be variations which will result in different interpretations.

7.5.1 MEANING OF ALTERATIONS

In *Bickmore* v *Dimmer* [1903] 1 Ch 158 Stirling LJ held that the term 'alterations' should be limited to alterations which would affect the form and structure of a building. Thus in *London County Council* v *Hutter* [1925] Ch 626 the erection of an electrically illuminated advertisement on the façade of the premises on 12 iron brackets, cemented into 23 holes cut into the stonework, amounted to a breach of a covenant: **'not to cut or maim any of the principal walls . . . or make or permit to be made any alteration in the elevation of the building'**. Conversely, in *Joseph* v *London County Council* (1914) 111 LT 276 the erection of a lit advertisement on struts which were easily removed was held not to be an alteration.

7.5.2 ALTERATIONS TO FURTHER THE TENANT'S BUSINESS

A further point of difference between the two cases discussed in **7.5.1** was that in *London County Council* v *Hutter* the advertisement, which was one for gin for which the tenant had rented out the space, was in no way related to his business, whereas in *Joseph* v *London County Council* the advertisement was in furtherance of the tenant's business. The courts have shown themselves ready to construe a covenant, or in some cases to imply a covenant, which gives business efficacy to a lease. Such a construction would make the tenant in *Joseph* a candidate for more sympathetic treatment.

7.5.3 THE MEANING OF 'STRUCTURE'

It may not always be entirely clear what is included in the 'structure' of a building, so that a covenant **'not to cut or maim any of the principal walls or timbers, roof or foundations'** is a clearer and more comprehensive form of covenant than one which is simply **'not to make any structural alterations'**.

In *Lilley and Skinner Ltd* v *Crump* (1929) 73 SJ 366 it was necessary to decide whether making two openings in a wall between premises was an 'alteration' (which was only prohibited without the landlord's consent) or was a cutting or maiming, which was absolutely prohibited. Rowlatt J held that it was an alteration. In *Joseph* v *London County Council* (1914) 111 LT 276 it was said that an alteration meant an alteration to the fabric of the building.

It is quite usual for covenants against alterations to distinguish between structural alterations, against which there may be an absolute covenant, and minor alterations, which may be carried out with the landlord's consent. An example of such a covenant would be:

> **Not to cut, maim or injure or suffer to be cut, maimed or injured any of the structure or the roofs, walls, timbers, wires, pipes, drains, appurtenances, fixtures or fittings thereof, and not without the previous consent in writing of the landlord to make or suffer to be made any alteration or addition to the demised premises or any part thereof.**

There is no legal definition of 'structure', although it was considered by the Court of Appeal in the context of the Housing Act 1961, s. 32 (now the Landlord & Tenant Act 1985, s. 11) in its application to dwellinghouses in *Campden Hill Towers Ltd* v *Gardner* [1977] QB 823. There, Megaw

LJ expressed the opinion that it might be part of a building which affected the safety of it, or would materially affect its use as a dwellinghouse. In *Irvine* v *Moran* [1991] 1 EGLR 261, Forbes QC sought to follow this approach and said that the structure of a dwellinghouse consists of 'those elements which give it its essential appearance, stability and shape' and is 'a material or significant element in the overall construction', although not necessarily load-bearing.

Covenants against alterations are onerous covenants which will be construed against the landlord, so that in the case of any doubt, 'structure' is likely to be interpreted in favour of the tenant.

7.5.4 'ELEVATION' OF A BUILDING

Sometimes a covenant may expressly prohibit alterations to the 'elevation' of a building. In *Joseph* v *London County Council* (1914) 111 LT 276 it was held that the elevation of a building meant the front view of it.

7.6 Absolute and Qualified Covenants: Landlord and Tenant Act 1927, Section 19(2)

A covenant against alterations may be an absolute one, where the tenant covenants not to carry out alterations at all, or a qualified one, where the tenant covenants not to carry out alterations without first obtaining the landlord's consent in writing (see for an example the clause in **7.5.3**).

The importance of this is that the qualified form of the covenant will almost always be caught by the Landlord and Tenant Act 1927, s. 19(2), which provides that consent to '*improvements*' shall not be unreasonably withheld.

It also provides that the landlord may require payment of costs and a reasonable sum for his consent to any improvements which damage or diminish the value of the demised premises, or any neighbouring premises belonging to the landlord, if reasonable and the improvements do not add to the letting value. In these circumstances, the landlord may also require an undertaking to reinstate the premises.

7.6.1 'IMPROVEMENTS'

Although the Landlord and Tenant Act 1927, s. 19, refers to improvements, the courts have interpreted this liberally and in a way which favours the tenant.

In *Balls Brothers Ltd* v *Sinclair* [1931] 2 Ch 325, the tenant under a lease which included a covenant not to make any alteration or addition without the written consent of the landlord was refused consent to move a staircase. Luxmoore J took the view that the covenant was within s. 19(2). As the section protected the landlord's interests by providing for reinstatement and a reasonable sum payable to him for any diminution in value, 'improvement' must be looked at from the tenant's point of view.

This view was taken by the majority of the Court of Appeal in both cases of *F. W. Woolworth and Co. Ltd* v *Lambert* [1937] Ch 37 and *Lambert* v *F. W. Woolworth and Co. Ltd* [1938] Ch 883. In this case, the tenant was also the tenant of premises at the rear of the demised premises. It wanted to extend its shop by joining the two premises together. The alterations needed to achieve this involved considerable demolition of a wall at the rear of the demised premises and removal of a staircase and staff accommodation into the adjacent premises at the rear. The facts were considered by the Court of Appeal twice over (the decision in the first case in 1936 as to what amounted to improvements being *obiter*). The majority of the court in both cases felt that the alterations were 'improvements' within s.19(2) as this was to be decided from the tenant's point of view, but Greene LJ in the earlier case and Slesser LJ in the later case felt that they could not fall within s.19(2) as they could not possibly be improvements to the 'demised premises' which were the subject-matter of the covenant.

The work was only an improvement when taking into consideration the additional use of the adjoining premises.

7.6.2 BURDEN OF PROOF UNDER SECTION 19(2)

The Landlord and Tenant Act 1988 requires a landlord to give written reasons for refusing consent to assign where the covenant is a qualified one and it is implied that the landlord's consent shall not be unreasonably withheld. The Act does not apply to qualified covenants against alterations, however, and the onus of proving an unreasonable refusal is therefore on the tenant.

In the first *Woolworth* case [1937] Ch 37, the landlord had demanded a sum of £7,000 for his consent to the alterations. The tenant's action for a declaration that the landlord's consent had been unreasonably withheld was dismissed as the tenant failed to satisfy the court that this sum was unreasonable. Moreover, the court held that it had no jurisdiction to decide what would have been reasonable by referring it to an official referee unless both parties agreed to this. The wording of the section does not confer this remedial right upon the court, unlike s. 19(3) relating to user, which expressly contemplates a determination by the court of what is a reasonable sum.

In the second *Woolworth* case [1938] Ch 883, the landlord refused consent to the alterations without giving any reasons, and this was in itself held to be unreasonable. This would seem in part to shift the burden of proof of unreasonableness from the tenant to the landlord.

7.6.3 UNDERTAKING TO REINSTATE

The Landlord and Tenant Act 1927, s. 19(2), also allows a landlord to require an undertaking from the tenant to reinstate the premises where this would be reasonable and the improvement does not add to the letting value. The Law Commission has suggested that the requirement that the improvement does not add to the letting value of the premises should be abolished as the landlord may want the premises restored to their original layout in order to occupy them itself, in which case the letting value is irrelevant.

An assignee or subtenant would be bound by such a covenant only if it were drafted so as to become a term of the lease, so a landlord should require any assignee or subtenant to covenant directly with the landlord to reinstate.

If the lease includes a covenant to **'deliver up'** the premises in the same state as at the commencement of the term, however, the landlord will be able to sue not only the original tenant, but also an assignee for damages on a breach of the covenant at the end of the lease. To sue on such a covenant before the end of the lease it would have to be a covenant to **'keep and deliver up'** the premises in the same state as at the commencement of the term.

If there is no covenant in the lease and no undertaking to reinstate, then the landlord will have no remedy, as an undertaking to reinstate will not be implied (*Never-Stop Railway (Wembley) Ltd* v *British Empire Exhibition (1924) Incorporated* [1926] Ch 877).

In *James* v *Hutton and J. Cook and Sons Ltd* [1950] 1 KB 9 it was held that damages recoverable by a landlord for breach of an undertaking to reinstate should be assessed according to the usual rule of compensation for damages for breach of contract. In that case, the tenant had put in a new shop window, but there was no evidence that this was less desirable than the original one or any indication that the landlord did in fact intend to reinstate the old shop window. Damages recoverable were limited to the diminution in value of the reversion, and as there was no diminution, the landlord recovered only nominal damages.

7.6.4 REASONS FOR REFUSING CONSENT

A landlord's reasons for refusing consent to improvements may be many and varied. In *Woolworth (No. 2)* Slesser LJ said that 'many considerations, aesthetic, historic or even personal, may be relied upon as yielding reasonable grounds for refusing consent'. He pointed out that the wider the court's interpretation of 'improvement', the more necessary it is to protect a landlord who has grounds for objecting.

Although the Landlord and Tenant Act 1927, s. 19, specifically allows the landlord to have the premises reinstated if the improvement diminishes the letting value, this presumably does not mean that an undertaking to reinstate in other circumstances would necessarily be unreasonable.

7.6.5 CONDITIONS ATTACHING TO CONSENT

Conditions imposed on the granting of consent, like the grounds for refusing consent, may also take account of a wide range of matters, and are not limited to matters contemplated by s. 19(2) itself.

The licence granting consent to alterations will almost certainly include conditions as to how, and possibly when, the work is to be done. It will require that the landlord shall approve the plans and specifications, and that the tenant will obtain planning permission and approval under the Building Regulations if necessary. It will often require the tenant to carry out the work in a workmanlike manner within a certain time, and not in such a way as to cause a nuisance or annoyance to nearby owners or occupiers.

The tendency is for alterations covenants to become more comprehensive, so that the covenant itself may specify these requirements as conditions for consent. Such a covenant might be:

> **To carry out approved alterations for which consent is given in a good and workmanlike manner, with materials of good quality, and to the satisfaction of the landlord.**

For the reasons mentioned in **7.7.2** and **7.8.1** care should be taken in drafting such a licence to make the requirements of the landlord permissive rather than obligatory.

7.7 Compensation for Improvements: Landlord and Tenant Act 1927, Part I and Landlord and Tenant Act 1954, Part II

The underlying objective of this legislation is to allow a tenant to recover compensation for 'proper improvements' which have been made by the tenant, or the tenant's predecessor in title, and which add to the letting value of the premises. The provisions do not cover trade or tenants' fixtures, which are removable by the tenant (see **3.4**). The rationale for compensation is that the landlord will benefit from the improvements, so it is available only where a business tenancy comes to an end and the tenant quits. The tenant will usually be entitled to a new tenancy under the Landlord and Tenant Act 1954, Part II, so that the provisions will not apply.

7.7.1 EFFECT OF AUTHORISED IMPROVEMENTS MADE UNDER THE ACT

The legislation has a more practical significance in that it may operate to authorise improvements which are prohibited under the terms of the lease.

Any authorisation (whether by non-objection by the landlord or by certification by the court) is taken to override even an absolute covenant against alterations. The procedure is therefore used by tenants as an alternative to an application to the landlord for consent to alterations.

The landlord may resist the claim by offering to effect the alterations personally and an increased rent (to be fixed by the court in default of agreement) may be charged to cover the cost.

The Landlord and Tenant Act 1927, s. 16, allows for the landlord to be reimbursed for any increased expenditure as a result of improvements made under the Act. This would presumably cover any increased insurance premium or business rates in the unusual circumstance of these being payable by the landlord and not by the tenant.

7.7.2 QUALIFYING TENANCIES

The Landlord and Tenant Act 1927, s. 17, sets out the requirements for compensation to be claimed.

The tenant must be the tenant of a holding (which does not have the same definition as in the Landlord and Tenant Act 1954) under a lease or an agreement for a lease. The premises must be used wholly or partly for trade, business or a profession, and the improvements must relate to that part of the premises so used. Mining and agricultural tenancies are excluded, as are lettings to a tenant during a period of employment by the landlord, or during a period when the tenant holds an office or appointment from the landlord if the tenancy states this in writing.

It includes improvements made pursuant to any statutory requirements (see **7.3**) if made after 1 October 1954, but excludes improvements made pursuant to a contract for valuable consideration. Thus, where a tenant covenanted in a sublease to install a lavatory, this sufficed to disqualify the improvement for compensation, even though the obligation was to someone other than the landlord (*Owen Owen Estate Ltd* v *Livett* [1956] Ch 1).

One way in which a landlord may avoid the compensation provisions therefore is to insert some consideration for consent to the alterations in the licence and to put the tenant under an obligation to carry them out. Waiver of an absolute covenant against alterations may be sufficient consideration, but waiver of a qualified covenant is probably not. Obligations imposed merely as part of the consent, such as obtaining the landlord's approval of the plans, are unlikely to be regarded as consideration, provided they are basically permissive in nature (*Godbold* v *Martin The Newsagents Ltd* (1983) 268 EG 1202).

The Landlord and Tenant Act 1954 prohibits any contracting out of these provisions.

7.7.3 CONDITIONS FOR CLAIM

The conditions which the tenant must satisfy are set out in the Landlord and Tenant Act 1927, s. 3.

The tenant must serve a written notice, together with plans and specifications, on the landlord. If the landlord is not the freeholder, then the tenant should serve notice also on the superior landlord to allow a claim for compensation against it also in due course.

The landlord may object to the improvements within three months, but if the landlord fails to serve a notice of objection within this time then the improvements are to be treated as authorised.

If the landlord does object then the tenant must ask the court to certify the improvements. The court must do this if the court is satisfied that:

(a) they will add to the letting value at the end of the tenancy; and
(b) they are reasonable and suitable to the character of the premises; and
(c) they will not diminish the value of any other property belonging to the landlord or a superior landlord.

The landlord and any superior landlord have a right to be heard by the court, and the court may impose conditions or require modifications of the plans.

To qualify for compensation, the tenant must obtain the court's certification of the improvements before they are completed (*Hogarth Health Club Ltd* v *Westbourne Investments Ltd* [1990] 1 EGLR 89).

A tenant who makes a claim for compensation at the end of the tenancy must do so in the prescribed form and within the prescribed time-limits. The tenant must give details of the cost of the improvements and the date when they were carried out. The amount of compensation is limited to the 'net addition' to the value of the holding, thus allowing for the fact that not all the improvements may add to the letting value.

7.8 The Effect of Alterations on Rent

Improvements may increase the market rental value of the property, and this could obviously operate unfairly on a tenant who has paid for the alterations in the first place. The tenant could effectively be paying for the alterations again in the increased rent. The Landlord and Tenant Act 1954, s. 34, therefore provides for disregard of improvements made by the tenant on fixing the rent under a new lease under Part II of the Act. It is common for a rent review clause also to provide that improvements effected by the tenant are to be disregarded in assessing a new rent.

7.8.1 DISREGARD UNDER THE LANDLORD AND TENANT ACT 1954

The Landlord and Tenant Act 1954, s. 34(1)(c), provides that in fixing a rent under a new tenancy under the Act there shall be disregarded 'any effect on rent of any improvement carried out by the tenant or a predecessor in title of his otherwise than in pursuance of an obligation to his immediate landlord'.

In *East Coast Amusement Co. Ltd* v *British Transport Board* [1965] AC 58, the House of Lords held that this applied only to improvements carried out during the currency of the lease to be renewed. Section 54 was therefore amended by the Law of Property Act 1969, s. 1(1), by the addition of subsection (2), which provides that an improvement qualifies to be disregarded if it was effected within 21 years before the application for a new tenancy, that the holding has been subject to a business tenancy ever since then, and that the tenant did not quit at the end of any of the tenancies. This effectively abrogates the decision in *East Coast Amusement Co. Ltd* v *British Transport Board*

Because alterations may therefore have an effect on rent for up to 21 years after completion, a careful record should be kept of any alterations carried out.

The section applies to alterations made by a tenant or his predecessor in title. It was held in *Euston Centre Properties Ltd* v *H. & J. Wilson Ltd* (1981) 262 EG 1079 that this did not include improvements carried out by the tenant when he was a licensee only, and such improvements should be ignored.

The obligation to the landlord will probably have to be more than requirements imposed upon the tenant in the licence as to the way in which the alterations are effected (*Godbold* v *Martin The Newsagents* (1983) 268 EG 1202).

Many leases contain a covenant by the tenant to comply with requirements as to the state of premises laid down in any statute (see the clause in 7.3). Such a covenant would put the tenant under an obligation to the landlord to carry out the alterations in addition to any statutory obligation, and such alterations would therefore fall outside the disregard provision of s. 34(1)(c) (*Forte and Co. Ltd* v *General Accident Life Assurance Ltd* [1986] 2 EGLR 115).

7.8.2 DISREGARD UNDER A RENT REVIEW CLAUSE

A rent review clause will often include a provision that improvements made by the tenant shall be disregarded when fixing a new rent. Sometimes this will incorporate the wording of the Landlord and Tenant Act 1954, s. 34(1)(c), specifically or by reference to the section, for example:

> **There shall be disregarded such matters as would by virtue of section 34(i)(a) to (c) inclusive and section 34(2) of the Landlord and Tenant Act 1954 be disregarded were the tenant applying for a new tenancy under that Act on the review date.**

From the tenant's point of view, it may be important to ensure that the reference to the section is to its amended form, including subsection (2). In *Brett* v *Brett Essex Golf Club Ltd* [1986] 1 EGLR 154 a reference only to s. 34(1)(c) in a lease made in 1978 was construed (when looked at in the light of other provisions in the lease where the draftsman had expressly mentioned amended legislation) as being a reference to the unamended section, and this discounted earlier improvements. In that case, a nine-hole golf-course made by the tenant on adjoining land, not held by him under the same lease, had been added to the holding by the 1978 lease. It was held that this could not constitute an improvement to the demised premises as it was not part of the premises as originally demised.

If the rent review clause does not provide for improvements to be disregarded then they will be taken into account (*Ponsford* v *HMS Aerosols Ltd* [1979] AC 63).

7.9 Improvements in Short Leases Taxable as Premiums

In a lease not exceeding 50 years where the tenant covenants to effect improvements, the landlord will be liable to pay income tax or corporation tax on the increase in value of the premises, less one 50th for every year of the tenancy after the first year. A covenant to reinstate the premises will apparently avoid this liability however.

EIGHT

RESTRICTIONS ON THE USER OF LEASEHOLD PROPERTY

A landlord will invariably want to take a covenant from a lessee as to the user of the demised premises.

The landlord may have various reasons for this, such as to preserve the letting value of the premises and of the reversion, to avoid complaints from any neighbouring tenants, or to comply with any restrictions as to user which affect the landlord, such as restrictive covenants on the freehold title and planning requirements. Both the landlord and the tenant will be greatly concerned with matters entirely extraneous to the lease which affect the user of the demised premises, and the first part of this chapter considers these matters and their bearing on the drafting of user clauses in leases.

The form of user covenants in leases is important not only as regards the use to which the demised premises may be put, but also because of the effect of user covenants on the interpretation of other covenants, such as covenants against disposition and rent review. It is necessary, therefore, to consider the nature and effect of user covenants on these matters.

It is possible too that there may be other covenants in a lease which affect user, and the scope and effect of these covenants will be considered.

8.1 Matters Extraneous to the Lease which may Affect the User of Demised Premises

8.1.1 RESTRICTIVE COVENANTS ON THE FREEHOLD TITLE

Restrictive covenants on the freehold title will be binding on a tenant or a subtenant only if such person has notice (*Mander* v *Falcke* [1981] 2 Ch 554). Notice is given by entering such covenant as a minor interest in the charges register of the freehold title at HM Land Registry (if the freehold title is registered) or (in the case of a post-1925 restrictive covenant if the freehold title is unregistered) as a class D(ii) land charge. Restrictive covenants are, however, binding on squatters regardless of notice (*Re Nisbet and Potts' Contract* [1906] 1 Ch 386).

A tenant who takes a lease under an open contract has no right to call for the freeholder's title in either registered or unregistered land (see **2.1.3**). It is quite possible that there will be restrictive covenants on the freehold title which affect its use, and a tenant should therefore always ensure that the contract includes a clause for deduction of the freehold title. In unregistered land, a prospective tenant will not be able to search the land charges register without the names of estate owners against whom to search. In registered land, the covenants will appear in the charges register of title; but without sight of the office copy entries, the tenant will not know about them.

8.1.2 PROCEDURES FOR DEALING WITH RESTRICTIVE COVENANTS AFFECTING LAND

8.1.2.1 Application for declaration

Because the law relating to the passing of the benefit and burden of restrictive covenants to subsequent landowners is complicated, and many such covenants are old ones (sometimes even imposed in the 19th century!) it is possible to make an application to the court for a declaration as to whether any particular land is in fact affected by a covenant and by whom such a covenant would be enforceable (Law of Property Act 1925, s. 87(4)).

8.1.2.2 Waiver

If there have been continuous breaches of a restrictive covenant over a long period in which the person entitled to the benefit of the covenant has acquiesced, or if there is any other conduct from which an inference of waiver of the covenant can be drawn, then it will no longer be enforceable. Even though the court may not be prepared to enforce it by granting an injunction, damages may be obtainable (*Shaw* v *Applegate* [1977] 1 WLR 970).

8.1.2.3 Discharge or modification

Under the Law of Property Act 1925, s. 84, as amended by the Law of Property Act 1969, 'any person interested' may apply to the Lands Tribunal for the discharge or modification of a restrictive covenant affecting freehold land or a lease of over 40 years of which 25 years have elapsed. The grounds for an application are:

(a) Under s. 84(1)(a) that the restriction should be deemed obsolete because of changes in the character of the property or the neighbourhood, or for other circumstances.

(b) Under s. 84(1)(aa) (widened by Law of Property Act 1969) that the continued existence of the covenant would impede the reasonable user of the land. The Lands Tribunal here must be satisfied that those entitled to the benefit of the covenant do not receive practical benefits from it, or that it is contrary to the public interest. The Tribunal should have regard to the development plan under the town and country planning legislation and to any planning applications granted or refused.

(c) Under s. 84(1)(b) where the persons entitled to the benefit agree, expressly or impliedly, to the discharge or modification of the covenant.

(d) Under s. 84(1)(c) that the proposed discharge or modification will not injure those entitled to the benefit of the covenant.

8.1.2.4 Indemnity policy

A purchaser can take out an indemnity policy against the possibility of being sued for breach of a restrictive covenant. For a fairly recent covenant, the cost of this may be prohibitive; but for an older covenant it may be more reasonable, and this course of action may save the time which a hearing by the Lands Tribunal would necessarily involve.

8.1.3 RESTRICTIVE COVENANTS IN A HEAD LEASE

Unless the contract for the sublease stipulates otherwise, the only title for which a subtenant may call is the immediate head lease from which the sublease is to be created (see **2.3**). A subtenant is, however, bound by restrictive covenants in the head lease and in any other superior lease. In unregistered title, the restrictive covenants are not registrable under the Land Charges Act 1972. In registered title, they will be referred to in office copy entries by reference to the lease.

Ideally, therefore, in the case of a sublease, the sublessee will want to see all superior leases. In a contract for the purchase of a term under a sublease there should always be provision for inspection of any head lease.

A tenant should ensure that covenants in a head lease are repeated in any sublease, as otherwise the tenant might become liable to the landlord for breach of a covenant in the head lease which cannot be enforced against the subtenant. An additional safeguard for a tenant is also to take a covenant from the subtenant to perform all the covenants in the head lease.

From the point of view of the landlord, an exhaustive form of user clause, whereby the tenant covenants 'not to use or permit or suffer the premises to be used . . .' is desirable, as this may extend the landlord's right of action against the tenant to cover the acts of any subtenant. There are conflicting judicial opinions, however, as to whether the granting of a sublease under which the subtenant is not expressly bound by the covenants in the head lease amounts to 'permitting' a breach of a user covenant in the head lease. The scope of a covenant against 'permitting' a certain user of premises was considered in *Norton* v *Charles Deane Productions Ltd* [1970] EGD 268.

A landlord would have a right to sue a subtenant for damages for breach of a restrictive covenant in a head lease. As the enforceability of such covenants does not depend upon the doctrine of privity, however, the landlord can obtain forfeiture only against the head tenant. The wording of the covenant in the head lease is therefore important. The wider the wording of the covenant, the easier it will be to establish a breach.

8.1.4 RESTRICTIONS UNDER THE TOWN AND COUNTRY PLANNING ACTS

It is important to ensure that premises can be used for a prospective tenant's business purposes and any valid planning permissions and any conditions attached should be inspected. A condition restricting user to a named use may prevent a change even within a use class (*City of London Corporation* v *Secretary of State for the Environment* (1971) 23 P & CR 108). A tenant should be aware, however, that a covenant restricting user to a particular use class is not a warranty by the landlord that such user is legal (*Hill* v *Harris* [1965] 2 QB 601). The landlord will often cover the point with an express declaration however, such as:

> **Nothing contained in this lease or in any consent granted by the landlord under this lease shall imply or warrant that the demised premises may be used under the Planning Acts for the purpose herein authorised or any purpose subsequently authorised and the tenant hereby acknowledges and admits that the landlord has not given or made at any time any representation or warranty that any such use is or will be or will remain a permitted use under the Planning Acts.**

If there is no planning permission but an established use, it may be possible to apply for a certificate of lawfulness of an existing use (see **2.6.10**).

Any 'material change' of user requires planning permission; but this will not always be necessary if the new use is within the same class under the Town and Country Planning (Use Classes) Order 1987 (see **2.7.2**).

The intention of the order is to allow for some flexibility in use within the different classes. Also, a change of use of a subsidiary part of the premises, where the use is ancillary to the main use of the premises, will not constitute a material change requiring permission. Abandonment of a permitted use may, however, constitute a change and result in a planning permission no longer being valid.

Planning controls are enforceable against the occupier of premises, but the Town and Country Planning Act 1990 provides that an enforcement notice may also be served upon the landlord of premises. The landlord therefore has an interest in ensuring that there is no breach of any planning requirements and may require a covenant from a tenant to comply with any planning conditions and not to carry out any development without consent. An example of such a covenant would be:

> **To comply at the tenant's expense in all respects with the Planning Acts and to indemnify the landlord against any breaches thereof and not to apply for any consents whatsoever under the Planning Acts without the prior approval of the landlord.**

The covenant may be more specific in requiring the tenant to maintain the established use, or to use the premises only for purposes within a particular use class. An example of such a covenant would be:

Not to use the demised premises or any part thereof nor permit or suffer the same to be used otherwise than as offices within class B1 of the Town and Country Planning (Use Classes) Order 1987.

Such covenants would maintain the letting value of the premises and the value of the reversion for the landlord. In addition to any planning enforcement against the tenant, the landlord would then also have a right of forfeiture for a breach of such a covenant.

In *Brewers Co.* v *Viewplan plc* [1989] 2 EGLR 133 a reference to the 1972 Use Classes Order was not construed as a reference to the 1987 Order which replaced it, but see **2.7.7** for a fuller discussion of this.

Many advertisements are also subject to planning controls under the Town and Country Planning (Control of Advertisements) Regulations 1984, and it is therefore advisable for the landlord to extend the covenant to comply also with any regulations made under the Town and Country Planning Acts. Provided that any advertisement does not infringe the regulations, user for a particular business would usually include advertisements usual to that type of business.

8.1.5 LICENSING OR REGISTRATION OF CERTAIN USES

Certain use of premises requires either a licence or registration under the relevant statutes. For example, a licence is necessary under the Firearms Act 1968 to sell firearms; and a justices' licence is necessary to sell alcohol. Nursing homes are required to be registered under the Registered Homes Act 1984, and premises used for the manufacture of sausages and ice-cream under the Food Act 1984.

A landlord of such premises will usually require a covenant in the lease that the tenant will obtain any necessary licence or registration, and will do nothing to prejudice any such licence once granted. An example of such a covenant would be:

At all times to observe and comply with the provisions of or imposed under any statute, licence or registration regulating or permitting the use of the demised premises for the purpose for which they are for the time being used and the requirements of any competent authority in that connection and at the expense of the tenant to do all that is necessary to obtain, maintain and renew all licences and registrations required by law for the use of the demised premises for that purpose.

8.1.6 COVENANTS IN RESTRAINT OF TRADE

A covenant which imposes an excessive restraint of trade may be illegal under the general law of contract. Such covenants are sometimes taken by a vendor on the sale of freehold business premises, or by a mortgagee on the grant of a mortgage on freehold or leasehold business premises. Although in theory they might be included by a landlord in a lease, in practice a tenant is unlikely to accept a lease of premises which unduly restricts its business.

Generally, such covenants are unenforceable insofar as they exceed what is necessary to protect the business interests of the covenantee. In *Amoco Australian Pty Ltd* v *Rocca Bros Motor Engineering Co. Pty Ltd* [1975] AC 561, the Privy Council held that covenants by a sublessee that a service station would buy only the products of its landlord (a petroleum company) were void as being in restraint of trade. In *Alec Lobb (Garages) Ltd* v *Total Oil (Great Britain) Ltd* [1983] 1 WLR 87, however, it was held that only clauses in a lease which were void as being against public policy should be struck out, and that all the other clauses in a lease should stand. It seems unlikely, therefore, that normal user clauses in a lease would be affected by clauses in excessive restraint of trade.

8.2 User Covenants in a Lease

8.2.1 FORM OF COVENANT

A covenant as to user may be:

(a) 'wide', i.e. one which prohibits only certain types of use; or
(b) 'narrow', i.e. one which prohibits all uses except for certain specified ones.

8.2.2 ABSOLUTE AND QUALIFIED USER COVENANTS

A user covenant may be:

(a) absolute, i.e. one which does not provide for any change in use; or
(b) qualified, i.e. one which allows a change of use with the landlord's consent.

An example of an absolute user clause would be:

Not to use or permit or suffer to be used the demised premises or any part thereof other than as an office in connection with the tenant's business.

An example of a qualified user clause would be:

Not to use the demised premises or suffer the same to be used except as an office in connection with the tenant's business without the landlord's consent in writing.

A fully qualified user covenant is one which adds the words implied into covenants against assignment by the Landlord and Tenant Act 1927, s. 19(1), that such consent shall not be unreasonably refused. An example of this would be:

Not without the landlord's consent which shall not be unreasonably refused to use or permit or suffer the demised premises or any part thereof to be used other than as solicitors' offices or for any other use within class A2 of the Town and Country Planning (Use Classes) Order 1987.

Unless these words are expressly added to the covenant, there is no requirement that the landlord's refusal to consent to a change of user be reasonable. Furthermore, no such term will be implied (*Guardian Assurance Co. Ltd* v *Gants Hill Holdings Ltd* (1983) 267 EG 678), unless perhaps the covenant is a negative and specific one of a regulatory nature, such as the approval of plans (*Cryer* v *Scott Bros (Sunbury) Ltd* (1988) 55 P & CR 183).

A tenant with merely a qualified (as distinct from a fully qualified) covenant against a change of user is therefore in much the same position as a tenant with an absolute covenant as regards obtaining the landlord's consent; although, in the case of a qualified covenant, the compensation provisions of s. 19(3) apply.

In the case of a fully qualified covenant, the tenant is obviously in a much stronger position to contest the landlord's grounds for refusal of consent. In *Anglia Building Society* v *Sheffield City Council* (1983) 266 EG 311, where there was a fully qualified covenant against change of use, the user covenant was for use as a travel and employment agency and theatre ticket bureau. The Council refused consent to an assignment to a building society on the ground that service use would depress the rents in a nearby shopping area. Such refusal was held unreasonable: for the landlord to require user as a retail shop would in fact have given it an advantage not reserved to it in the original lease. This was the same ground upon which the court found refusal to consent to assign to be unreasonable in *Bromley Park Garden Estates Ltd* v *Moss* [1982] 1 WLR 1019; and it is thought that much the same criteria of reasonableness would apply to fully qualified covenants against change of use as in the case law on refusal of consent to assign. The Landlord and Tenant Act 1988, which requires a landlord to give reasons in writing for a refusal of consent to assign, does not, however, apply.

A further difference is that, because s. 19(1) does not apply to user covenants to make them fully qualified, it is open to the parties to stipulate what shall be regarded as a reasonable refusal. If grounds for reasonable refusal are specified, however, the landlord's reasons must then fall within them. In *Berenyi* v *Watford Borough Council* (1980) 256 EG 271, it was expressly provided that the landlord's consent should not be regarded as being unreasonably withheld on certain grounds. The court found that the real reason for withholding consent to a change of user was increased vehicular access to the premises if they were used by more than one occupier. As this was not among the grounds set out, it was not available to the landlord as a ground for objection when the court of first instance had reached a conclusion, on the evidence, that this was not a valid reason.

8.2.3 PROVISIONS OF THE LANDLORD AND TENANT ACT 1927, SECTION 19(3) AS TO QUALIFIED COVENANTS

Section 19(3) provides that, in the case of qualified user covenants, the landlord shall not demand any money 'whether by way of increase of rent or otherwise', for consent to a change of use. There can be no contracting out of this provision.

The landlord may nevertheless require the expenses of any necessary licence or consent, and a 'reasonable sum' for any diminution in the value of the demised premises or any neighbouring premises belonging to the landlord. The subsection also provides for the court (probably only the High Court and not the county court) to determine what is a reasonable sum; and, if this is paid by the tenant, then the landlord is bound to grant consent. Section 19(3) does not apply, however, where the change of use involves structural alteration to the premises, which is covered by s. 19(2); and neither does it apply to agricultural or mining leases.

8.2.4 INTERPRETATION OF USER COVENANTS

The interpretation of user covenants has given rise to some litigation and careful consideration should therefore be given to their drafting in regard to the user allowed.

From a tenant's point of view, a wide user clause will allow some flexibility in trading, and may make it easier to assign the lease or to sublet. A wide clause may, however, have an adverse effect on rent review. It has already been mentioned (**8.2.2**) that a tenant with merely a qualified (as opposed to a fully qualified) covenant as to change of user is not likely to be in any better position than a tenant with a user covenant which is absolute.

From a landlord's point of view, it will be particularly desirable to restrict and maintain control of user if the landlord has leased other units or shops which may be in competition with the tenant. The case of *Basildon Development Corporation* v *Mactro Ltd* [1986] 1 EGLR 137 concerned an action brought by a landlord to restrain a supermarket from selling goods which would compete with the businesses of other tenants, and possibly cause such tenants financial hardship. The more restrictive the user, however, the more adverse its effect on any rent review: see **9.4.4.3**(a).

A landlord will also be concerned to ensure that the tenant's user does not infringe any of the restrictions binding on the landlord as to user of the premises referred to in **8.1**.

8.2.5 INTERPRETATION OF EXACT TERMS USED

Problems may arise in the interpretation of the words used, either because the description of the business is general (e.g. 'supermarket'), or because the meaning of certain trades may change with time so as to infringe upon other trades. It would obviously be unwise to use words often found in older leases — such as 'draper', 'hosier' and 'haberdasher' — which have little meaning today. It has been held, however, that user as a hairdresser covered the sale of contraceptives (*Bier* v *Danser* (1951) 157 EG 552) and that user as 'a garage with car sales and vehicle repairs' included the sale of vehicle accessories, but not sweets and confectionery (*Atwal* v *Courts Garages* [1989] 1 EGLR 63).

It was held in *Texaco Antilles Ltd* v *Kernochan* [1973] AC 609 that user words should be construed as at the date they are used. In that case, restrictive covenants imposed in 1925 restricted user to a public garage; they were held to include use also as a filling station, which would have been usual in 1925. In *Basildon Development Corporation* v *Mactro Ltd* [1986] 1 EGLR 137, which concerned a user covenant in a lease, it was conceded by counsel that the relevant date for determining the meaning of use as a food and drink supermarket and purposes incidental thereto was the date the lease was granted. Doubts were, however, expressed in the Court of Appeal as to whether this should be the sole test, and it was thought that other circumstances might also be relevant.

The courts have been reluctant to find that general descriptions of trade import an exact meaning which should remain unchanged for all time. Thus, in *Stevenage Development Corporation* v *Baby Carriages and Toys (Stevenage) Ltd* (1968) 207 EG 531, it was held that 'nursery goods' did not include baby clothes. In the *Mactro* case, it was said that 'supermarket' was a technical word and that the goods sold by a 'supermarket' might well change.

8.2.6 ANCILLARY USE OF PART OF THE PREMISES

A further cause of litigation has arisen where the tenant has used some part of the premises let for an ancillary use not specifically covered by the user covenant. What proportion of the premises used, or the business carried on, may relate to a purpose ancillary to the main one without constituting a breach of the user covenant?

In *Calabar (Woolwich) Ltd* v *Tesco Stores Ltd* (1977) 245 EG 479, the use of premises was restricted to a supermarket and the sale of certain ancillary goods. The sale of freezers, which constituted 15 per cent of the business carried on, was held not to be sufficient to constitute a breach.

In *Montross Associated Investments SA* v *Moussaieff* [1990] 2 EGLR 61, the use of premises as offices in connection with the business of high-class retailers of jewellery was held to satisfy a user covenant in a lease to use premises for the retail sale of high-class jewellery.

8.2.7 COVENANTS TO KEEP A BUSINESS OPEN

A landlord with several units in a shopping centre will be anxious to maintain the shopping attractions of the whole centre, and to this end covenants have been included in the leases of this type of property to keep a business open and to trade during normal shopping hours. An example of such a covenant might be:

> **To keep each level of the demised premises having any frontage to a pedestrian mall open for trade to the general public during normal shop hours as defined in the lease and to trade actively and continuously throughout substantially the whole of the demised premises and not to permit the demised premises to remain vacant.**

The clause will usually allow for closed periods if the premises are damaged or altered, or where it would be contrary to any local by-law to open. Such covenants have caused problems for tenants where their business has not thrived, and the courts have had to consider to what extent they are enforceable.

It now seems to be established that the courts will not grant a landlord an order for specific performance of any such covenant (*F.W. Woolworth plc* v *Charlwood Alliance Properties Ltd* [1987] 1 EGLR 53). Indeed, if the tenant's business were failing, any such order would be in vain. The courts have, however, been prepared to award damages for breach of such a covenant (*Transworld Land Co. Ltd* v *J. Sainsbury plc* [1990] 2 EGLR 255).

8.3 Covenants in a Lease, Other than User Covenants, which May Affect User of the Premises

In addition to user covenants, a lease may include other covenants which affect the use of the premises. Examples of these would be a covenant:

(a) not to cause a nuisance or annoyance to the landlord or to the owners or occupiers of neighbouring premises; or
(b) not to carry on a noxious or offensive trade; or
(c) not to use the premises for illegal or immoral purposes.

All three of these requirements may form the subject-matter of a separate covenant, or may be found included in one covenant as follows:

> **Not to use or permit or suffer the use of the demised premises or any part thereof for any dangerous, offensive, noxious, noisome, illegal or immoral activity or in any manner that may become a nuisance or annoyance to the landlord or to the owner or occupier of any neighbouring premises.**

A very usual covenant as to user is one by the tenant not to use the premises in such a way as to vitiate, or increase the premiums on, any insurance policy. Such a covenant might be:

> **Not to do or permit to be done anything that will or may render void or voidable any policy of insurance covering the demised premises [or any neighbouring premises] or increase the premium payable thereon.**

8.3.1 COVENANTS AGAINST NUISANCE OR ANNOYANCE

The landlord may be sued by nearby owners or occupiers for any acts of the tenant's which amount to a nuisance. It is desirable, therefore, to safeguard the landlord's position by including in the lease a covenant by the tenant not to cause a nuisance or annoyance to the landlord or to any neighbouring owners or occupiers. The wording of such covenants may differ quite widely. For example, the tenant may additionally covenant not to cause grievance or inconvenience, and the covenant may extend expressly to noise.

It is doubtful whether 'nuisance' should be restricted to a tortious act; but, in any event, the word 'annoyance' has been held to be wider than 'nuisance'. In *Tod-Heatly* v *Benham* (1888) 40 Ch D 80, it was held that a hospital for ear, nose and throat, skin and eye infections was likely to cause a reasonable apprehension of the risk of infection, and was therefore an infringement of a covenant against causing an annoyance or grievance to neighbours without any proof of damage. From a landlord's point of view, therefore, the covenant should be worded as widely as possible.

8.3.2 COVENANTS AGAINST NOXIOUS TRADES

The actual wording of covenants against noxious trades may vary and may also specify, for example, 'noisome' or 'dangerous' trades. Covenants in some older leases often add a list of prohibited trades to the end of a general covenant. Each covenant will, of course, fall to be interpreted according to its exact wording.

It is possible that a trade which is not in itself offensive may nevertheless be so in a residential locality. Thus in *Duke of Devonshire* v *Brookshaw* (1899) 81 LT 83, a fried fish shop emitting smells was held to be a breach of a covenant against carrying on an offensive trade.

Statutes may define certain trades as being offensive or dangerous. For example, certain offensive trades were listed in the Public Health Act 1936. The statutory definition will not be binding upon the court, but is likely to have some persuasive value.

8.3.3 COVENANTS AGAINST IMMORAL OR ILLEGAL USER

Such covenants may be of assistance to a landlord where shop premises are used to sell pornographic films or literature, or club premises for prostitution or illegal gambling. In such cases, the continuing 'stigma' attaching to premises may be grounds for refusing an application by a tenant for relief against forfeiture (*British Petroleum Pension Trust Ltd* v *Behrendt* (1986) 52 P & CR 117). If, however, the immoral user is by a subtenant without the tenant's knowledge, and the tenant takes steps to stop it on becoming aware of it, then relief is likely to be granted (*Glass* v *Kencakes Ltd* [1966] 1 QB 611).

8.4 The Effect of User Covenants on Other Provisions in the Lease

When drafting a user covenant, it is important to consider its effect on the operation of other provisions in the lease, and in particular on covenants against assignment and underletting and on rent review. The landlord may have to weigh the increased control which could be obtained from a strict user covenant, possibly preserving the value of the reversion, against the depressing effect which such a covenant might have on rent review. Similarly, any benefit to the tenant of a wider user covenant may be offset by a possible increase in rent on review.

It is proposed to consider the possible effects in the light of the cases on the subject.

8.4.1 EFFECT OF USER COVENANTS AGAINST ASSIGNMENT OR UNDERLETTING

A qualified covenant against assignment or underletting (which in practice will usually also be against 'parting with possession of the whole or any part of the demised premises' and will therefore include a licence) is governed by the Landlord and Tenant Act 1927, s. 19(1). This implies into the covenant that the landlord's consent may not be unreasonably withheld. This section was given more muscle to coerce reluctant landlords by the Landlord and Tenant Act 1988, which requires the landlord to give, within a reasonable time, written reasons for any refusal of consent, and exposes the landlord to the risk of an action in tort for failure to do so.

As has already been mentioned, s. 19(1) does not apply to user covenants, so that the only cases where there will be grounds to consider reasonableness of a refusal to grant consent to a change of user will be where the user covenant is fully qualified — that is, where it is expressly stated in the lease that the landlord's consent to a change of user will not be unreasonably refused.

A covenant against assignment or underletting is taken to protect the landlord from having either an undesirable tenant or an undesirable user of the premises. It is inevitable, therefore, that the courts have also had to consider user clauses in cases dealing with an unreasonable refusal of consent to assign.

Where a proposed assignment will necessarily involve breach of a user covenant, it will be reasonable for the landlord to refuse consent (*Wilson* v *Fynn* [1948] 2 All ER 40). Where, however, the proposed assignment may or may not result in a breach of the user covenant, refusal to consent will be unreasonable, as it was said in *Killick* v *Second Covent Garden Property Co. Ltd* [1973] 1 WLR 658 that the landlord would still have a remedy against an assignee for a breach of the user covenant, if it occurred.

The narrower the user clause, the more difficult the tenant may find it to assign or sublet. At the extreme end of the spectrum, a covenant restricting user of the premises to the tenant's business only makes the lease virtually unassignable (*Granada TV Network Ltd* v *Great Universal Stores Ltd*

(1963) 187 EG 391). Even where there is a very narrow user clause restricting user to a few specified purposes, it may still be reasonable for the landlord on grounds of user, to refuse consent to assign to an assignee who proposes to comply with the user covenant (*Bates* v *Donaldson* [1896] 2 QB 241).

In *International Drilling Fluids Ltd* v *Louisville Investments (Uxbridge) Ltd* [1986] Ch 513, Balcombe LJ formulated certain propositions from the cases on refusal of consent to assign (see **5.8.1.4**). He came to the conclusion that the general principle — that a landlord need consider only his own interests in deciding whether or not to grant consent — should be qualified to require also a consideration of the tenant's interests where the detriment to the tenant of a refusal far outweighs the benefit to the landlord. In that case, the tenant had vacated the premises and, after a year of marketing the property, had found only one interested assignee. The permitted user of the premises was for offices with ancillary showrooms, and the proposed assignee wanted to use the premises for serviced office accommodation. Although this was within the user clause, evidence was given that it could adversely affect the value of the landlord's reversion. There was no evidence, however, that the landlord intended to sell or mortgage the reversion, and the landlord was fully covered for rent by a covenant from the assigning tenant, which was financially sound. Although a refusal of consent might have been reasonable on the ground of some slight benefit to the landlord, this was outweighed by the hardship to the tenant, which was paying rent on vacant premises for which it was difficult to find an assignee. Balcombe LJ therefore concluded: 'it is not reasonable for the landlord to refuse consent to an assignment on the grounds of the proposed user (being within the only specific type of use), where the result will be that the property is left vacant and where (as here) the landlord is fully secured for payment of the rent'.

In the *International Drilling Fluids* case, the Court of Appeal considered *Premier Confectionery (London) Co. Ltd* v *London Commercial Sale Rooms Ltd* [1933] Ch 904, a decision at first instance by which, therefore, it was not bound. In that case, a tenant of two separate leases, granted consecutively, of a shop and an adjoining kiosk, sought consent to assign the leases separately. User of both was restricted to the sale of tobacco. Despite the very narrow user restriction which there was no question of the proposed assignee breaking, the landlord's refusal of consent to assign was held to be reasonable. Commenting in *International Drilling Fluids*, Balcombe LJ said that, insofar as this case might be authority for the proposition that it must always be reasonable for a landlord to refuse consent to assign for the purpose of a single permitted user, he would not be prepared to follow it. It is possible, however, to distinguish *Premier Confectionery*, as the landlord's concern there was that, if the leases were assigned separately, the two businesses would be in competition with each other, which could affect the tenant's ability to pay rent. It was therefore for the benefit of both the landlord and the tenant to refuse consent to assignment.

It has already been mentioned that a landlord cannot, by refusing consent to assign on grounds of user, seek to obtain an advantage not reserved in the original lease (*Anglia Building Society* v *Sheffield City Council* (1983) 266 EG 311).

8.4.2 EFFECTS OF A USER COVENANT ON RENT

A user covenant will be a relevant consideration when fixing a new rent under a rent review clause or on the granting of a new lease under the Landlord and Tenant Act 1954. It was held in *Plinth Property Investments Ltd* v *Mott, Hay and Anderson* (1978) 38 P & CR 361, that an arbitrator was right to take such a covenant into account, as the landlord could demand a considerable sum to waive it.

In *Bovis Group Pension Fund Ltd* v *G.C. Flooring and Furnishing Ltd* (1984) 269 EG 1252, the rent review clause directed the arbitrator to fix a rent on the basis of office user for which planning permission had not been obtained. It was held that this, rather than the actual user, was the user which the arbitrator should consider. Nor will an actual user which is in contravention of planning permission be taken into account: e.g. residential property being used partly for offices. In *C and A Pensions Trustees Ltd* v *British Vita Investments Ltd* (1984) 272 EG 63, the landlord sought to widen the user covenant by unilaterally authorising further uses of the premises. It was held that, for the purposes of rent review, this too should be disregarded.

It has been pointed out that a tenant with a qualified user covenant is in no better position as regards obtaining the landlord's consent to its relaxation than a tenant whose covenant is absolute. However, the fully qualified form of covenant (where the landlord's consent to change of user is not to be unreasonably withheld) should have a less depreciatory effect on rent.

In seeking to obtain the best of both worlds, landlords have tried to avoid the depressing effects on rent of strict user covenants by inserting a provision in the rent review clause that rent shall be assessed on the basis of some hypothetical user. The fact that planning permission has not been obtained for such hypothetical user will presumably not invalidate such a basis of review: *Bovis Group Pension Fund* v *G.C. Flooring and Furnishing Ltd* (1984) 269 EG 1252). However, from a landlord's point of view, the clause could be made more watertight by providing that the premises are assumed to be suitable for the hypothetical use and that the use is assumed to be lawful. It will be recalled that *Hill* v *Harris* [1965] 2 QB 601 (**8.1.4**) decided that there was no such assumption of lawful use with regard to a tenant's actual proposed use. It is, of course, quite conceivable that a tenant would argue strongly about the inclusion of such provisions.

A landlord should, nevertheless, be wary of extracting from a tenant covenants which are extreme. A hypothetical use which is too far removed from the real lease runs the risk of being totally disregarded. A variation from the hypothetical use which favoured the tenant occurred in *Basingstoke and Deane Borough Council* v *Host Group Ltd* [1988] 1 WLR 348, where the rent review clause provided for a new rent to be fixed on the basis of an empty site, with user limited to that of a public house to be built by the original tenant. The Court of Appeal ignored the hypothetical user and decided that the tenant should pay for the public house which it had. Similarly, a restriction to use by one tenant only (making the premises unassignable) may be opened up on rent review to include all user of the same type as the tenant's (*Law Land Co. Ltd* v *Consumers' Association Ltd* (1980) 255 EG 617). The curious result is that this form of extreme restriction may have a less depreciatory effect on rent than a restriction to certain specified trades or businesses! The courts have, however, been even-handed about this, and in *Jefferies* v *O'Neill* (1983) 46 P & CR 376, where the realities of the situation were that the demised premises could be used only by the particular tenants, it was held that rent review should be on the basis prescribed in the lease of 'a willing tenant'. The tenants in that case were a firm of solicitors who had taken a lease of adjoining premises at first-floor level, and had extended their offices by breaking through from their own existing offices. The sole access was from their offices, and they were, therefore, the only possible tenants.

In *S.I. Pension Trustees Ltd* v *Ministerio de Marina de la República Peruana* [1988] 1 EGLR 119, the user covenant which was to be taken into account on the hypothetical letting, for the purposes of rent review, covered office use for mortgage finance and insurance consultancy. The licence to assign to a diplomatic mission restricted use to this. It was held, however, that the reference in the rent review clause to the provisions of the lease meant the original provisions as to user and not the more restricted variation in the licence to assign.

NINE

RENT AND RENT REVIEW

9.1 Introduction

9.1.1 THE NATURE OF RENT

Rent was at one time an incident of tenure and represented consideration for the leasehold estate in the land. For this reason, rent was originally known as rent service. In recent years, however, there has been an increasing tendency to emphasise the contractual nature of a lease, rather than the estate which the contract creates. The payment of rent is an important part of that contract.

Nevertheless, the notion that the rent is payable for an estate in the land is still to be found in certain areas of the law relating to leases, and it is for this reason, for instance, that a tenant is still liable for rent even if the premises on the land are destroyed. The lease should therefore contain a provision that rent will be suspended (wholly or partially) for any time during which the premises are unusable as a result of damage, and the landlord may want to include loss of rent as one of the insurable risks. A clause providing for the suspension of rent is as follows:

> **Provided that if the demised premises or any part thereof shall be destroyed or damaged by fire or any other risk for which the landlord has insured so as to be unfit for occupation and use then the rents hereby reserved or a fair proportion thereof according to the nature and extent of the destruction or damage shall be suspended until the demised premises or the destroyed or damaged portion shall be rendered fit for occupation and use.**

A clause providing for insurance covering three years' loss of rent is included in **11.2.1**.

It is only fairly recently that the House of Lords accepted in *National Carriers Ltd* v *Panalpina (Northern) Ltd* [1981] AC 675 that the doctrine of frustration, which applies to terminate a contract, might also apply to terminate a lease: see **12.7**).

9.1.2 CERTAINTY AS TO RENT

9.1.2.1 Rent in money, services, or kind

Although rent is almost invariably a money payment nowadays, it may be in kind, and the most common example of rent in kind is a service tenancy (see **1.1.5**). Whatever form the rent takes, however, it must be certain or capable of being rendered certain, even if it is work (*Barnes* v *Barratt* [1970] 2 QB 657).

9.1.2.2 Formula for determining rent

A formula for arriving at a figure for rent is sufficiently certain, even if there is no actual machinery for determining it, as it was held by Megarry J that the court then has jurisdiction to determine it (*Brown* v *Gould* [1972] Ch 53). For example, it may be agreed that rent shall be fixed by a third party, a means of fixing rent which is frequently adopted if the parties fail to agree on a rent review.

In the absence of such a formula, and on a failure of the parties to agree, it is possible that the lease will be void for uncertainty. Thus in *King's Motors (Oxford) Ltd* v *Lax* [1970] 1 WLR 426, the lease contained an option to renew at a rent to be agreed between the parties, but with no indication as to the criteria. The option was held to be void.

If there is an existing lease, however, it will be more difficult to find that it is void for uncertainty on this ground. In *Beer* v *Bowden* [1981] 1 WLR 522 there was a complete hiatus as to rent on an extended lease when the parties failed to agree. The tenant had, however, remained in possession for some two years. The judge took a robust approach, deriving some support from a provision that the tenant's improvements should not be taken into account in deciding a new rent. He held that it must have been intended that the tenant should pay some rent, and ordered that the rent be fixed by the master after hearing expert evidence.

9.1.3 TERMINOLOGY RELATING TO DIFFERENT RENTS

Rent service: The correct name for rent payable to the landlord under a lease is rent service. It can be distinguished from a rentcharge, this being a rent issuing out of and payable on freehold land.

Different terms are used to distinguish different types of rent.

Rack rent: a rent of the full annual value of the property. If the rent is fixed during a period of rent restriction, it will be the highest rent that it is possible to reserve at that time and not the full market rent (*Newman* v *Dorrington Developments Ltd* [1975] 1 WLR 1642)

Ground rent: a small annual rent which arises where the landlord has in effect capitalised part of the rack rent otherwise obtainable by taking a premium (i.e. a capital sum) when the lease is granted. A ground rent is therefore less than the rack rent.

Best rent: the highest rent which can reasonably be expected to be obtained for the premises.

Peppercorn rent: a nominal rent which it was often considered wise to reserve to ensure that the transaction was a lease.

Dead rent: the basic minimum rent payable on a mining lease, whether the mine is worked or not. There will usually be an additional rent fluctuating according to the amount of mineral mined.

9.1.4 FLUCTUATING RENTS

Sometimes rent will be fixed by reference to other fluctuating factors. It is common practice in mining leases for rent to vary according to the amount of mineral mined.

9.1.4.1 Turnover rents

Turnover rents are rents based on a proportion (usually a percentage) of the trade turnover for a business. The basis for calculation of the proportion must be carefully stated in the lease, although there should be provision for varying this if there is a material change of use, as the calculation suitable for a low-turnover/high-profit business may be very different from that suitable for a high-turnover/low-profit business.

A tenant should ensure that any turnover elements in the rent are linked to net turnover and not gross turnover. This is to avoid the type of problem which arose in *Tucker* v *Granada Motorway Services Ltd* [1979] 1 WLR 683, where an increased tax on tobacco showed an increased gross turnover on sales but did not affect net turnover.

There should also be a provision for production of accounts and a certificate of turnover.

Such a lease may provide for a minimum rent, being a proportion of the open market rent, to be payable in any event, and the landlord may wish to include a provision that the open market rent shall be payable if the tenant ceases trading.

The following clause is a rudimentary example of a reservation of a basic rent and additionally a turnover rent, being a percentage of net profits over a certain figure (although the full clause would contain definitions of turnover and provision for certification by an accountant):

> **YIELDING AND PAYING therefor by equal quarterly payments in advance a basic rent of [sum] per annum and in addition [x per cent] of the net turnover for the year preceding the rental year exceeding [£x,000].**

9.1.4.2 Rents variable with rents from subleases (geared rents)

Another form of fluctuating rent is a rent to be fixed by reference to rent received on subleases. This type of rent is sometimes used in building leases where the lessee will be unable to afford much rent initially, but will eventually benefit when there is an income from the property. In such an arrangement, it is important to synchronise the rent review in the head lease with rent reviews in the subleases. If the rent review dates for the subleases vary, it may be preferable to provide that the rent on the head lease shall be a percentage of the rent on the subleases as they vary from time to time. This is fully dealt with in **5.9.2.4** and a precedent given for synchronisation of rent reviews.

9.2 The Reservation of Rent

9.2.1 EXPRESS RESERVATION

Rent must be reserved in the lease expressly. A reservation of rent will not be implied, although it may be possible to seek rectification of a lease if it is clear that there was an enforceable agreement to include a rent reservation which has been omitted from the lease itself. In addition to the reservation of rent, the landlord should take a covenant from the tenant to pay the rent. There is then privity of contract between the original landlord and the original tenant, and the landlord may therefore sue the tenant on any such covenant throughout the duration of the term (see **6.1.1**).

The definition of a 'term of years' in the Law of Property Act 1925, s. 205(1), specifically states 'whether or not at a rent' and in *Ashburn Anstalt* v *Arnold* [1989] Ch 1, the Court of Appeal confirmed that rent is not essential for a lease. In practice, there will be very few leases which do not reserve a rent, and any such arrangement is more likely to indicate a licence (see **1.1.4**).

9.2.2 WHEN PAYABLE

Rent will be payable in arrear unless the lease specifically states that it shall be payable in advance. Most leases do provide for rent to be payable in advance on the usual quarter days (25 March, 24 June, 29 September and 25 December).

9.2.3 DEDUCTIONS

The tenant's covenant to pay rent usually provides that the rent reserved will be paid '**without any deductions**', so that the rent reserved is a net rent.

Even where the lease contains such a proviso, however, the tenant may make certain deductions authorised by statute. Such deductions include:

(a) landlord's tax recovered from the tenant;
(b) rent paid by a subtenant directly to the landlord to avoid distress on the tenant's default;
(c) charges on the premises payable by the landlord;
(d) compensation for improvements due from the landlord under the Landlord and Tenant Act 1927; and
(e) the cost of repairs on which the landlord has defaulted and which the tenant has carried out (see **10.3.3**).

9.2.3.1 Excluding tenant's right to set-off

A covenant by the tenant to pay rent 'without any deductions' will not be sufficient to exclude the tenant's equitable right to set off damages for breach of the landlord's repairing covenant. Thus in *Connaught Restaurants Ltd* v *Indoor Leisure Ltd* [1993] 46 EG 184, where the tenant's covenant was **'to pay the rents at the times and in manner aforesaid without any deductions . . . and if so required by banker's standing order'**, Waite LJ said:

> The term 'deduction' is one of those words for which the convenience of flexibility has been achieved at the price of some inherent ambiguity. Draftsmen who are concerned to exclude the tenant's equitable right of set-off would therefore be well advised to do so explicitly.

It was held in *Electricity Supply Nominees Ltd* v *IAF Group plc* [1993] 1 WLR 1059 that an exclusion of the right to set off such damages against rent did not fall within the Unfair Contract Terms Act 1977. The reason is that rent is an integral part of the creation of a lease, which is an interest in land, and the Act does not apply to 'any contract so far as it relates to the creation or transfer of an interest in land or to the termination of such an interest' (Unfair Contract Terms Act 1977, sch. 1, para. 1(b)). The relevant wording in the *Electricity Supply Nominees Ltd* case was more specific than that in *Connaught Restaurants Ltd* v *Indoor Leisure Ltd*, as the tenant covenanted: **'to pay rent and all other sums payable under this lease at the time and in the manner hereinbefore provided without any deductions or set-off whatsoever'**. This was held to cover the equitable right to set off damages for a landlord's breach of repairing covenant, so that the tenant was not entitled to deduct these damages from the rent.

9.2.4 APPORTIONMENT

Rent is apportionable, and should therefore be apportioned at the commencement and termination of the tenancy. To avoid any dispute, the lease should expressly provide (and most leases do) for a proportion of the rent to be payable as from the date of the lease, or the date when the tenant takes occupation of the premises. This would be effected by the following clause:

> **YIELDING AND PAYING therefor the rent of [£X,000] or such other rent as may from time to time be agreed or determined, payable by equal quarterly instalments in advance on the usual quarter days the first of such payments or a proportionate part thereof to be made on the date hereof and the last payment being (if appropriate) of a proportionate sum.**

9.2.5 OTHER MONETARY PAYMENTS

It is also usual for the lease to provide that any premiums for insurance payable by the tenant, or any service charge, shall be paid as rent, and therefore recoverable as rent (see **11.1.4**) and these too should be apportioned. A clause providing for this would follow the rent clause and might read as follows:

AND ALSO YIELDING AND PAYING as additional rent (i) a fair proportion of the amount paid by the landlord for insuring the building and the loss of rent and other risks hereunder in accordance with the landlord's covenant and (ii) the service charge payable hereunder.

9.3 The Payment of Rent

Rent may be tendered in the same way as any other debt, but in practice the parties will usually agree to payment by another method, such as by cheque or by standing order (see clause in **9.2.3.1**). Even then, rent paid by cheque is not regarded as paid until the cheque is cleared (*Official Solicitor* v *Thomas* [1986] 2 EGLR 1 where it was said that tender does not discharge a debt and it was open to the landlord to refuse to cash a cheque, even though the parties had agreed that this was the way in which rent should be paid). In *Stoneman* v *Brown* [1973] 1 WLR 459, however, Lord Denning MR was prepared to regard payment as made when the letter containing the cheque was posted.

Rent is payable to the landlord or the landlord's agent and any service charge should be made similarly payable if it is to be paid as rent.

9.4 Rent Review

9.4.1 INTRODUCTION

Until fairly recently, rising property values and inflation have meant that a landlord who wanted the investment advantage of a fairly long term had to include in the lease a rent review clause in order to maintain the real value of the rent received. During the 1980s leases would often provide for a rent review every three years, and three or five-yearly reviews are now quite common, although older leases may have seven-yearly reviews.

9.4.1.1 Upwards and downwards review

Many rent review clauses provide for an upwards only review. In *Boots the Chemists Ltd* v *Pinkland Ltd* [1992] 2 EGLR 98, however, the judge refused to make a rent review clause in a new lease under the Landlord and Tenant Act 1954 an upwards only review clause. He took account of the fact that rents obtainable have fallen more recently, felt that the future was unpredictable, and held that the rent review clause in the new lease should be one allowing for adjustment of the rent either way. In *Blythewood Plant Hire Ltd* v *Spiers Ltd* [1992] 2 EGLR 103, however, an upwards only rent review clause was included in a new lease under the Landlord and Tenant Act 1954, as it was said that the landlord's interest would otherwise be adversely affected.

An example of an upwards only rent review clause would be one which provides for the rent on review to be:

a rent equal to the rent previously payable hereunder or such revised rent as may be determined as herein provided whichever is the greater.

The Joint Committee of the Law Society and the Royal Institution of Chartered Surveyors has produced model forms of rent review clauses which provide a choice of upwards and/or downwards review.

9.4.1.2 Drafting rent review clauses

Rent review clauses are a constant source of litigation between landlord and tenant, and should therefore be drafted as carefully and precisely as possible. A rent review clause needs to provide for the following matters:

(a) the period of rent reviews;
(b) how the rent review procedure is to be commenced and its mechanism;
(c) the formula by which a new rent is to be fixed;
(d) a procedure for determining any dispute;
(e) an interim rent pending agreement on a new rent.

Each of these may be considered in turn.

9.4.2 THE PERIOD OF RENT REVIEWS

This will depend upon the rate of inflation when the lease is granted. Nowadays, five-year three-yearly rent reviews are usual.

If the lease bears a different date from the commencement of the term, then it may be preferab state specifically the date of the first rent review to avoid any ambiguity as to whether time is to from the date of the lease or the commencement of the term.

It could be dangerous to state specified dates for the rent review throughout the term of the le however, as it could result in any 'hypothetical' lease (see **9.4.4.3**), which was assumed to be a l for 25 years, say, from the review date, being a lease without any rent reviews for the last part o term. Thus a 20 lease granted in 1990, with review dates in 1995, 2000 and 2005, would have two review dates left in a hypothetical lease for the same term by 2000. It is probably prefer therefore to state the periods of review after the first review date, e.g. on the fifth and t anniversaries of the commencement of the term.

From a landlord's point of view, a rent review at the end of the term is desirable, as any new agreed will apply during an interim period before a new lease under the Landlord and Tenant 1954 takes effect and will save the landlord applying for an interim rent.

9.4.3 INITIATING REVIEW AND THE MECHANISM FOR DETERMINING A NEW RE

9.4.3.1 Initiating review

A lease will usually provide that a rent review procedure is to be started by the landlord giving no to the tenant of the review and might be expressed thus:

> **The landlord may call for a review of the rent payable hereunder from the end of review year by serving notice to that effect on the tenant not earlier than six mo prior to the review date**

Sometimes this will be a 'trigger' notice stating what the landlord proposes that the new rent be.

> **The open market rental value [to be ascertained by the rent review] shall be such an sum as shall be specified in writing signed by or on behalf of the lessor and poste recorded delivery to the tenant at the demised premises.**

Although it is usually in the landlord's interest to initiate the procedure, it may also be in the ten interest if an assignment is contemplated or some idea of future financial liabilities is required. tenant should therefore consider a provision which allows it to serve notice initiating the procec either as an alternative to the landlord's notice, or if the landlord fails to do so within a certain ti

9.4.3.2 Time not presumed to be of the essence

It used to be thought that time was of the essence for such a notice, but the House of Lords ca *United Scientific Holdings Ltd* v *Burnley Borough Council* [1978] AC 904 established that there presumption that time is not of the essence in such clauses, so that a failure to give notice wit specified time will not be fatal for the landlord. This presumption may be rebutted.

9.4.3.3 Making time of the essence

(a) *Counter-indication in review clause.*

First, the review clause may itself make time of the essence. This can be done expressly (see clause in **9.4.3.4**), and it may be either of general application or selective, i.e. applicable to only parts of the review procedure. Thus a rent review clause may provide that time shall be of the essence only as regards one particular step in the procedure, such as a tenant's counter-notice. A provision that the rent is to be conclusively presumed as stated in the landlord's notice unless the tenant serves a counter-notice within a certain time could have this effect (*Amalgamated Estates Ltd* v *Joystretch Manufacturing Ltd* (1980) 257 EG 489). This case also demonstrates clearly that the requirements for a counter-notice must be carefully complied with, and a letter merely inquiring as to the landlord's method of calculation of a proposed rent will not suffice as a counter-notice.

If it is intended that time is to be of the essence as regards one particular step only, this must be made clear. In the absence of a clear statement to this effect, time may, by association, become of the essence for other parts of the procedure too. Thus in *Art and Sound Ltd* v *West End Litho Ltd* [1992] 1 EGLR 138 a clear statement that time was to be of the essence with regard to an agreement between the parties was construed as applying also to an arbitrator's determination.

That time is to be of the essence may also be inferred. An inference to this effect may be made if the rent review clause sets out a very specific timetable stating the times within which each step should be taken, as in *Trustees of Henry Smith's Charity* v *AWADA Trading and Promotion Services Ltd* (1983) 47 P & CR 607. Even a specific timetable, however, may be held to be merely prescriptive and not mandatory, and so may fail to make time of the essence. If a particular consequence is stated to occur in the event of failure to act within a given time-limit, this is an indication that the wording was intended to be mandatory rather than prescriptive. Such a consequence might, for instance, be a deeming provision as to rent. Even such a default clause must, however, be read in the light of all the terms of the lease: see dicta of Millett J in *Power Securities (Manchester) Ltd* v *Prudential Assurance Co. Ltd* [1987] 1 EGLR 121.

In *Mecca Leisure Ltd* v *Renown Investments (Holdings) Ltd* (1984) 271 EG 989 a similar procedure to that in *Henry Smith's Charity* was set out, but Eveleigh LJ said in that case that each rent review clause should be construed on its own merits and that 'deeming' provisions as to time in other cases are therefore not likely to assist in construing such clauses in other leases. It is obvious from this that even a very slight variation in wording may result in a different construction of such clauses, and if it is intended that time should be of the essence, then it is desirable to state this unequivocally.

(b) *Tenant's break clause linked to review.*

Secondly, there will be a presumption that time is of the essence if the tenant has a right to terminate the lease under a break clause which is linked to the rent review (*Coventry City Council* v *J. Hepworth and Son Ltd* (1982) 46 P & CR 170). The presumption here is that the tenant should be able to exercise the break clause in the light of the new rent, so that a limit specified for operation of the break clause may also imply a time limit for the rent review procedure. Care should therefore be taken in drafting any break clause procedure to ensure that it does not have the inadvertent effect of making time of the essence in a related rent review clause.

If, however, the rent review procedure is not entirely within the control of the landlord, as (for example) where there is provision for arbitration which could take longer then any specified time-limit, then there may not be a sufficient link between the two clauses to make time of the essence for the rent review (*Metrolands Investments Ltd* v *J.H. Dewhurst Ltd* (1984) 49 P & CR 334).

(c) *Service of notice*

Thirdly, it is always open to one party or the other to serve a notice making time of the essence. Any such notice should state very clearly that this is the party's intention, so that the notice will not merely be regarded as another stage in the procedure.

9.4.3.4 Where 'time of essence' provision cannot be relied on

(a) *Waiver.*

Any provision which does make time of the essence may not be readily waived and will not be treat as having been abandoned without very clear evidence of this (*Patel* v *Peel Investments (South) L* [1992] 2 EGLR 116). In that case there was provision for the tenant to elect for arbitration:

> **by notice in writing to the lessor not later than three months after the lesso notification [of the new rent] in writing (time in this respect to be of the essence hereo**

The landlord inadvertently served two notices and there was correspondence for over a year, bu was held not to amount to a waiver of the time-limit for the tenant's notice.

(b) *Undue hardship on tenant: Arbitration Act 1950, s. 27.*

The court has power to dispense with strict time-limits under the Arbitration Act 1950, s. 27 there would otherwise be 'undue hardship'. In *Patel* v *Peel Investments (South) Ltd* [1992] 2 EG 116, the tenant was out of time and bound to pay a rent 30 per cent above the market rent wh had been specified in the landlord's notice. The hardship which this would cause the tenant such that the tenant's application for arbitration was allowed under s. 27. It was said in the c that the expression 'undue hardship', which is required to invoke the section, should not construed narrowly, particularly if the amount of hardship on the party seeking to invoke it is q out of proportion to that party's degree of fault.

The jurisdiction under s. 27 applies, however, only where there is an arbitration clause, and wh the failure to observe the time-limit was in the appointment of the arbitrator or in 'some other s to commence arbitration proceedings'. In *Richurst Ltd* v *Pimenta* [1993] 1 WLR 159, it was h that this did not cover the landlord's initial notice of rent review, at which time there was no ques of any dispute referable to arbitration. Although the landlord was found to be deserving of re and his notice was only three weeks outside the time-limit, the court felt that it could not inv the section to refer the review to arbitration. Conversely, in *Pittalis* v *Sherefettin* [1986] QB 868, Court of Appeal held that a tenant's counter-notice was within s. 27 being 'effectively the first s in the arbitration proceedings'.

9.4.4 THE FORMULA BY WHICH A NEW RENT IS TO BE FIXED

It is important that the method for the calculation of the new rent should be stated as precise possible, making it clear what matters are to be taken into consideration and what are to be ign in arriving at a figure.

The usual figure which the parties are setting out to ascertain is the rent which the premise likely to command in an open market at the review date. This will usually be expressed in a cl such as:

> **The market rent of the demised premises means the best yearly rent at which demised premises might reasonably be expected to be let in the open market by a wi landlord to a willing tenant at the relevant review date with vacant possession for a t of years equal to the residue of that hereby granted on a lease containing the same te and conditions (save as to the amount of rent) as are contained herein.**

9.4.4.1 A market rent: 'open market rent'

The rent itself may be expressed to be an 'open market rent' or a 'full market rent', and the c have indicated that whichever expression is used will make little difference to the actual marke obtainable. This is the rent which a willing tenant would be expected to pay to a willing landlord for the property on the open market.

A tenant should perhaps be wary of the 'best' market rent, which could conceivably include a rent obtainable from some particular tenant due to peculiar circumstances, although in practice most rent review clauses do refer to the 'best' rent.

Also, subject to contra-indications, a 'reasonable' rent will be ascertained by *objective* standards and may take account of circumstances which are not at all reasonable to consider as between the parties. Thus in *Ponsford* v *HMS Aerosols Ltd* [1979] AC 63 the House of Lords found that it was 'reasonable' to take into account improvements to the premises, even though these had been paid for by the tenant. The result was that the tenant was effectively paying for them twice over. In order to avoid such an unfair result, the rent should have been expressed to be **'reasonable as between the parties'**, or **'in all the circumstances'**.

9.4.4.2 The hypothetical tenant: 'a willing tenant'

The rent review clause will generally provide for the rent to be assessed as the rent which some willing hypothetical tenant would pay for the property on the open market. The tenant is not, however, to be assumed to be among the hypothetical bidders (*F.R. Evans (Leeds) Ltd* v *English Electric Co. Ltd* (1977) 36 P & CR 185). Thus the reality that tenants in a particular trade, for instance, are experiencing financial difficulties is irrelevant. Nor will a direction that the property is assumed to be let with vacant possession mean that the *actual* tenant is to be included as a bidder for the premises.

9.4.4.3 The hypothetical lease: 'on a lease containing the same terms and conditions'

The problems associated with the valuation of premises for rent review have mainly arisen on the terms of the hypothetical lease under which the willing tenant will hold. Obviously the terms of the hypothetical lease are of prime importance as regards its value.

(a) *Presumption of realism.*

Landlords have shown considerable ingenuity in the invention of terms for hypothetical lettings, which may vary quite substantially from the terms of the real letting. The courts have frequently shown a dislike for pure fantasy, however, and the general tendency is to adopt a realistic approach wherever possible, on the ground that this is more likely to give business efficacy to any agreement. In *Basingstoke and Deane Borough Council* v *Host Group Ltd* [1988] 1 WLR 348 Nicholls LJ said

> . . . the parties are to be taken as having intended that the notional letting postulated by their rent review clause is to be a letting on the same terms (other than as to quantum of rent) as those still subsisting between the parties in the actual existing lease.

The lease in that case provided for rent review, in certain circumstances, on the basis of a vacant site, whereas in fact the lease was of a public house erected on the site by the tenant. The Court of Appeal held that the notional letting should be one with the same user as the actual letting.

If the hypothetical lease is on the basis of assumptions about user which are not entirely fictional and removed from reality, however, then the hypothetical lease may be taken as being a lease with the hypothetical user. In *Sheerness Steel Co. plc* v *Medway Ports Authority* [1992] 1 EGLR 133 rent review was to be on the basis that the premises were let for industrial purposes whereas in fact the sole industrial use for which they were suitable was steel rolling. It was held that for the purposes of rent review the hypothetical lease should assume user for *any* industrial purposes. Similarly, where the hypothetical lease required an assumption of user for retail purposes generally, this was held to prevail over the user clause in the actual lease which limited shop premises to the sale of high class china (*Postal Properties Ltd* v *Greenwell* [1992] 2 EGLR 130).

In *Laura Investment Co. Ltd* v *Havering London Borough Council (No. 2)* [1993] 1 EGLR 124 t lessee of five acres of undeveloped land was required to underlet various plots with the lesso consent. Hoffmann J, having decided at a previous hearing ([1992] 1 EGLR 155) that rent revie was to be on the basis that buildings erected on the land were to be included in the hypothetic lease as there was no requirement to disregard improvements, then decided that the rent revie should take into account the underleases which the tenant had granted. The tenant was obliged underlet the various plots and the landlord, whose consent to underletting was required, coul ensure that the underlettings were at market rents and not at premiums. This decision wa consistent with that of Peter Gibson J in *Forte and Co. Ltd* v *General Accident Life Assurance L* [1986] 2 EGLR 115 who decided that a rent review should not be on the basis of vacant possessio but should take into account a sublease of part of the premises, made before the review and whic would continue for some time after it.

In *Law Land Co. Ltd* v *Consumers' Association Ltd* (1980) 255 EG 617 the terms of the leas restricted user to that of the tenant's undertaking but directed rent review to be on an open mark basis. The Court of Appeal held that the only feasible basis for a hypothetical tenant was to assum a lease which did not restrict the user of the premises at all. In *Plinth Property Investments Ltd* v *Mot Hay and Anderson* (1978) 38 P & CR 361 it was held that a restriction in the lease to use the premise as offices in connection with the tenant's business of consulting engineers could be taken int account. The curious paradox of these two cases is therefore that a virtually total restriction on use may have to be completely disregarded for the purposes of a hypothetical lease and so have a les depreciating effect on rent review than a more moderate one.

(b) *Length of hypothetical term: 'for a term of years equal to the residue of the term hereby granted'.*

Another matter which requires consideration is the length of the hypothetical term which is to b applied for the purposes of rent review. If the hypothetical lease is to be for the unexpired remainde of the *actual* term, this could depress the rent towards the end. Conversely, if it is to be taken as th full term of the lease at every rent review, this could inflate the rent.

Given ambiguity of meaning, it would seem from *Lynnthorpe Enterprises Ltd* v *Sidney Smith (Chelsea) Ltd* [1990] 2 EGLR 131 that the court will again construe the hypothetical lease as closely a possible to the actual lease. In that case, a hypothetical tenancy for 'a term of years equivalent t the said term' was held to be one which commenced at the time of the actual lease and wa commensurate with it, and not one which commenced at the date of the rent review.

Stephen Tromans has suggested that a compromise on the length of the hypothetical term migh be the remainder of the actual term with a minimum of 10 years (Tromans, *Commercial Lease* (London: Sweet & Maxwell, 1987), p. 53).

(c) *Assumptions and disregards.*

All rent review clauses are likely to include certain matters to be assumed as between the landlord and the tenant, and others which are to be disregarded, in arriving at the market rent. The possible effect of these on the particular property should be carefully considered from the point of view of both landlord and tenant.

(i) Disregard of rent: '**save as to the amount of rent**'.

Sometimes a rent review clause will provide for a new rent to be fixed having regard to all the terms of the letting '**other than as to rent**'. Taken literally, such a clause could mean that the hypothetical lease had no provisions for rent at all, and that even a forfeiture clause for non-payment of rent did not exist. Such a construction is obviously absurd and the phrase requires further definition, such as 'other than as to rent currently payable'.

If such wording is to be regarded as excluding all future rent reviews, then the landlord will clearly be entitled to a much larger rent than if it is merely the rent for the next three or five years which is being determined. In *British Gas Corporation* v *Universities Superannuation Scheme Ltd* [1986] 1

WLR 398 Browne-Wilkinson V-C indicated that business efficacy should generally require such words not to exclude future rent reviews, although he conceded that certain clear words requiring future rent reviews to be disregarded, as distinct from a disregard of all provisions as to rent, might still have to be construed in this way. The later case of *Equity and Law Life Assurance Society plc* v *Bodfield Ltd* [1987] 1 EGLR 124 was a case where the Court of Appeal agreed with the construction to give commercial meaning to the clause, while adding that an express exclusion of such a construction would nevertheless have to be interpreted as drawn.

(ii) Assumption of vacant possession and letting as a whole: **'disregarding any effect on rent of the fact that the tenant has been in occupation of the demised premises'**.

An assumption of vacant possession, and that the property is to be let as a whole, could adversely affect the landlord of a large office block, which might only be readily occupied in smaller units. It might well be to the landlord's advantage to take into account existing subleases on a rent review of this type of property. On the other hand, an assumption of vacant possession of a smaller single unit would be reasonable. 'Vacant possession' implies that the tenant's fixtures are to be excluded, which is fair to the tenant, but it may also imply a free fitting-out period, as it was held to do in *99 Bishopsgate Ltd* v *Prudential Assurance Co. Ltd* [1985] 1 EGLR 72. Any such assumption of vacant possession should therefore expressly exclude this possibility.

If the premises, or part of them, are sublet, or the tenant is under an obligation to sublet, then the court may deem it inappropriate to assume vacant possession (see *Laura Investment Co. Ltd* v *Havering London Borough Council (No. 2)* [1993] 1 EGLR 124 and *Forte and Co. Ltd* v *General Accident Life Assurance Ltd* [1986] 2 EGLR 115).

(iii) Disregard of rent-free periods: **'disregarding any rent-free period or concession or inducement which would or might be given to an incoming tenant on the grant of a new lease of the demised premises'**.

In *City Offices plc* v *Bryanston Insurance Co. Ltd* [1993] 1 EGLR 126 the rent review clause provided for the market rent to be ascertained by reference to a hypothetical lease which assumed that the premises were suitable for immediate occupation but disregarded any rent-free periods which the hypothetical landlord might offer to the hypothetical tenant. It was held that this should be construed as meaning that the rent should be payable immediately from the rent review date and that there should be no such period in the hypothetical lease which would inflate the rent for the remainder of the rent review period, thereby giving the landlord a higher than market rent.

(iv) Assumption that planning consent obtained: **'upon the assumption that the demised premises may be lawfully used as [hypothetical use for which planning consent is assumed to have been obtained]'**.

A direction that rent is to be determined on the assumption that a particular planning use has been obtained for the property, which has not in fact been obtained, will require a rent to be ascertained on that basis rather than on the basis of the actual user (*Bovis Group Pension Fund Ltd* v *G.C. Flooring and Furnishing Ltd* (1984) 269 EG 1252). Such an assumption must not, however, require any feat of imagination as regards the physical layout of the premises, however unsuitable it is for the supposed use (*Orchid Lodge (UK) Ltd* v *Extel Computing Ltd* [1991] 2 EGLR 1162).

(v) Assumption of tenant's compliance with covenants in the lease: **'disregarding any failure by the tenant to comply fully with the obligations on its part herein contained'**.

A common assumption in rent review clauses is that the tenant has complied with the covenants in the lease. This is desirable as regards repairing covenants, as otherwise the tenant will obtain an advantage on rent review from breach of any repairing covenants. Any assumption that the premises are reinstated if damaged or destroyed should, however, be carefully considered in conjunction with clauses for reinstatement and suspension of rent. If the tenant is to accept such an assumption, it is desirable that the landlord should not have sole control over the reinstatement.

(vi) Disregard of tenant's improvements: '**disregarding any effect on rent of an**y **improvement carried out by the tenant otherwise than in pursuance of an obligation t**o **the landlord**'.

Although the assumption of repairs will be made to deny the tenant the advantage of a reduced ren for disrepair, the rent review procedure will usually require a disregard of any improvements mad by the tenant. This is to avoid the tenant effectively paying twice over for these — initially for th improvements themselves, and subsequently in an increased rent which the premises the command.

The tenant should ensure that the disregard covers not only improvements made by him, but als by the tenant's predecessors in title and persons deriving title under him, such as subtenants, t whom the tenant may in fact have given consideration for the improvements.

The tenant should also ensure that the disregard extends to improvements made by him or predecessor in title when in occupation of the premises under a previous lease or licence. In *Brett Brett Essex Golf Club Ltd* [1986] 1 EGLR 154 the tenant had constructed a six-hole golf-course c adjoining land which was not at the time part of the demised premises, but subsequently becam part. The rent review clause adopted the disregard of improvements under the Landlord and Tena Act 1954, s. 34, and it was held that the improvements to the nearby land which was not part of th demised premises at the time could not be disregarded.

It is usual for the landlord to limit the disregard of improvements to those made with the landlord prior consent. The purpose of such a provision (which is included in the model clause of the Joi Committee) is to avoid future disputes as to what improvements the tenant has made. Th assumption that the tenant has complied with the covenants in the lease will not, however, cov this provision (*Hamish Cathie Travel England Ltd* v *Insight International Tours Ltd* [1986] 1 EGL 244).

There may, however, be an exclusion from the disregard of improvements made pursuant to obligation (as there is in the Joint Committee's model clause), because the landlord may have giv consideration for them. The tenant, for instance, may have been allowed a rent-free period f fitting out the premises, or a reduction in rent for the improvements.

Any such clause requires caution in subsequently drafting a licence to carry out work, which mu be drafted in permissive terms and not in an obligatory form if the improvements are still to f within the disregard (*Godbold* v *Martin The Newsagents Ltd* (1983) 268 EG 1202).

A further illustration of the caution required in drafting a licence for improvements is the case *Historic Houses Hotels Ltd* v *Cadogan Estates* [1993] 30 EG 94 where the rent review clause requi a disregard of improvements other than those made pursuant to an obligation to the landlord, b then added that on completion of the work, 'all . . . covenants and provisions contained in the sa lease . . . shall be applicable to the said premises in their then altered state . . . as if the said premi in their then altered state had originally been comprised in the said lease'. Knox J followed t decision in *Godbold* that the licence to carry out work was essentially permissive and not obligato He then found that the further clause in the licence requiring the terms of the lease to apply on assumption that the alterations had been made at the beginning of the term was limited to apply terms other than rent review. The parties' intention had been to exclude non-obligat improvements, and this was not changed by the licence to assign.

The better practice might be nevertheless to limit the exclusion from the disregard to improveme which the tenant is under an obligation *under the terms of the lease* to carry out.

If the tenant has covenanted to comply with statutory requirements, such as fire or health and sa regulations, then work carried out pursuant to these is work carried out under an obligat imposed on the tenant by the lease (*Forte and Co. Ltd* v *General Accident Life Assurance Ltd* [19 2 EGLR 115). The tenant should therefore also argue for this type of work to be disregarded.

(vii) Disregard of goodwill: '**disregarding any goodwill attached to the demised premises by reason of the tenant carrying on thereat the business of the tenant**'.

A rent review clause should also stipulate a disregard of any goodwill relating to the tenant's business, which would obviously penalise a successful business, and of the tenant's occupation. If the tenant occupies other premises near to the demised premises, such as other units in a shopping precinct, then its occupation of those premises should also be disregarded as failure to do so could artificially inflate the rent.

A shorthand for the assumptions and disregards to be made is sometimes used by adopting those set out in the Landlord and Tenant Act 1954, s. 34, which apply when fixing the rent for a new lease under the Act. This may not be entirely suitable. The section refers to rent for 'the holding', which may differ from the premises. It also refers to improvements by the 'tenant', which would not cover improvements (for which the tenant may have given consideration) by a subtenant or licensee. The section in its original form was limited to repairs carried out during the term of the lease, which may be inappropriate. Although amended in this respect by the Law of Property Act 1969 to disregard improvements within 21 years of the application, the court may construe any particular lease as referring to the unamended form of the section as it did in *Brett* v *Brett Essex Golf Club Ltd* [1986] 1 EGLR 154.

9.4.5 A PROCEDURE FOR DETERMINING ANY DISPUTES

The rent review clause may require an arbitrator or an independent expert valuer to determine the rent in the first place, or it may provide for the parties to try first to agree a new rent between themselves with resort to an arbitrator or valuer if they are unable to do so. In any event, the clause should provide some way of resolving disputes.

The clause should provide how the independent valuer or the arbitrator is to be appointed, and it is usual to provide for appointment by the President of the Royal Institution of Chartered Surveyors. An example of such a clause would be:

> **. . . if the landlord and the tenant shall not have agreed the open market rent three months before the relevant review date each party may request the open market rent to be determined by a surveyor to be agreed upon in writing by the landlord and the tenant and in default of such agreement to be nominated by the President for the time being of the Royal Institution of Chartered Surveyors upon application of the landlord to be made not earlier than two months before the relevant review date.**

The Joint Committee's model form of clause provides for resolution of disputes by an arbitrator alone, by an independent expert alone, or by whichever of the two the landlord chooses. There are, however, important differences between an arbitrator and an independent expert.

9.4.5.1 Differences between arbitratrator and independent expert

An arbitrator essentially decides an issue between the parties and will give a decision somewhere between the limits of the parties' differences, whereas an independent expert will be expected to apply his or her knowledge and skill to a problem, and may provide an answer entirely outside the limits of the dispute between the parties.

An arbitrator, who is conducting a judicial process, is answerable to the court and must observe the rules of natural justice, whereas an expert valuer can decide how to exercise his skills. In *Henry Sotheran Ltd* v *Norwich Union Life Insurance Society* [1992] 2 EGLR 9 an arbitrator issued directions for written representations. The tenants requested that he should hear oral evidence, but the arbitrator refused. It was held that this was misconduct and the case was referred to another arbitrator. In *Jones* v *Sherwood Computer Services plc* [1992] 1 WLR 277, however, the Court of Appeal held that the court had no jurisdiction to interfere with the finding of an expert where the contract under which he was appointed stated that his finding should be 'final'.

On the other hand, an arbitrator enjoys judicial immunity whereas an expert can be sued fo negligence. In practice, however, negligence may be extremely difficult to prove. An arbitrator ha authority to call witnesses and to order discovery of documents, and may state a case to the cour on a point of law which may arise during the hearing. Although an expert may hear evidence, ther is no power to compel witnesses and his position is not judicial.

Arbitration is likely to be a more expensive process than a determination by an expert, and so i more justifiable for large office blocks and precincts. If the property is a smaller single unit the determination by an expert valuer may be more appropriate.

9.4.5.2 Effect of court judgment

A judgment of a court on the construction of a rent review clause in proceedings relating to particular review did not preclude the question being brought before the court on a subseque review where a later case in the Court of Appeal was decided in a different way (*Arnold* v *Nation Westminster Bank plc* [1991] 2 AC 93).

9.4.6 INTERIM RENT PENDING DETERMINATION OF A NEW RENT

9.4.6.1 Commencement of revised rent

The rent review clause should provide for the revised rent to be made payable from the review dat even though no final determination of it may be made for some time after this. From a tenant point of view, it may be desirable to argue that any increase in the rent shall be recoverable only f a limit of one year from the rent review date. In any event, provision should be made for the existi rent to be paid during any interim period (see clause in **9.4.6.2**).

9.4.6.2 Interest on rent payable from review date

If, as a result of review, the rent is increased, and the increase takes effect retrospectively to t review date, the tenant will have additional rent to pay in respect of the intervening period. The re review clause often provides for interest to be payable on such additional rent. It is advisable make this calculable according to the base rate of a bank. If the rent review clause provides f downward, as well as upward, rent review, then the tenant should be able to recover a overpayment of rent, together with interest, as from the review date.

A clause dealing with back payment of the revised rent and interest might be as follows:

If on the relevant rent review date the open market rent shall not have been agreed determined as aforesaid the yearly rent reserved hereunder immediately before t relevant rent review date shall continue to be payable until the determination of t open market rent pursuant to [reference to clause containing rent review procedu but so that immediately on demand after such determination the excess difference any) over the amount actually so reserved and the amount which would have be payable had the determination been made before the relevant rent review date shall paid by the tenant to the landlord together with interest thereon at the rate specifi herein and if not so paid shall be recoverable as rent in arrear.

9.4.7 ENDORSEMENT OF REVIEW RESULT ON LEASE

The result of any rent review should be endorsed on the lease and signed by the landlord, the ten and any surety. There will usually be a clause providing for this as follows:

Upon the determination of the rent payable after any rent review date a memorand in the form required by the landlord recording the amount of such rent shall endorsed on this lease and counterpart thereof and signed by or on behalf of the par hereto.

9.5 Distress

9.5.1 INTRODUCTION

Distress is a common law remedy available to a landlord where the rent is unpaid. It entitles the landlord to enter the premises leased, to seize the goods which are found there, and to hold them until the arrears are paid. The landlord has a statutory right to sell the goods five clear days after they have been seized in order to pay off the arrears and costs. A landlord who sells must obtain the best price (Distress for Rent Act 1689).

9.5.2 DISTRESS FOR SUMS OTHER THAN RENT

The right to distrain is an incident of the relationship of landlord and tenant, and (unlike the right of re-entry for breach of covenant) does not need to be expressly reserved to the landlord in the lease. At common law, distress is available only in respect of arrears of rent. It would appear, however, that the landlord may distrain for other sums unpaid (e.g. payments of a service charge, or of insurance) if these other sums are expressed in the lease to be recoverable as rent: (*Concorde Graphics Ltd* v *Andromeda Investments SA* (1982) 265 EG 386). The landlord's right to distrain in such cases is not an incident of the landlord and tenant relationship, but a contractual right.

In drafting the lease, therefore, the landlord should consider carefully the respective merits of expressing such other payments to be recoverable as rent or not. This is discussed further at **11.1.4**. A form of wording making a service charge recoverable as rent is set out at **9.2.5**.

9.5.3 WHEN DISTRESS IS AVAILABLE

Distress is, for the most part, available only during the subsistence of the tenancy in respect of which the arrears are owed. A landlord has a right to distrain against a tenant only if the relationship of landlord and tenant exists between them both at the time that the rent accrues due and at the time that the distress is levied. Thus, an assignee of the landlord's reversion may distrain for arrears of rent which accrue due while the assignee is landlord, but not for arrears which accrued due before the reversion was assigned.

If a tenant of business premises protected by the Landlord and Tenant Act 1954, Part II, is holding over after the expiry of the contractual term, the landlord is entitled to distrain, during the continuation tenancy, in respect of rent due before, as well as during, the period of holding over.

By statute, a landlord is entitled to distrain for arrears within six months of the termination of the tenancy (other than by forfeiture) so long as the tenant remains in possession (Landlord and Tenant Act 1709, s. 6). This right could be useful to a landlord of business premises if the tenant remains in possession after the termination date where a new lease has not been granted. The landlord cannot, however, distrain for arrears under the old tenancy after a new one has been granted.

The landlord has a right to distrain for rent even if there is no legal lease, provided (under the principle of *Walsh* v *Lonsdale* (1882) 21 ChD 9) the tenant is in occupation under a valid contract to grant a lease.

9.5.4 DISTRESS WHERE TENANT IS BANKRUPT OR IN INSOLVENT LIQUIDATION

The limits on distress in these circumstances are discussed in **Chapter** 14.

9.5.5 RENT INCREASED RETROSPECTIVELY UNDER REVIEW CLAUSE

At common law, a sum can comprise rent only if its amount can be calculated precisely on the day that it falls due. This means that the landlord cannot distrain at common law for backdated rent, simply because it is not strictly speaking rent. Thus if, on review, rent is increased retrospectively to the review date, the increased amount cannot be subject to common law distress (*C.H. Ba Ltd* v *Memorial Enterprises Ltd* [1974] 1 WLR 728). It is possible, however, that the landlord c rely on a contractual right to distrain for such additional 'rent', if this is provided for expressly the lease.

9.5.6 MEANS OF LEVYING DISTRESS

The landlord may levy distress in person or through a certificated bailiff, i.e. one certificated by county court (Law of Distress Amendment Act 1888, s. 7). The former method is not, of cour available if the landlord is not an individual but a corporation. A certificated bailiff acts as the ag of the landlord, who may therefore be liable for the bailiff's wrongful acts.

9.5.7 GOODS WHICH MAY BE DISTRAINED

Only goods, i.e. choses in possession, may be distrained. The landlord cannot distrain agai choses in action: it is not possible, for instance, to distrain on share certificates.

The landlord has a right to distrain upon all goods found on the premises, whether they belong the tenant or to a third party. A third party may, however, avoid distress by removing its go before the commencement of the distress. Even after distress has begun, a third party may be a to avoid the distress by serving a notice upon the landlord (see **9.5.7.2**).

9.5.7.1 Privileged goods

Certain types of goods can never be distrained. These include:

(a) tenant's fixtures;
(b) items in use at the time of the distress;
(c) items on the premises for a temporary purpose of trade, such as goods left for repair.

Certain types of goods can be distrained only if the distress cannot be satisfied by distraining up other goods on the premises. These include tools of trade (including the books of a professio person) not exceeding a value of £150 (Law of Distress Amendment Act 1888, s. 4).

9.5.7.2 Goods of third parties

Subject to the exceptions relating to privileged goods, the goods of a third party which are on tenant's premises may be subject to distress at common law. The third party can avoid distress his own goods by paying the landlord the rent due and then claiming an indemnity against the ten (*Exall* v *Partridge* (1799) 8 TR 308). Furthermore, if some of the tenant's goods are charged t third party, the landlord should levy distress first against goods not so charged.

Under the Law of Distress Amendment Act 1908, a third party may protect its goods by serv upon the landlord or the landlord's bailiff a written notice specifying the goods and stating that tl are the property of the third party and that the tenant has no property or beneficial interest in goods. If the person serving the notice is a subtenant, his relief from distress is conditional upon paying the rent under the sublease direct to the head landlord. The effect of the service of a no by a subtenant is to create the relationship of landlord and tenant between the subtenant and head landlord until the rent arrears are paid. Until such time, the tenant's right to the rent from sublease passes to the head landlord.

Some goods of third parties are, however, excluded from the protection of the Act. These inclu

(a) goods within the reputed ownership of the tenant;
(b) goods which belong to the tenant's spouse or business partner;
(c) goods which are in a company's offices and which belong to the company, where premises themselves are leased to a tenant who is a director, officer or employee of that compa

9.5.8 DISTRESS AND SET-OFF

It is uncertain whether a tenant may resist distress by relying on a right of set-off, e.g. for the cost of making good breaches by the landlord of a repairing covenant. McLouglin argues that set-off should not be a defence, since otherwise, where there is room for argument as to the extent of the set-off, it would be dangerous to exercise the right to distrain. He considers that any right to set-off 'operates only to reduce the overall indebtedness of the tenant to the landlord, but not so as to limit the right to distrain' (McLoughlin, *Commercial Leases and Insolvency* (London: Butterworths, 1992), p. 59).

9.5.9 DISTRESS AS WAIVER OF RIGHT TO FORFEIT

Since distress is available only during the subsistence of the relationship of landlord and tenant, a landlord who distrains for rent is affirming the continued existence of the lease and will therefore waive a right to forfeit the lease for the non-payment of the rent. If, however, the lease provides that the landlord's right to forfeit arises only if there is insufficient distress on the premises, the levying of distress will not itself effect a waiver of the right to forfeit. Similarly, a landlord who is proceeding for forfeiture and arrears of rent under the Common Law Procedure Act 1852 will first need to levy distress in order to meet the requirement of s. 210 that 'no sufficient distress was to be found on the demised premises'.

TEN

REPAIRING OBLIGATIONS IN A LEASE

10.1 Wording and Scope of Repairing Covenants

It is important to consider whether a landlord or a tenant should undertake the liability for repairs, as in the absence of any covenant as to repairs, very few obligations are implied in the case of commercial leases.

The obligation to repair will be a matter for negotiation if the premises to be let are a single unit, although in practice it is usual for the landlord to require the tenant to repair and to redecorate. The covenant for redecoration usually requires outside painting to be carried out every three years and interior painting every five or seven years and in any event during the last year of the term. Such a covenant by the tenant would read:

To paint the outside wood, iron and other work of the demised premises with two coats at least of good quality paint in a proper and workmanlike manner once in every third year of the term and also during the last year thereof;

To paint all the inside wood, iron and other work and the walls and ceilings inside the demised premises with at least two coats of a good quality paint in a proper and workmanlike manner once in every five years of the term and also during the last year thereof.

If the premises are a unit in a larger building (or estate) then it is usual to provide for the tenant to undertake repairs to the unit which is exclusively demised to him and for the landlord to undertake repairs to the structure and common parts. The unit will usually be referred to as 'the demised premises' and it then becomes important to know the extent of the demise (see **3.2.2**). The landlord's expenditure in this respect will be recoverable from the tenant as part of the service charges (see **11.1.2**).

An example of a short form of repairing covenant by the tenant relating to the interior of the unit would be:

At all times during the said term to keep the interior of the premises (including all windows and window frames, doors and door frames) and the interior surfaces of all ceilings, walls and floors and the conduits exclusively serving the premises in good and substantial repair (damage by the insured risks excepted) and in a clean and tidy condition and to renew or replace such parts thereof as may be necessary and to decorate in a good and workmanlike manner with good quality materials the interior at least once in every five years during the term and in any event during the last year of the term.

The landlord's covenant relating to the main structure and exterior of the building might be:

To keep in repair the structure of the building, the roof including all external and load-bearing walls, the outer faces of all walls enclosing the building and the outer walls separating the unit from any access corridor, the foundations and main beams of the building and common parts and all pipes, wires, drains, party-walls, sewers, channels, sanitary apparatus, passages, stairways, entrance ways and other things used or capable of being used in common.

It is important that a realistic estimate of the cost of repairs over the period of the lease be made and a proportionate annual charge included in the service charge, as any sudden increase in service charges may not be permitted in a new lease under the Landlord and Tenant Act 1954 (see **11.1.1** and **15.2.6.4**).

This chapter will consider the effect of different wording found in repairing covenants, the scope of repairing covenants and the remedies available to both the landlord and the tenant for breach of a repairing covenant by the other. Before doing so however, it is pertinent to mention such implied obligations on the landlord and the tenant as there are under common law or statute.

10.1.1 IMPLIED OBLIGATIONS AS TO REPAIR ON THE PART OF THE LANDLORD

Although statute law implies many repairing obligations on the part of a landlord of a dwellinghouse, there is no corresponding legislation with regard to commercial premises. However, it is probable that certain repairing obligations imposed in case law relating to dwellinghouses might also be held to apply to business premises.

In *Liverpool City Council* v *Irwin* [1977] AC 239 the House of Lords held that the council, which was the landlord of a block of flats, was under a duty to take reasonable care to maintain the stairs, lifts, lighting and rubbish chutes, all of which were essential to the enjoyment of the flats. Without the maintenance of these rights, the leases lacked business efficacy. It should be noticed, however, that the obligation was not an absolute one to maintain in any event, but merely to take reasonable care to do so. In that case, it was found as a fact that the disrepair was caused by vandals and the landlord had discharged its duty of care.

This obligation appears to have been extended in *King* v *South Northamptonshire District Council* [1992] 1 EGLR 53 in which the Court of Appeal held that there was an implied obligation on the part of the landlord to maintain an access way to the rear of a terrace of houses which was important to their enjoyment. The court indicated, however, that the layout of the terraces on the estate was a significant factor in this case.

In *Barrett* v *Lounova (1982) Ltd* [1990] 1 QB 348 the tenant had covenanted to repair the interior of the demised premises but there was no provision in the lease for external repairs. The exterior was in such a bad state of repair that the roof leaked so that it was impossible for the tenant to comply with her covenant. The court held that the tenant's covenant implied an obligation on the part of the landlord to repair the exterior, such an implication being necessary to give business efficacy to the tenant's covenant.

In *Gordon* v *Selico Co. Ltd* [1986] 1 EGLR 71 a landlord was held liable in nuisance for damage to a tenant's flat caused by dry rot and water escaping from the common parts of a building which he was liable to repair.

The Defective Premises Act 1972, s. 4(1), makes a landlord liable for injury to a person or property due to the defective state of premises if the landlord has a right to enter and repair the premises and knows of the want of repair. The liability is to the tenant as well as to visitors to the premises (*Smith* v *Bradford Metropolitan Council* (1982) 44 P & CR 171). This liability would always seem to apply in the case of a weekly tenancy (*McAuley* v *Bristol City Council* [1992] QB 134).

The Health and Safety at Work etc. Act 1974 imposes obligations on a person in control of business premises to take reasonable care to ensure that there are adequate and safe means of access to and egress from the premises and that any plant and machinery on the premises are safe.

It is an actionable nuisance under the Public Health Acts 1936 and 1961 if premises are prejudicial to health by reason of matters such as defective wiring or damp.

10.1.2 IMPLIED OBLIGATIONS AS TO REPAIR ON THE PART OF THE TENANT

There are no obligations to repair as such implied on the part of the tenant but a tenant is liable for waste. Different types of waste apply to different kinds of tenants. The most heinous kind of waste is voluntary waste, which consists of acts of wanton destruction, and all tenants, whatever their term, are liable for this. Permissive waste is damage caused by neglect or a failure to act, and tenants for a fixed term and most periodic tenants are liable for this, although not weekly tenants.

All tenants, including weekly tenants, are liable to use the demised premises in a tenant-like manner. This liability was described by Lord Denning MR in *Warren* v *Keen* [1954] 1 QB 15 by reference to a number of homely illustrations such as cleaning the chimneys and the windows, mending fused lights and unblocking the sink.

A fairly recent case where there was liability for waste with regard to holes in a wall due to fixtures having been removed is *Mancetter Developments Ltd* v *Garmanson Ltd* [1986] QB 1212 which is discussed at length in **7.1.3**. The circumstances of the case were such that there was no liability on the covenants in the lease, but the court was able to find liability in waste, which is a tort.

10.1.3 THE EFFECT OF DIFFERENT REPAIRING COVENANTS

Just like any other covenant, a repairing covenant will fall to be interpreted on its own particular wording. Although the most usual form of covenant will be 'to maintain and repair', there may be variations on this such as 'to yield up the premises in good repair' or 'to put into good repair'. The former refers to a requirement that the premises should be in good repair at the termination of the tenancy, and consequently, if this is all the covenant requires, the landlord will have no right to serve a notice of dilapidations on such a covenant until the end of the tenancy.

The wording 'to put into repair' may import something more than mere maintenance and may impose a liability to put into repair something which is in a state of disrepair at the time of the lease. It is possible that this may be implied in any event from a straight repairing covenant if the property is in a bad state of repair at the commencement of the lease (*Proudfoot* v *Hart* (1890) 25 QBD 42). The word 'replace' may also import something wider than a straight covenant to maintain and repair, and in *Elite Investments Ltd* v *T.I. Bainbridge Silencers Ltd* [1986] 2 EGLR 43 it was held that it was wide enough to require the tenant to replace the roof of a large industrial unit which had been deteriorating and in a bad state of repair when the premises were leased.

A comprehensive form of repairing covenant from a landlord's point of view would be:

> **To put and keep the whole of the demised premises in good and substantial repair and condition (damage by any insured risk excepted unless and to the extent that any act or omission of the tenant renders the insurance money irrecoverable) and to yield up the same (and all fixtures annexed thereto) in such good and substantial repair and condition to the landlord on the termination of the term hereby granted however determined.**

10.1.4 STANDARD OF REPAIR REQUIRED BY A REPAIRING COVENANT

A specification of 'good' repair or 'excellent' repair, or a covenant 'well and substantially' to repair, will add nothing to the general requirement to repair.

Sometimes a repairing covenant will add a proviso that 'fair wear and tear' shall be excepted from the repairing liability. It was held in *Regis Property Co. Ltd* v *Dudley* [1959] AC 370 that the exception covers damage caused by natural deterioration from weather and normal usage, assuming that the tenant uses the premises in a tenant-like manner. It will not cover damage caused by the negligence of the tenant or the tenant's visitors, nor will it cover damage resulting from the original want of repair which fell within the exception. So Lord Denning said in *Regis Property Co. Ltd* v *Dudley* 'If a slate falls off through wear and tear and in consequence the roof is likely to let through the water, the tenant is not responsible for the slate coming off but he ought to put in another one to prevent further damage'.

The test to be applied to the standard of repair required by a repairing covenant was laid down in *Proudfoot* v *Hart* (1890) 25 QBD 42. The premises should be in such a state of repair as would be acceptable to a reasonably minded tenant, bearing in mind their age and character and their locality at the date of letting. As the date of the lease is the relevant date, it is possible that a sublease with an identical repairing covenant to a head lease may nevertheless impose a different standard of repair if the locality, for example, has changed since the head lease was granted.

10.1.5 SCOPE OF A REPAIRING COVENANT

The wording of the repairing covenant will be primarily relevant in indicating the extent of the liability.

If the premises leased are a single unit then the tenant will probably have covenanted to repair and maintain the whole of it. It would be prudent to consider whether the tenant is also intended to maintain any access to the premises and services, such as drainage, water and electricity supplies. If these supply the premises exclusively then the landlord will want to make the tenant alone liable for these, but if they are shared with other premises, then the tenant should pay a proportionate part. Covenants should be taken from the tenant to reflect these liabilities. Such a covenant might be:

to contribute a fair proportion according to use of the cost of repairing, maintaining, cleansing and renewing all party-walls, party structures and yards, gardens, ways, sewers, drains, pipes, conduits and wires used by the occupier of the demised premises in common with the occupier of any other property, such fair proportion to be determined by the landlord's surveyor whose decision shall be final and binding on the parties.

If the demised premises are a unit in a larger building, then the usual repairing arrangements are that the tenant will repair and maintain the premises which are exclusively demised to him while the landlord will repair and maintain the structure, exterior and common parts, recovering the cost of this from all the tenants proportionately as part of the service charges (see examples at the beginning of **10.1**). If this arrangement is adopted, it is very important to define as clearly as possible the extent of the demised premises for which the tenant is solely responsible, and what is meant by 'structure' and 'exterior' for which the landlord is responsible. The lease should therefore specify whether the walls of the unit are within the demise and to be maintained by the tenant, whether they are party-walls with an adjoining unit to be maintained by two tenants jointly, or whether they are part of the structure of the building to be maintained by the landlord.

The term 'structure' does not have any precise legal definition, but in *Irvine* v *Moran* [1991] 1 EGLR 261 Forbes QC thought that the structure of a dwellinghouse referred to in the Housing Act 1961, s. 32, meant 'those elements of the overall dwellinghouse which give it its essential appearance, stability and shape', excluding fittings, equipment and decoration, but not confined to outside and load-bearing walls, roof and foundations.

In *Brown* v *Liverpool Corporation* [1969] 3 All ER 1345 (a case on a landlord's implied obligation to repair the exterior of premises under the Housing Act 1961, s. 32) it was held that steps giving essential access to the front of a property were part of the exterior.

A further problem which has given rise to litigation is the difficulty of deciding whether any particular work is a 'repair', or whether it is so extensive as to amount to the construction of something new which is therefore outside the scope of a usual repairing covenant. In *McDougall* v *Easington District Council* [1989] 1 EGLR 93 the Court of Appeal reviewed the decisions on what was within the scope of a 'repair' and identified three different criteria which the courts have applied. These are:

(a) The extent of the renewal involved. Although all repair involves renewal, it should only be renewal of subsidiary parts and not of the whole. Thus, in *Torrens* v *Walker* [1906] 2 Ch 166 the rebuilding of the front and back walls of a house which had been demolished was held to be outside the scope of a repairing covenant.

(b) Whether the work carried out would produce something quite different from the demised premises as originally let. Thus, in *Halliard Property Co. Ltd* v *Nicholas Clarke Investments Ltd* (1984) 269 EG 1257 a tenant who had covenanted to repair was not liable to rebuild an unstable, jerry-built shed at the rear of the premises, as the new building which would have been erected in its place would have been entirely different from that included in the demise. In *Post Office* v *Aquarius Properties Ltd* [1987] 1 All ER 1055 it was held that a tenant was not liable under a repairing covenant to remedy a structural defect whereby a porous concrete floor in a basement allowed seepage which caused flooding, as this would have been to create an entirely different building. The covenant to repair does not involve work required to correct a design defect and so produce a building of a different design.

(c) The cost of the work compared to the value of the building and the effect of the work on its value and life span. In *Ravenseft Properties Ltd* v *Davstone (Holdings) Ltd* [1980] QB 12 extensive structural work was required to stop stone cladding from falling from the façade of a building owing to the way in which the building had been constructed without expansion joints. The building (in Kensington High Street, London) was worth £3 million, and the work, which involved putting in the expansion joints, cost £55,000, which was less than 2 per cent of the value of the whole building. It was therefore held to be within the scope of the tenants' repairing covenants. On the other hand, in *Brew Brothers Ltd* v *Snax (Ross) Ltd* [1970] 1 QB 612 extensive work to the foundations of a building, the repair of drains and rebuilding of a wall would when completed have cost the same as the value of the building, and it was held that this was outside the scope of a repairing covenant.

In *McDougall* v *Easington District Council* [1989] 1 EGLR 93 the landlord replaced a flat roof with a pitched one, altering the front and rear elevations, and replaced door and window frames in a house, thereby increasing its value by 80 per cent. This was held to be too extensive to be covered by a repairing covenant and amounted to renewal.

10.1.6 OTHER MAINTENANCE

In addition to repairs, the parties should consider whether other related matters, such as landscaping, the erection and maintenance of signs and advertisements on an estate, the cleaning of windows, brickwork and drains and the replacement of electrical equipment, should be covenanted for. Obviously requirements will vary according to the premises and the user of them. However, a lease of a unit in a shopping precinct, for example, might well include covenants by the tenant to cover all these things.

10.1.7 NOTICE OF WANT OF REPAIR

A landlord's liability to repair generally only arises when the landlord receives notice of the want of repair. Whether sufficient notice has been received will be a question of fact in each case, but two cases may be contrasted by way of illustration.

In *O'Brien* v *Robinson* [1973] AC 912 the tenants of a flat had complained in the course of court proceedings for rent some three years earlier that the ceiling of their flat shook badly when the tenants above were dancing in the course of riotous parties. This was held not to constitute sufficient notice to the landlord of a latent defect in the ceiling which subsequently caused it to collapse. On the other hand, in *Sheldon* v *West Bromwich Corporation* (1973) 25 P & CR 360 where a plumber employee of the corporation was sent to investigate noises in the tenant's water system and reported back that there was rust in the water tank, this was held to be sufficient notice of the want of repair to make the landlord liable for the subsequent damage when the water tank burst.

The Defective Premises Act 1972, s. 4(1) (see **10.1.1**), imposes a statutory liability on landlords to repair, but s. 4(2) provides that this shall only apply if the landlord knows, or ought to have known, of the defect. The landlord should therefore consider taking a covenant from the tenant to give notice of any such defect, which might be in the following form:

> **Forthwith on becoming aware of the same, to give written notice to the landlord of any defect in the demised premises which might give rise to an obligation on the landlord to do or refrain from doing any act or thing so as to comply with the duty of care imposed on the landlord pursuant to the Defective Premises Act 1972, and to display and maintain in the demised premises all notices which the landlord may, from time to time, reasonably require to be displayed in relation thereto.**

In *Loria* v *Hammer* [1989] 2 EGLR 249 the tenant of one of four flats in a house carried out repairs to a leaking roof which was causing damage and sought to recover the cost from the landlord. The landlord, who had covenanted to keep the roof (*inter alia*) in repair, pleaded that he had not received notice of the defect. The court held that this was irrelevant where his liability to repair was independent of any notice and related to common parts of a building retained by him. In this case, moreover, the landlord was unable to recover the cost of repairing the ensuing damage to the tenant's flat by an increase in the service charge (which covered repairs to the common parts) as to allow him to do so would have been to allow him to recover the costs of his own wrongdoing. If this case is to be followed, then a clause similar to the one above, imposing liability on the tenant to inform the landlord of the want of repair to any common parts, would seem to be a wise precaution for a landlord.

10.2 Landlord's Remedies for Breach of a Tenant's Repairing Covenant

Where the tenant covenants to repair, it is usual to covenant also to allow the landlord to enter to view the state of repair and make good any want of repair if the tenant fails to do so. A typical covenant of this type would be:

> **To permit the landlord to enter the premises for the purposes of examining the state and condition thereof, the tenant forthwith making good any defects in the same which are the responsibility of the tenant hereunder in accordance with a notice to that effect given by the landlord, and in default the landlord shall be entitled to make good any such defects and charge the cost thereof to the tenant.**

A landlord may serve a notice of dilapidations on a tenant specifying the repairs which the landlord alleges are required to comply with a tenant's repairing covenant. The notice should be drawn up by a surveyor. If a notice under the Law of Property Act 1925, s. 146 (see **10.2.2**), is to be served, the notice of dilapidations should be attached to it. A landlord has various remedies for breach of a tenant's repairing covenant, but in most cases they are restricted by statute.

10.2.1 DAMAGES FOR BREACH OF A REPAIRING COVENANT

The breach of a repairing covenant is in effect a breach of contract for which the tenant is liable to the landlord in damages. The damages are limited however by the Landlord and Tenant Act 1927,

s. 18(1), which provides that the damages shall not exceed the diminution in value of the reversion as a consequence of the disrepair. It follows from this that if the property is to be demolished or developed, then damages may not be recoverable at all. Where a tenant will be entitled to a new lease under the Landlord and Tenant Act 1954 and the open market rent is to be fixed with disregard to the state of repair, then again the landlord will not be entitled to damages (*Family Management* v *Gray* (1979) 253 EG 369). However, in *Crown Estate Commissioners* v *Town Investments Ltd* [1992] 1 EGLR 61 the tenant had sublet parts of the premises to sublessees, whose repairing covenants were less onerous than the tenant's in that they were not responsible for external repairs, and other parts of the premises were vacant, which could cause a diminution in the value of the reversion.

In the case of a lease of seven years or more with three years or more of the term unexpired, the Leasehold Property (Repairs) Act 1938 applies, and in order to claim damages for breach of a repairing covenant, the landlord must first comply with the procedure laid down in the Act which is discussed in **13.4.5.2**.

10.2.2 ACTION FOR FORFEITURE

A landlord may only forfeit the lease for breach of a repairing covenant if there is a proviso for forfeiture in the lease.

Before commencing forfeiture proceedings, the landlord must first serve a notice under the Law of Property Act 1925, s. 146, and, if the lease is within the Leasehold Property (Repairs) Act 1938, the notice must state the tenant's right to serve a counter-notice under that Act. This procedure is fully dealt with in **13.4**.

Because of the court's extensive powers to grant relief to a tenant against forfeiture, a well-drawn lease will include a covenant by the tenant to pay any costs incurred by the landlord in connection with the service of a s. 146 notice and schedule of dilapidations, and a claim for such costs will still be good even though there is a requirement to comply with the 1938 Act. A usual covenant of this type would be:

To pay all costs (including solicitors' costs and surveyors' fees) incurred by the landlord of and incidental to the preparation and service of:

(a) a notice under section 146 of the Law of Property Act 1925 notwithstanding that forfeiture is avoided otherwise than by order of the court and
(b) a schedule of dilapidations recording breaches of the tenant's covenant to keep and to yield up the demised premises in repair.

10.2.3 LANDLORD'S REMEDIES FOR BREACH OF A COVENANT AS TO DECORATIVE REPAIRS

If the s. 146 notice served by the landlord relates to decorative repairs, then the Law of Property Act 1925, s. 147, provides that the court may grant relief to the tenant if satisfied that the notice is unreasonable having regard to all the circumstances of the case, and in particular to the length of the term unexpired. The section does not apply:

(a) where there is a breach of an express covenant to put the premises into a decorative state of repair;
(b) to any matter necessary or proper to keep the property in a sanitary condition or to maintain or preserve the structure;
(c) to any statutory liability to keep a house fit for habitation;
(d) to any covenant to yield up the premises in a specific state of repair at the end of the term.

The section does not apply to a covenant to carry out exterior decoration.

Relief may be whole or partial, and it is usual for the court to grant relief on conditions.

10.2.4 LANDLORD'S RIGHT TO ENTER AND CARRY OUT REPAIRS

The lease may reserve the right to the landlord to enter and carry out repairs if the tenant fails to do so, or there may be an implied right to do so under the common law or statute (see **10.1.1**).

If the lease additionally gives the landlord the right to recover the cost of the repairs, then the cost may be recoverable from the tenant as a contract debt and not as damages. This is important as there are cases at first instance where it has been held that the procedure under the Leasehold Property (Repairs) Act 1938 does not apply to recovery of a contract debt, which is different from damages (*Elite Investments Ltd* v *T.I. Bainbridge Silencers Ltd* [1986] 2 EGLR 43). From a landlord's point of view, it is therefore important to include in the lease a right to recover as a debt the costs of any repairs which the landlord has a right to carry out. The decisions are, however, only at first instance, and a landlord might still be well advised to serve the necessary notice to comply with the procedure under the 1938 Act except in circumstances of extreme urgency.

The problems which can arise if a right to recover the cost of repairs is not reserved as a debt are illustrated by the case of *SEDAC Investments Ltd* v *Tanner* [1982] 1 WLR 1342. The lessors had reserved a right to enter and carry out repairs themselves if the lessees failed to do so. They were informed by the lessees that fragments of stonework from the demised building were falling on to a pavement, and they therefore carried out the necessary repairs to stop the danger as a matter of urgency. Their solicitors subsequently served a s. 146 notice on the lessees, who served a counter-notice under s. 1(2) of the 1938 Act. It was held that the procedure clearly contemplated the breach of a repairing covenant not yet remedied. As no s. 146 notice had been served, the lessees had been deprived of their right to serve a counter-notice, which meant that the court had no jurisdiction to give leave to the lessors to proceed in an action for damages.

The other advantage of a right to enter and carry out repairs and to recover the cost as a contract debt is that the Landlord and Tenant Act 1927, s. 18(1), will not apply to limit the sum to the diminution in value of the reversion as it does to a sum claimed as damages. A clause which suggests that the sum might be recoverable as a debt rather than as damages is the following covenant by the tenant:

> **Upon failure to comply within one month (or such lesser time as is reasonable if the repairs are urgent) with a written request by the landlord to carry out the repairs specified therein (being repairs which the tenant has covenanted to carry out), to permit the landlord to enter the demised premises with workers and others to execute the works required to comply with such request and the cost thereof shall be a debt immediately payable by the tenant to the landlord.**

10.2.5 LANDLORD'S RIGHT TO ENTER AND VIEW THE STATE OF REPAIR

Whenever a landlord is responsible for repairs to demised premises, there is a right implied at common law that the tenant will allow the landlord to enter and view the state of repair. This applies whether the obligation to repair arises under common law or statute. The rationale for this was explained by Somervell LJ in *Mint* v *Good* [1951] 1 KB 517 in relation to a weekly tenant as being a right necessary to give business efficacy to the agreement.

In *Saner* v *Bilton* (1878) 7 ChD 815 it was held that a covenant by a landlord to keep the structure of a warehouse in repair implied a licence by the tenant to permit the landlord entry for a reasonable time to carry out the necessary repairs.

If the demised premises are a unit in a building, then it will be necessary to reserve the right to the owners of neighbouring or adjoining premises also to enter to carry out repairs. Rights of entry for the landlord and the neighbouring owners can be reserved in one tenant's covenant as follows:

> **To permit the landlord and its agents and workers and the tenants and occupiers of any other parts of the building or of any adjoining or neighbouring premises at any time**

during the term at reasonable hours in the daytime and upon prior notice (except in case of emergency when no notice need be given) to enter upon the demised premises for the purpose of inspecting and executing repairs or alterations of or upon such other parts of the building or such other adjoining or neighbouring premises, the persons exercising such rights making good all physical damage to the demised premises thereby occasioned.

10.3 Tenant's Remedies for Breach of the Landlord's Repairing Covenants

Although an account is given here of the remedies which have been recognised as available to tenants for breach of their landlords' repairing covenants, it must be remembered that the suitability of the different remedies will vary with the circumstances, and in particular whether the property leased is a separate unit, or a unit in a building or on an estate.

10.3.1 DAMAGES FOR BREACH OF COVENANT

A tenant's damages are assessed on the normal contractual basis of foreseeability, even though there may be no privity of contract between the parties. Although the cases mostly relate to dwellinghouses, some of the heads of damages would seem to be equally applicable to business premises.

In *Calabar Properties Ltd* v *Stitcher* [1984] 1 WLR 287 the Court of Appeal held that the damages which a tenant of a dwellinghouse could recover for breach of a repairing covenant were for (*inter alia*) alternative accommodation when the property was uninhabitable, discomfort, loss of enjoyment and diminution in the market value. In addition, as regards business premises, if the premises have to be vacated, it might presumably be possible to recover damages for loss of business and goodwill, although it might be difficult to quantify the latter. In *McGreal* v *Wake* (1984) 13 HLR 107 damages were awarded for storage of furniture while repairs were being carried out and for making good decorations afterwards, and both of these heads could be applicable to business premises.

In *Mira* v *Aylmer Square Investments Ltd* [1990] 1 EGLR 45 the tenant of a long lease of a flat claimed damages for the reduced rent which he obtained on a subletting due to construction works carried out by the landlord which caused noise and dirt and amounted to a breach of the landlord's implied covenant for quiet enjoyment. It was held that damages were recoverable as in contract under the first head of *Hadley* v *Baxendale* (1854) 9 Exch 341 even though there was no privity of contract between the parties. The possibility of the rent on a subletting being reduced was damage which the landlord ought to have known was likely to occur as a result of the breach of covenant, as the lease was a long lease.

Applying these principles to business leases, where underletting is extremely common, would suggest that a tenant would have a good claim for damages for a reduced rent obtainable on a subletting due to a breach of a repairing covenant.

10.3.2 SPECIFIC PERFORMANCE OF THE COVENANT

This remedy was first recognised as applicable to a breach of a repairing covenant in the lease of a dwellinghouse in *Jeune* v *Queens Cross Properties Ltd* [1974] Ch 97 and was given statutory force in relation to dwellinghouses by the Landlord and Tenant Act 1985, s. 17. In *Jeune* the want of repair was to a common part of a building which was divided into flats, and the remedy would seem to be as applicable to the common parts of a building or an estate as to the part actually demised. It has been applied also to the supply of services such as the repair of boilers on an estate (*Parker* v *Camden London Borough Council* [1986] Ch 162) and the repair of lifts (*Peninsular Maritime Ltd* v *Padseal*

Ltd (1981) 259 EG 860, in which the Court of Appeal confirmed an interlocutory mandatory injunction for the repair of lifts).

10.3.3 RIGHT TO CARRY OUT REPAIRS AND SET OFF COST AGAINST RENT

This right was recognised in *Lee-Parker* v *Izzet* [1971] 1 WLR 1688. Where the landlord has defaulted on his repairing covenant, the tenant may carry out the repairs personally and set off the cost against future rents. The right should be exercised by the tenant with caution. It would be advisable, for instance, to obtain two or three estimates for the work to be done before proceeding, and to limit the cost as far as possible. The repair must be one which is covered by the landlord's repairing covenant, and the landlord must first have been given the opportunity of carrying it out.

Additionally, there may be a right in equity to set off an uncertain estimated sum for repairs against a landlord's claim for arrears of rent if the two claims are closely connected. Thus in *British Anzani (Felixstowe) Ltd* v *International Marine Management (UK) Ltd* [1980] QB 137 the plaintiff, who was a lessee under a building lease, agreed to build two warehouses and to sublet them to the defendant. The agreement contained an undertaking by the plaintiff to put right any defects in the buildings within two years. There was a defect in the flooring of one of the warehouses, and when the plaintiff sued the defendant for unpaid rent, the defendant counterclaimed for the cost of putting right the defective floor. It was held that although this was a claim for unliquidated damages under the agreement as to building and not in the lease itself, there was such a close connection between the lease and the agreement that the defendant's claim went to the foundation of the plaintiff's claim for arrears of rent and was fair and just.

10.3.4 APPOINTMENT OF A RECEIVER

The Supreme Court Act 1981, s. 37(1), allows the court to appoint a receiver to collect rents and service charges and to use them to carry out repairs to premises. The order may be made where it is just and convenient to do so. There is further statutory provision for this as regards dwellinghouses in the Landlord and Tenant Act 1987, Part II.

The difficulties experienced with regard to enforcing a landlord's repairing covenants on the retained parts of a block of flats is unlikely to be experienced with business premises, however. The landlord will usually only reserve minimal ground rent on residential blocks of flats where the long leases are sold for a premium, and therefore retains very little interest in the property, whereas business premises are usually let at realistic market rents and the landlord's interest is a real one.

ELEVEN

SERVICE CHARGES AND INSURANCE

11.1 Service Charges

Where the premises let are part of a larger building or estate which includes other units, such as an office in an office block, a shop in a shopping precinct or an industrial unit on an industrial estate, the landlord will retain the common parts, and provision will need to be made for their repair and maintenance. The landlord may also provide services to be used by all the tenants, such as heating and hot water for offices and cleansing and signs for shopping precincts and industrial estates, and the landlord will want to charge for these. It is to cover the expenditure on such matters that the lease of such a unit will provide for a service charge to be payable by the tenant.

11.1.1 IMPOSITION OF A SERVICE CHARGE

It should be noted that if the lease does not provide for the payment of a service charge by the tenant, then no charge will be payable and in the absence of common mistake, rectification of the lease will not be available (*Riverlate Properties Ltd* v *Paul* [1975] 1 Ch 133). It might be possible to impose one however, on the renewal of a lease, particularly where the original lease is an old one where the landlord did not originally provide such sophisticated services. In *Hyams* v *Titan Properties Ltd* (1972) 24 P & CR 359 the court permitted a variation from a fixed service charge to one based upon the proportion of expenditure in a new lease under the Landlord and Tenant Act 1954. Any variation must be fair and reasonable, however, and in *O'May* v *City of London Real Property Co. Ltd* [1983] 2 AC 726 the House of Lords held that the burden of proof to show that any variation is fair and reasonable is on the party seeking it. In that case the landlord sought to impose a fluctuating service charge, of undefined risk and cost to the tenants, in a new lease under the Landlord and Tenant Act 1954, offering as compensation a reduction in the rent. The rent reduction was fixed at 50p per week, and it was held not to be an adequate compensation for the comparatively unlimited risk which the landlord sought to impose on the tenants.

The absence of any services would of course indicate a lower rent, and the misrepresentation of a service charge to an assignee-purchaser has been held to be misrepresentation giving rise to a claim for damages (*Heinemann* v *Cooper* [1987] 2 EGLR 154, in which an assignee recovered £3,000 damages on a 62-year lease in which the service charges were about £800 per annum instead of £200 per annum, which was the sum indicated by the vendor-assignor).

It was held in *Finchbourne Ltd* v *Rodrigues* [1976] 3 All ER 581 that a service charge must be fair and reasonable, and that a covenant by tenants to pay a service charge could not give a landlord an unfettered right to spend whatever he liked on maintenance and then charge the tenants for this. This does not require the landlord to accept the lowest quotation for services however (*Bandar Property Holdings Ltd* v *J.S. Darwen (Successors) Ltd* [1968] 2 All ER 305, in which a tenant was held liable to pay the slightly larger premium for insurance arranged by the landlord than the quotation for identical insurance which the tenant had obtained).

11.1.2 MATTERS TO BE COVERED BY A SERVICE CHARGE

In order to minimise the risk of disputes, it is important to define as clearly and exhaustively as possible exactly what matters are to be covered by the service charge. To this end, the lease will need to include in the definition section a definition of terms such as 'the block', 'the centre', 'common parts', 'the refuse area', 'the parking area'. These are all likely to be parts not included in any individual demise and therefore retained by the landlord and for which the landlord undertakes the responsibility for maintenance. In the absence of a covenant to do so, the landlord will not necessarily be liable to maintain these parts, even though the tenant covenants to pay a service charge. In *Duke of Westminster* v *Guild* [1985] QB 688 the tenant had covenanted to contribute towards the cost of a drain serving the demised premises, but it was held that although the tenant's easement of drainage gave him the right to enter and repair the drain, it could not impose an obligation on the landlord to do so in the absence of an express covenant. There may be an implied liability to take reasonable care to maintain services, such as safe access and lighting, necessary to give business efficacy to an agreement (*Liverpool City Council* v *Irwin* [1977] AC 239) and to repair a right of access which it might reasonably be expected that the property would enjoy (*King* v *South Northamptonshire District Council* [1992] 1 EGLR 53).

In addition to the maintenance of the common parts, the landlord will usually undertake to provide services for the whole block, and it is equally important to state clearly what services will be provided and to define them as precisely as possible. For example, it is advisable to specify the dates and hours between which heating will be provided and the temperature of any hot water supplied. In the lease of a unit in a large block, provision for apportionment and payment of service charges and the services covered by it are usually set out in a schedule to the lease. Services provided by the landlord are likely to include the repair, redecoration and cleansing of the common parts of the building or precinct, heating and lighting and the maintenance of machinery for these, security and emergency services, staffing, refuse disposal, the provision of signs, furniture and facilities, landscaping, management, and publicity. The landlord will be responsible for paying VAT and possibly for creating a reserve fund.

From a landlord's point of view, the covenant as to the provision of services should be qualified to exclude a failure which is beyond the landlord's control, such as heating during a severe fuel shortage. A comprehensive form of exemption for the landlord would be:

The landlord shall not be liable and the tenant shall have no claim against the landlord for:

(a) any interruption in any of the services by reason of necessary repair or maintenance of any installation or apparatus or damage thereto or destruction thereof by fire or other cause beyond the landlord's control or by reason of mechanical or other defect or breakdown or frost or unavoidable shortage of fuel or labour or

(b) any act, omission or negligence of any employee of the landlord in the performance of any duty relating to the provision of the services or any of them.

The landlord's covenant should therefore be to provide services as far as is practicable, so as not, for instance, to be liable for a mechanical failure of plant, although in *Yorkbrook Investments Ltd* v *Batten* [1985] 2 EGLR 100 it was held that such wording would not exempt the landlord from liability if the heating boiler frequently failed because it was antiquated and unserviceable and had exceeded its expected functioning time.

It was recommended by the Joint Subcommittee of the Law Society and the RICS on Model Clauses in Commercial Leases that there should be provision for variation of a percentage or proportionate service charge (see the precedent below) to allow for additional units being added or new services to be provided and services no longer required to be dropped. The definitions of the common parts and any list of services should be subject to some variation to cover this. Any such variation should be reasonable.

A general clause allowing for new services to be added to the service charges would be:

Any additional costs and expenses which the landlord may incur in providing such other services and in carrying out such other works as the landlord may deem desirable or necessary for the benefit of the building or any part of it, or for securing or enhancing any amenity of or within the building.

A provision for the variation of the calculation of service charges would be:

If in the reasonable opinion of the landlord as substantiated by written evidence and calculations it should at any time and for any reason become necessary or equitable to do so by reason of any change in the comparative floor areas of the demised premises and other premises in the building the landlord may recalculate the percentage payable in respect of the demised premises and will notify the tenant accordingly and the revised percentage shall have effect from the date of the event giving rise to the need for such recalculation: Provided always that any such recalculation shall be made on the same basis of comparative floor areas as has been applied for the current percentage and in no circumstances shall any such calculation result in the landlord being entitled to receive more than the actual cost of the matters which caused the percentage recalculation.

From the landlord's point of view, provision should cover the capital expenditure as well as the running cost of any new service, as a clause allowing for additional services may be strictly construed by the courts. In *Mullaney* v *Maybourne Grange (Croydon) Management Co. Ltd* [1986] 1 EGLR 70 it was held that the costs of replacing wooden window frames with double-glazing units was not covered by an allowance for the costs of 'additional services or amenities'.

Depending on the nature of the property, the landlord may have statutory obligations for the safety of the retained parts (fire arrangements such as sprinklers or handrails for staircases). There will be cleansing requirements and, particularly for shopping precincts, landscaping and attractive features such as seats, fountains and Christmas decorations. In some cases, a resident caretaker or security staff may be required, and the service charge should cover any accommodation costs and wages of such persons.

The landlord will not be able to charge interest on money which has had to be borrowed to carry out expensive repairs to something covered by the service charge unless this is specifically allowed for in the service charge covenant. In *Boldmark Ltd* v *Cohen* [1986] 1 EGLR 47 a provision that the landlord could charge **'such sums as the landlords may from time to time expend in respect to the general administration and management of the block'** was held not to cover interest on money borrowed. The judge indicated that a provision for charging interest might have been sensible, although the Joint Subcommittee were of the opinion that any such interest charges should be borne by the landlord. For this reason, and also to avoid a sudden exceptionally heavy service charge in any one year for the tenants, it may be advisable to establish a reserve or sinking fund to cover such matters, based upon a realistic expectation of the useful life of equipment and anticipated repair and redecoration of property. A clause providing for a reserve fund would be for the service charges to cover:

such annual provision as the landlord may, in its absolute discretion, decide as being proper and reasonable for the establishment and maintenance of a reserve fund for the replacement of any boilers, plant, machinery, apparatus and equipment.

The landlord should ensure that the management costs of any service charges are also covered by the service charge covenant. This will include the costs of producing accounts and a certificate of expenditure and the fees of a management company or other person who deals with the day-to-day running of the property. A clause allowing for the recovery of these costs would be:

The landlord shall be entitled to include in the service charge the fees of any accountant or other person engaged by the landlord in connection with the provision of services and a certificate of expenditure.

11.1.3 MEANS OF APPORTIONING SERVICE CHARGES

There are three main methods of calculating an individual tenant's share of a total service charge.

First, there may be an equal apportionment at the outset when units are first let. This type of fixed charge is only likely to be found in older leases, and in *Hyams* v *Titan Properties Ltd* (1972) 24 P & CR 359 the Court of Appeal permitted a change to a proportionate charge on renewal of a lease. If this type of charge were to be applied today, it would seem to be essential to have some formula for reviewing any such apportionment allowing for change of circumstances.

Secondly, apportionment may be on the basis of rateable values, but this too is not likely to achieve a fair result as the rateable values may change and will take into account amenity value such as ground-floor accommodation as opposed to 11th floor.

Thirdly, apportionment may be on the floor area of space demised to each tenant. If this is the basis then it is advisable to state in the lease how the area is to be calculated. The following clause would indicate this:

The annual amount of the service charge payable by the tenant shall be such proportion of the total cost thereof to the landlord as the superficial floor area of the demised premises bears to the total lettable floor area of the [building] excluding any common parts or access ways thereof

None of these methods will be entirely fair as they will not take into account the use of the services made by any particular tenant. It may therefore be advisable to include in the service charge clause provision for charging for additional services. This will be important if insurance premiums are included in the service charge and one tenant is carrying on a high-risk trade requiring an additional premium. For this reason, it is preferable to deal with the payment of insurance premiums separately from service charges.

In some cases, service charges may need to be calculated at two tiers. For example, on an industrial estate, there may be an overall service charge for the roads, lighting and signing on the estate to be apportioned between the buildings on the estate, and another service charge to be apportioned between the tenants of individual units in the different buildings. This would obviously lead to a very complicated calculation, and would probably be best avoided if possible.

If the property is mixed, such as shops with offices or residential accommodation over, then there may be some merit in merely providing in the lease that the tenant shall pay a 'fair proportion' of the total service charge. In this case, it would be prudent to provide for determining any dispute as to a fair proportion by reference to the landlord's surveyor. An example of this would be:

to contribute a fair proportion according to use of the cost of services used by the occupier of the demised premises in common with the occupiers of any other properties, such fair proportion to be determined by the landlord's surveyor whose decision shall be final and binding on the parties hereto.

See the case discussed below of *Concorde Graphics Ltd* v *Andromeda Investments SA* (1982) 265 EG 386 for the capacity in which the landlord's surveyor may be called upon to act.

The lease should provide for the landlord to pay the appropriate percentage of service charge for any period during which any unit is not let. It should also give the landlord access to the demised premises for the purpose of repairing any common parts, or repairing or renewing services for which the landlord undertakes responsibility. An example of such a clause would be:

To permit the landlord to enter the demised premises to carry out any works or repairs to the building or the conduits serving the same as the landlord may require, the landlord making good any damage to the demised premises thereby caused.

The lease should contain a provision for resolving any disputes concerning the service charge. It is important that the landlord should comply strictly with any procedure laid down as otherwise costs may not be recoverable. The procedure would usually give the tenant the right to inspect receipts and so verify the landlord's certificate of costs, and require the tenant to give notice of objection to the service charge demanded within a specified time. If the parties are unable to agree, then it should be possible to refer the matter to some third party. A third party who is to arbitrate between the landlord and the tenant should be entirely independent. Thus, in *Concorde Graphics Ltd* v *Andromeda Investments SA* (1982) 265 EG 386, where the landlord's managing agents and the landlord's surveyor were essentially the same person, it was held that he could not act in an arbitral capacity to resolve a dispute between the landlord and its tenants and the landlord must appoint another surveyor to do this.

If the third party appointed is acting in an arbitral capacity, then his decision must fall between the two figures claimed to be correct by the landlord and the tenant. If he is acting as an expert, however, then he may settle on a figure outside these boundaries. If the calculation of the service charge is complex and requires some specialised knowledge, then it may be preferable to provide for the determination of a dispute by an expert rather than an arbitrator.

The tenant will generally only be liable for the service charge costs during the term of the lease. In *Capital and Counties Freehold Equity Trust Ltd* v *BL plc* [1987] 2 EGLR 49, the tenant had covenanted to pay expenses which 'may . . . during the said term be expended or incurred or become payable'. The landlord had contracted with a builder to carry out repairs and decorations, but the work was not to be done until after the end of the term. It was held that the tenant was not liable for the cost of this as it was not covered by the covenant.

If the service charge includes an element of reserve or sinking fund then, on sale of the lease, a purchaser should ideally pay for the tenant's contribution remaining in the fund. This can no doubt be part of the negotiations on the sale price. A purchaser should in any event enquire about provision for replacement of expensive items in the service charge.

An assignee of a lease is not liable for any arrears of service charge and it is important therefore that a landlord does not give consent to assignment until all arrears of service charge have been paid. It is thought that a refusal of consent on this ground would be reasonable.

11.1.4 RECOVERY OF SERVICE CHARGES

Service charges are usually made payable as additional rent (see below) in advance, the future year's expenditure being estimated on the previous year's. During the first year it can of course only be enlightened guesswork. At the end of the year, when accounts are rendered, an adjustment can be made by charging the tenants for any shortfall or setting off any surplus against the following year's demand. The following clauses would cover this procedure:

The tenant shall on the quarter days fixed for the payment of the rent pay in addition to the said rent such a sum in advance and on account of the service charge as the landlord or its managing agents shall from time to time specify at their discretion to be fair and reasonable.

As soon as practicable after the end of each landlord's financial year the landlord shall furnish to the tenant a copy of the certificate and account of the service charge payable by the tenant for the year, credit being given therein for the advance payments made by the tenant in respect of the said year and upon the furnishing of such account there shall be paid by the tenant to the landlord any balance of the service charge found

> **payable or there shall be allowed by the landlord to the tenant any amount which may have been overpaid by the tenant by way of advance payments as the case may require.**

The lease may contain a provision that interest should be payable on an unpaid service charge after a certain time, and if so it would seem fair that interest should also be payable to the tenant at the end of the year on any substantial overpayment.

As mentioned in **11.1.3**, the tenant should have a right to challenge any expenditure within a certain time-limit, and the lease should provide for this. Any provision in the lease that the certificate of costs prepared by a surveyor is to be regarded as 'final' cannot displace the court's jurisdiction to hear any dispute should any arbitral procedure prescribed by the lease fail to resolve it (*Re Davstone Estates Ltd's Leases* [1969] 2 Ch 378).

In *Morgan* v *Steiner* [1993] 33 EG 87 the tenants had covenanted to pay to the landlord **'all legal and other costs that may be incurred in obtaining the payment of maintenance contributions from any tenant in the building'**. It was held that this did not cover the landlord's costs of a tenants' action for the appointment of independent managing agents and a declaration of trust of the service charges paid.

It was held in *Electricity Supply Nominees Ltd* v *Thorn EMI Retail Ltd* [1991] 2 EGLR 46 that a tenant, from whom service charges had been recovered by the landlord, could recover these from a subtenant whose lease was extended under the Landlord and Tenant Act 1954 when the tenant's lease had expired. The basis of recovery was a quasi-contractual indemnity by the application of the rule in *Moule* v *Garrett* (1870) LR 7 Ex 101. (See further **6.5.2** and **12.1.1**.)

Service charges are nowadays almost always made payable as additional rent. Accordingly the landlord can distrain for non-payment of the service charge as for rent. It was held in *Concorde Graphics Ltd* v *Andromeda Investments SA* (1982) 265 EG 386 that a landlord cannot distrain for a service charge if any part of it is in dispute. It was also held that any overpayment of a service charge is a payment made under a mistake of law and not a mistake of fact, and is therefore irrecoverable by a tenant. It would therefore be advisable for a tenant in dispute with the landlord to pay any disputed sum into an account in the name of an independent third party pending settlement of the dispute.

A further possible advantage to the landlord of making a service charge payable as rent is that it is not necessary to serve a s. 146 notice before commencing forfeiture proceedings for non-payment. J.E. Adams has suggested, however, that the procedure for forfeiture for non-payment of rent is subject to so many statutory and equitable rights of relief for the tenant that ultimately the forfeiture route under the s. 146 procedure might be preferable. He suggests that the clause making the service charge recoverable as rent might therefore be modified to apply only to the right of distraint, so that it reads: **'and may, so far as a right of distraint is concerned, be recovered as if rent in arrear'**. The right to recover unpaid rent will definitely pass to an assignee on assignment of the reversion, whereas it is doubtful if the right to recover a covenanted payment would pass ('Precedents editor's notes [1993] Conv 11).

Because of the tax position with regard to service charges (see **11.1.5**) it is probably preferable that the accounting year for its calculation should be the same as the landlord's accounting year, and the lease should provide for this to be varied on notice to the tenants to allow for a change if the reversion is sold. This would be covered by the following clause:

> **The financial year for the purposes of the service charge shall be from the first day in January every year to the thirty-first day of December of that year or such other period as the landlord may, in its absolute discretion, from time to time reasonably determine.**

If a reserve or sinking fund is established, it is advisable that this should be constituted as a trust. The advantage of this is that the moneys will not then be available to the landlord's trustee in bankruptcy, and the tenants may also feel that the fund is safer. The following provisions allow for this:

So far as it shall be deemed prudent to make reasonable provision for future expenditure the landlord shall hold such reserve sum on trust for the joint benefit of the landlord, the tenant and other tenants within the building and shall place the same on deposit in a suitably designated account in a building society or invest the same in any other way authorised by law for the investment of trust funds with power to vary and transpose the same. Within the perpetuity period the landlord shall apply the said sums or the investments for the time being representing the said sums and the income thereof whenever necessary in or towards the purposes of [replacement or renewal or other matters for which the reserve fund is to be established]. The expression 'the perpetuity period' shall mean in relation to each such sum a period of eighty years from the date upon which the same shall have been set aside

If a trust is set up then ideally a separate deed should be drawn up to regulate the trust fund. It should specify the purposes for which the fund may be applied, allow for investment and an annual audit, specify the tenants as the beneficiaries and set out the basis for distribution of the fund on its termination, for example, if the property is destroyed. The Joint Subcommittee suggests that this should be between those who last contributed in the proportions in which they contributed.

Even if no trust fund is formally set up, it may be possible to imply a trust if the reserve funds are kept in a separate account which is designated as belonging to the tenants (*Re Chelsea Cloisters Ltd* (1980) 41 P & CR 98).

Provision should also be made for transfer of the fund to a new landlord on assignment of the reversion provided the new landlord enters into similar covenants to the present landlord's.

11.1.5 THE TAX IMPLICATIONS OF SERVICE CHARGES

A tenant will be able to set off service charges, along with rent, as expenditure against profits.

A landlord will be liable to tax under Schedule A on both rent and service charges. This means that any reserve, or sinking, fund can only be set up by the landlord out of net sums after deductions of tax. The landlord will also be taxable on any interest from such a fund. Moreover, it will not be possible to set off interest against expenditure until there is a year where expenditure is actually incurred, which may be some time.

VAT will be chargeable on services provided to the tenants (see **4.6**).

If a trust is established for the reserve fund, there would always be the possibility that the fund might some day revert to the tenants and it is unlikely therefore that they can be regarded as having parted with all interest in it. This may mean that the tenant cannot deduct as expenses from income any part of a service charge which is paid to a trust for the tenants. VAT would not be chargeable until such time as the fund was spent on the provision of services.

These matters need careful consideration in the drafting of the lease at the outset and may well become negotiating factors on an assignment of the lease or the reversion subsequently.

11.2 Insurance

Insurance is an important consideration which should be specifically dealt with in the lease. Apart from the actual covenant to insure, there are other matters which should be considered and provided for.

11.2.1 DIFFERENT WAYS OF EFFECTING INSURANCE

Insurance arrangements may vary according to the type of property, and in particular whether the property is a single self-contained unit or a unit in a block (in an office block, on an industrial estate or in a shopping precinct). In both cases, the landlord will want to arrange insurance cover, but in the latter type of property, insurance cover will be arranged for the whole block and premiums recovered from the tenants as part of the service charges or separately. It is probably preferable to charge separately for insurance cover as some tenants may carry on business with higher risk factors than others, and their share of the premium will be correspondingly larger. Also, this allows for an easy adjustment to the share of premium if there is a change of user and premises become a greater or lesser risk.

The tenant will want to know that premiums have been paid on the insurance policy and the landlord's covenant to insure usually provides for evidence of this, as in the following clause:

> **To keep the building insured against loss or damage by fire and such other risks as the landlord thinks fit and (upon payment by the tenant of any increased premium caused thereby) against such risks as the tenant may from time to time reasonably request for an amount equal to its full reinstatement cost (including all professional fees and the cost of any work which might be required by any statute) and three years' loss of rent in respect of the demised premises (the interest of the tenant if required being noted on the insurance policy) and to produce to the tenant on demand (but not more than twice in any one year) the policy of insurance (or a copy thereof) maintained by the landlord and the receipt for the last premium payable in respect of it.**

It is just possible that, in the case of individual self-contained premises, the landlord might be prepared to allow the tenant to insure, but will of course require proof that the premiums have been paid and will probably specify which insurance company the policy should be with. The landlord will therefore require a covenant from the tenant in the lease to this effect. This way of insuring could be of financial advantage to the tenant, who may be able to take out one policy to cover not only the demised premises, but also business risks.

If the tenant has taken a mortgage to purchase the lease, then the mortgagee may also insist on insuring the property, or at least on approving the insurers with whom the property is insured and the policy. This could mean that the property is insured twice over — an expensive practice for a tenant who cannot persuade either the landlord or the mortgagee to accept the other's insurer. In the event of a claim on the insurance in these circumstances, the insurer against whom a claim is made may claim a contribution from the other insurer.

11.2.2 MATTERS TO BE COVERED ON INSURANCE

Insurance should be to the full cost of reinstatement of the premises, to be agreed between the landlord and the tenant, or in default of agreement to be fixed by an independent surveyor. The covenant to insure should require the insurance moneys to be spent on reinstatement. There should be a clause therefore that the landlord:

> **shall promptly apply the proceeds of any insurance policy effected by the landlord covering the demised premises and all alterations and fixtures thereto in the rebuilding and reinstatement thereof.**

In the absence of any such covenant, the landlord is under no obligation to expend the insurance moneys on rebuilding, unless it can be shown that the insurance was effected to cover both the landlord's and the tenant's interests, although this may be implied if the tenant has paid the premiums (*Mumford Hotels Ltd* v *Wheler* [1964] Ch 117).

A covenant by the landlord to reinstate requires reinstatement to the same standard where premiums have been paid by the tenant. In *Vural Ltd* v *Security Archives Ltd* (1989) 60 P & CR 258 the premises were destroyed by fire, and the landlord was liable for the reinstatement of a wood parquet floor which was better for the tenant's business than the linoleum one which the landlord wished to have installed.

A covenant by the landlord to use insurance moneys to reinstate 'forthwith' was held in *S. Turner (Cabinet Works) Ltd* v *Young* (1955) 115 EG 632 to mean within a reasonable time.

It is important also that the insurance should cover rent and service charges if applicable during a period when the premises are unusable (see the clause in **11.2.1**), as rent is still payable even though the premises have been destroyed. (This is because a lease is an estate in the land, and the land is therefore regarded as the subject-matter of the lease, although in practice of course it is the premises on the land in which the tenant is interested.) Separate insurance is usually arranged for plate glass windows and the tenant may covenant to insure these. A typical clause for this would be:

To insure and keep insured for its full replacement value in some insurance office of repute all the plate glass in the demised premises.

The usual property insurance will cover (*inter alia*) damage from risks such as fire, earthquake, flood, subsidence, lightning, explosion, malicious damage and riot. It may also cover third-party risks (injury to third parties and sometimes also third-party property) arising out of accidents in the common parts of the building, precinct or estate.

The tenant will effect a separate insurance policy for its own business risks, including third-party cover for accidents or losses on its own premises.

As well as the buildings, the landlord will want to insure essential machinery and plant, such as lifts and central heating boilers and pipes. In the case of a block insurance, this will be recoverable also from the individual tenants either as part of the service charge or separately.

11.2.3 OTHER MATTERS WHICH SHOULD BE DEALT WITH IN AN INSURANCE COVENANT

In the case of a single unit, insurance is probably best effected in the joint names of landlord and tenant, and may provide for a third party, such as a mortgagee, to have an interest noted on the policy. A clause providing for this is:

The insurance policy is to be effected in the joint names of the landlord and the tenant with a note to be made on the policy of the names of such other persons interested in the demised premises as either the landlord or the tenant shall from time to time reasonably require.

Both parties will then have access to the insurance documents, it will be clear that insurance is to cover both parties' interests, and both parties will receive notice of discontinuance of the policy if it is allowed to lapse. This would avoid the disastrous kind of misunderstanding which occurred in *Argy Trading Development Co. Ltd* v *Lapid Developments Ltd* [1977] 1 WLR 444, where the tenant mistakenly believed that the landlord had insured as previously, although the tenant had covenanted to do so. In fact the policy had been allowed to lapse and the tenant was liable for the destruction of the premises by fire.

If insurance is effected in the name of one party only (usually the landlord) then the other party will require to have proof that the cover is satisfactory and that the premiums have been paid. The insurance covenant should therefore provide for production of copies of the insurance policy, and last receipt for premiums paid, on demand. A purchaser of leasehold premises or a mortgagee will also require to see these to be satisfied that the policy is extant and cover is adequate, and the tenant may be required to produce these on a sale. In a block insurance, the tenant's interest should be noted on the insurance policy, and the tenant should ensure that this is done.

A landlord who is insuring will also require a covenant from the tenant not to do any act or thing, or permit any act or thing to be done, which would either increase the insurance premiums or invalidate the insurance cover. An example of such a clause would be:

> **Not to use the demised premises either in such a manner as may render an increased premium to be payable for the insurance of the premises (and to reimburse the landlord in respect of any such increased premium that may become payable as a result) or in such manner as may render the insurance void or voidable.**

If the demised premises form part of a block then ideally the tenant will want to know that a covenant to this effect is included in all other leases of units in the block. An alternative to this would be for the landlord to covenant to allow to the tenant any increase in premium due to a high-risk user by another neighbouring tenant. An example of such a covenant would be:

> **To deduct from the amount of any premium for insuring the demised premises/building any increase therein attributable to the use to which any adjoining or neighbouring property of the landlord is put.**

The lease should make provision for ownership of the insurance moneys in the event that the property is destroyed but, for some reason, cannot be rebuilt. It is not unusual to provide that the moneys shall belong to the landlord, but it may be fairer to provide that they shall belong to them in proportion to the value of their respective interests. A clause to this effect would be:

> **In any case in which it is not possible within two years (or such longer period as may be agreed between the landlord and the tenant) to enter into a contract for the rebuilding or reinstatement of the demised premises, the insurance moneys and all interest earned thereon shall be divided between the landlord and the tenant in the ratio of the open market value of their respective interests in the demised premises immediately prior to the occurrence giving rise to the insured loss or damage (there being taken into account the likelihood of the tenant being able by virtue of any statutory provision to retain the use and occupation of all or any part of the demised premises after the expiry of the term hereby granted) and any dispute as to the division of such insurance moneys shall be determined by arbitration.**

The courts have occasionally had to consider the distribution of insurance moneys as between landlord and tenant where there is no provision for this in the lease. In the absence of any specific provision, it now seems that the moneys will be divisible between the landlord and the tenant according to the respective values of the reversion and the leasehold interest. This was the solution reached in *Beacon Carpets Ltd* v *Kirby* [1985] QB 755, in which the sum insured was not sufficient to rebuild the warehouse demised and the tenant did not wish to lease the smaller warehouse which the landlord proposed to build, so that the site was left vacant. The insurance covenant in the lease was by the landlord and the policy was in joint names. It was held that the lease contemplated that the insurance policy should be for the benefit of both parties, and they were therefore both entitled to the insurance moneys in proportion to the value of their respective interests.

TWELVE

TERMINATION OF THE LEASE BY MEANS OTHER THAN FORFEITURE

A commercial lease may come to an end in various ways other than by forfeiture: by effluxion of time, under the Landlord and Tenant Act 1954, through operation of a break clause, by surrender or merger; or by disclaimer. There are indications that two other methods of terminating leases also exist: frustration and acceptance of a repudiatory breach; but whether the latter will establish itself as an appropriate method remains unclear.

12.1 Effluxion of Time

Statute provides for a tenancy within Part II of the Landlord and Tenant Act 1954 to continue despite the fact that the term granted by the lease has expired. For a lease so protected, effluxion of time is therefore not a termination event: see **15.2.1**. Not all business tenancies, however, are afforded the protection of Part II: it applies only if the tenant occupies the premises for the purposes of a business carried on by him or for those and other purposes (Landlord and Tenant Act 1954, s. 23(1): see **15.1.2.2**). A tenant who has sublet the entire premises does not satisfy these requirements. Thus, if such a tenant has a fixed-term tenancy, it will terminate at the end of the contractually agreed term.

12.1.1 EXPIRY OF HEAD LEASE WHILE PREMISES SUBLEASED TO BUSINESS TENANT

A sublessee who is occupying the premises for the purposes of a business may itself have the protection of Part II. The position can therefore arise that the tenancy of a sublessee continues under Part II of the Act even after the expiry by effluxion of time of the reversion out of which it was created. Suppose, for instance, that A (a freeholder) leases premises to B, and B sublets the whole of them to C for the remainder of the term less one day. If C's subtenancy is protected by Part II of the Landlord and Tenant Act 1954, it will continue beyond the expiration of its contractual term and also beyond the expiration of B's head lease.

In order to prevent the covenants in C's sublease becoming unenforceable by reason of the destruction of B's reversion, the Landlord and Tenant Act 1954, s. 65(2), extends the effect of the Law of Property Act 1925, s. 139 (see **12.4.3**), to cases where B's tenancy merely determines. Thus s. 139 has the extended effect of treating A's freehold as the reversion of C's continuation tenancy for the purpose of preserving the same incidents and obligations as would have affected B's reversion had it not expired by effluxion of time. There is, however, a potential danger for B in this situation if, at the time of the expiration of its head lease, C is in breach of a covenant in the sublease. This was evident in *Electricity Supply Nominees Ltd* v *Thorn EMI Retail Ltd* [1991] 2 EGLR 46. In the head lease, B had covenanted (*inter alia*) to pay a service charge. B then subleased to C, and extracted from C a covenant in effect to pay B this charge. At the time B's head lease expired, C's payments of the service charge were nine months in arrears. A sued B for breach of its covenant in the head lease to pay this charge. B thereupon paid A the arrears and sought to recover them under the indemnity covenant in the sublease. However, the Court of Appeal considered (without expressing any concluded view) that the Law of Property Act 1925, s. 141, would apply in this situation: see *Re King* [1963] Ch 459 and **6.2.1.2**. This would transfer to A, from the date of expiry of B's head lease, the benefit of all the covenants in the sublease, including the benefit of the indemnity covenant. The result would be that B could not recover its payment by an action against C for breach of covenant.

In the event, the Court of Appeal held that B could recover from C under the principle of restitution known as the rule in *Moule* v *Garrett* (1872) LR 7 Ex 101: see **6.5.2**. This rule may not always be sufficient to satisfy B. Thus, if the rent payable under a sublease is more than that payable under the head lease, it will be A, not B, who stands to benefit by suing in respect of arrears under the sublease which are accrued due at the date of expiry of the head lease. B's best course is to bring any action against C before the expiry of the head lease, but this may not always be practicable, e.g. the amount of service charge due may not yet be calculated.

12.2 Landlord and Tenant Act 1954

The Landlord and Tenant Act 1954 provides specific means by which a tenancy protected within Part II can come to an end. It should be noted that a business tenancy within Part II does not come to an end merely because the contractual term has expired or because the landlord has served a notice to quit (whether to determine a periodic tenancy or to exercise a break clause in a fixed-term tenancy). The Act recognises a tenant's notice to quit or surrender and a forfeiture by the landlord as methods of terminating a business tenancy. Terminations and renewals under the Act are dealt with in **chapter 15**: see especially **15.2.2**.

Where the landlord and the tenant agree to the grant to the tenant of a future tenancy of the holding, on terms and from a date specified in the agreement, the current tenancy continues until that date but no longer, and is not a tenancy to which Part II of the Act applies (Landlord and Tenant Act 1954, s. 28).

12.3 Break Clause

A lease for a term of years may contain a proviso entitling either the landlord or the tenant (or both) to serve a notice to terminate the lease on a specified date or dates. Thus a lease for a term of 21 years may contain a proviso entitling either the landlord or the tenant (or both) to terminate the lease at the end of either the seventh or the 14th year. Such a proviso is known as a break clause.

A break clause in favour of a tenant is particularly useful if the tenant considers that there is a risk that it may not be able to continue to pay the rent or perform the other obligations of the lease. Whether a tenant can obtain a break clause depends, however, like so much in this area, on the bargaining strength of the parties. Since the recession of the early 1990s, tenants have been in a stronger position to demand such a clause.

A break clause exercisable by a tenant may be made conditional upon the tenant paying the rent reserved by the lease and observing and performing the covenants therein contained. If the lease does not specify who may exercise the break clause, it will be taken to be exercisable by the tenant alone.

The break clause must be exercised according to its terms. Thus, if it is stated to be exercisable by 'lessees', its exercise requires the authority of all the lessees (*Re Viola's Indenture of Lease* [1909] 1

Ch 244). Similarly, if the clause requires notice in writing, merely oral notice does not suffice. The clause will state the procedure to be followed: this will usually comprise the service of a notice by a specified date or within a specified period. It has been held that, in this context, time is of the essence (*United Scientific Holdings Ltd* v *Burnley Borough Council* [1978] AC 904). Thus the party wishing to exercise the break clause loses the right to do so once the specified date for service of the notice has passed.

A notice which contains a substantive error, such as the wrong date for termination, is invalid (*Hankey* v *Clavering* [1942] 2 KB 326). But a notice containing a mere clerical error which would not mislead a reasonable recipient, is not. Thus in *Carradine Properties Ltd* v *Aslam* [1976] 1 WLR 442, a notice was served in September 1974 which purported to determine the term on 27 September 1973. Since it was clear that the year stated was a clerical error for 1975, the notice was held to be good.

Where the lease imposes obligations upon the tenant at the end of the term, it is a matter of construction whether such obligations are imposed in the event of the earlier determination of the lease through the exercise of a break clause. Thus in *Dickinson* v *St Aubyn* [1944] KB 454, the lease contained a covenant by the tenant to paint 'in the last quarter of the said term'. It was held that this imposed an obligation to paint only during the last quarter of the full term, should the lease run that long. The earlier determination of the lease in that case therefore meant that the obligation to repaint never arose.

A break clause runs with the legal estate of the party entitled to it. It is therefore exercisable only by the person who is the landlord or the tenant (as the case may be) for the time being. Thus, for instance, an original tenant cannot exercise it after assignment of the lease. Similarly, a mere equitable assignee of either party, who does not have the legal estate vested in him, cannot exercise it (*Stait* v *Fenner* [1912] 2 Ch 504).

If A leases premises to B, and B subleases them to C, the exercise by B of a break clause in the head lease does not affect C's underlease. B's act is treated as a surrender (see **12.4.3**), and C's sublease continues (*Phipos* v *G. and B. Callegari* (1910) 54 SJ 635).

12.3.1 BREAK CLAUSES AND THE LANDLORD AND TENANT ACT 1954, PART II

Although the exercise of a break clause by a landlord is sufficient to bring to an end the term granted by the lease, statute has intervened in both residential and commercial leases to protect the position of the tenant. In the context of commercial leases, this protection is contained in the Landlord and Tenant Act 1954, Part II.

Section 24(1) provides that a tenancy protected within Part II 'shall not come to an end unless terminated in accordance with the provisions of this part of the Act'. This means that, where the tenancy is so protected, the service by a landlord of a notice in compliance with a break clause in the lease, whilst effective to determine the contractual term, does not terminate the lease for the purposes of Part II. A landlord seeking to effect a termination under the Act must also serve a notice under s. 25(2): see **15.2.2.1**. A single notice to terminate the tenancy may nevertheless suffice if it complies with both the break clause and the requirements of the Act (*Keith Bayley Rogers and Co.* v *Cubes Ltd* (1975) 31 P & CR 412). Where the terms of the break clause are such as to make such combined service impossible, two separate notices will have to be served.

It should, of course, be borne in mind that the protection afforded to tenants by the Landlord and Tenant Act 1954, Part II, means that even the service by the landlord of the requisite notices does not necessarily mean that the landlord will be able to remove a tenant who wishes to remain in possession. This is because the tenant has a right to serve a counter-notice expressing unwillingness to give up possession and to apply to the court for a new tenancy: see **15.2.2.1**. If the tenant does so, the landlord will be able to oppose a new tenancy only if he can establish one of the grounds set out in s. 30 of the Act: see **15.2.4**.

12.4 Surrender and Offer-to-Surrender Clauses

Surrender is the yielding up by the tenant of its lease to the person or body with the immediate estate in reversion. The result is to merge the estate surrendered into such reversionary estate. Thus if A, the freehold owner, leases premises to B, and B subleases them to C, A has the immediate estate in reversion on B's head lease, and B has the immediate estate in reversion on C's sublease. A surrender by C therefore causes C's estate to merge into the estate of B, and thereby cease to exist.

12.4.1 EXPRESS SURRENDER

An express surrender must be by deed, unless the lease is for a term of three years or less, in which case it must be in writing (Law of Property Act 1925, ss. 52 and 53(1)(a)). A surrender of even a lease for more than three years, however, may be effective in equity if in writing and for value: see *Megarry's Manual of the Law of Real Property*, 7th ed. Megarry and Thompson (London: Sweet & Maxwell, 1993), p. 332. The correct form of words for an express surrender is 'surrender and yield up' (Key and Elphinstone, *Precedents in Conveyancing*, 15th ed. (London: Sweet & Maxwell, 1953), vol. 1, p.1246; *Woodfall's Law of Landlord and Tenant*, 28th ed., release 28 (London: Sweet & Maxwell), vol. 1, para. 17.017).

12.4.2 IMPLIED SURRENDER

An implied surrender (sometimes called a surrender by operation of law) is a surrender which arises where the parties conduct themselves in a way which is inconsistent with the continued existence of the lease. A surrender by operation of law is not required to be by deed (Law of Property Act 1925, s. 52(2)(c)). Examples of an implied surrender include the acceptance by the tenant of a new lease to begin during the continuance of the old lease, and the grant by the landlord of a new lease to a third party with the lessee both consenting and giving up possession to the new lessee at the time it is granted. A mere oral agreement between the landlord and the tenant, however, that the tenant will surrender before the expiration of the contractual term does not constitute an implied surrender (*Take Harvest Ltd* v *Liu* [1993] AC 552, PC).

12.4.3 SURRENDER OF HEADLEASE: IMPACT ON SUBLEASE

If A leases freehold property to B, which B then sublets to C, the surrender of B's head lease during the subsistence of C's sublease destroys the estate which comprises the immediate reversion upon C's sublease. C's sublease, however, survives. The problem at common law was that it left C holding an estate carved out of A's freehold reversion, but with no privity of estate between A and C. This meant that not all the covenants in C's lease were enforceable as between A and C. Statute has remedied this by deeming C to be the immediate lessee of A. This provision (now contained in the Law of Property Act 1925, s. 139) means that, upon a surrender by B, A's estate is deemed to be the reversion of C's estate for the purpose of preserving the same incidents and obligations as would have affected the original reversion had there been no surrender. After B's surrender, therefore, covenants in C's sublease are enforceable between A and C.

If, however, the surrender by B were effected with a view to B's taking a new lease from A, B can surrender the head lease and take a new lease from A without having to surrender C's sublease; and B and C can enforce the covenants in C's sublease as if B's original lease had not been surrendered (Law of Property Act 1925, s. 150). This simplifies the granting of new leases upon a surrender, because it means that subtenants do not need to be involved.

12.4.4 OFFER-TO-SURRENDER CLAUSES

In the past, leases sometimes contained a clause whereby, if the tenant wished to assign the lease, it was first obliged to offer to surrender it to the landlord. The general aim of such clauses was explained by Lord Denning MR in *Greene* v *Church Commissioners for England* [1974] Ch 467 as being to preserve for the landlord the benefit of any rise in the letting value of the property leased. Without such a clause, in the event of a general rise in rents, the tenant could take the benefit by way of a premium upon assignment; whereas, by taking advantage of such a clause, it would be the landlord who would benefit by reletting at a higher rent.

Such clauses would specify a procedure, including the giving of notice, the time within which any acceptance by the landlord could be effected, and the method of ascertaining any consideration to be paid for the surrender. A typical clause would provide that, in the event of the landlord not accepting the offer to surrender, the tenant would have a qualified right to assign.

As explained elsewhere (see **5.6.2.2**), a clause in such a form does not infringe the Landlord and Tenant Act 1927, s. 19(1)(a) (which deems qualified covenants against assignment to be subject to a proviso that the licence or consent shall not be unreasonably withheld) because the subsection bites only when the tenant's right to assign (albeit a qualified right) has arisen. Under the clause, however, this right does not arise until after an offer to surrender has been made and has not been accepted by the landlord. The surrender mechanism therefore operates as a condition precedent to the right to assign. Such a clause was accepted as valid in *Adler* v *Upper Grosvenor Street Investment Ltd* [1957] 1 WLR 227 (which involved an obligation to offer to surrender the lease voluntarily) and this decision was affirmed in *Bocardo SA* v *S and M Hotels Ltd* [1980] 1 WLR 17: see **5.6.2.2**.

12.4.4.1 Offer-to-surrender clauses in business leases

The usefulness of offer-to-surrender clauses in the context of business leases is, however, curtailed by virtue of the Landlord and Tenant Act 1954, s. 38(1). This section is designed to invalidate provisions in a lease which seek to prevent a tenant from invoking the renewal machinery of Part II of that Act. The section provides that any agreement relating to a tenancy within Part II is (subject to specified savings) void insofar as it purports to preclude the tenant from making an application or request under Part II or provides for the termination or the surrender of the tenancy in the event of the tenant making such application or request.

The application of s. 38(1) to business tenancies was considered by Megarry VC in *Allnatt London Properties Ltd* v *Newton* [1981] 2 All ER 290; affirmed [1984] 1 All ER 423. There the lease contained an absolute prohibition against assignment and an offer-to-surrender clause. If the landlord rejected the offer (or failed to accept it within 21 days) the tenant could assign subject to the qualified consent of the landlord. The tenant made an offer to surrender in accordance with the clause, which the landlord accepted. The tenant then purported to withdraw the offer when he realised that the payment he would receive under the clause would be less than a quarter of what he might expect to obtain by way of premium from an assignee. The landlord claimed specific performance of the agreement and damages.

Megarry VC found that, although the agreement did not in terms preclude the tenant from applying for a new tenancy, it did have that effect. This was sufficient for him to hold that s. 38(1) rendered the agreement to surrender void. Nevertheless, his Lordship held that s. 38(1) did not strike down the machinery requiring the tenant to offer to surrender: an offer to surrender was not an agreement to surrender, and the section invalidated only the latter. The consequence was that the tenant never acquired a qualified right to assign.

This decision, leaving both parties stymied, means that offer-to-surrender clauses are seldom found in new leases of business premises. Furthermore, apart from invalidity under s. 38 of the Landlord and Tenant Act 1954, an agreement pursuant to an offer-to-surrender clause contained in an older lease may well be void for non-compliance with the formalities prescribed by the Law of Property (Miscellaneous Provisions) Act 1989, s. 2: see Law Commission Report No.208 (1992), *Business Tenancies: a Periodic Review of the Landlord and Tenant Act 1954*, at paras 3.16–3.19.

Voluntary surrender (i.e. a surrender not pursuant to an offer-to-surrender clause) is a method of terminating a tenancy within Part II of the Landlord and Tenant Act 1954, by s. 24(2) of the Act.

Even a voluntary surrender or agreement to surrender is ineffective for this purpose, however, unless the tenant has been in occupation under the tenancy for at least one month before the instrument was executed (s. 24(2)(b)).

12.5 Merger

Merger is the converse of surrender, and occurs where the tenant acquires the reversion immediately expectant upon its lease. The general rule is that the lease determines through being merged (or drowned, as it is sometimes expressed) in the reversion.

Merger can occur only where the two estates are both legal or both equitable, and only where they become vested in one person in the same right. Thus merger will not occur if, for example, the lessee takes a conveyance of the freehold in the name of another as trustee for himself (*Belaney* v *Belaney* (1867) LR 2 Ch App 138).

Equity took a more restrictive view of merger than the common law, and in certain instances would not treat merger as having occurred. Thus, equity looked to the intention of the party acquiring the reversion. In the absence of evidence of intention, equity presumed that merger had not occurred if it was either in that person's interests or if it was consistent with his duty. Furthermore, equity would not treat merger as occurring where, although the same estate became vested in the same person, this was in different capacities: such as a lessee who acquires the immediate reversion of his lease as personal representative. The equitable rules are now of general application: the Law of Property Act 1925, s. 185, states that there is no merger by operation of law of any estate the beneficial interest in which would not be deemed merged or extinguished in equity. Thus, if a tenant acquiring the reversion does intend to merge the two estates, its best course is to state this intention in writing.

Where merger does occur, it has the effect of destroying covenants in the lease, even if they affect other land of the covenantor. Thus in *Golden Lion Hotel (Hunstanton) Ltd* v *Carter* [1965] 1 WLR 1189 the lessor had covenanted in the lease not to build on an adjoining plot. The lessee purchased the reversion, merger occurred, and the covenant was destroyed. Thereafter the purchaser of that adjoining plot could not be prevented from building.

12.5.1 IMPACT OF MERGER ON SUBLEASES

The position of a sublessee on merger of the head lease is essentially the same as on surrender. The position at common law was that merger did not destroy a sublease created out of the merged leasehold estate, but that the covenants in the sublease were thereafter unenforceable. As in the case of surrender, however, the common law has long since been amended by statute. The Law of Property Act 1925, s. 139, applies also to merger. Thus if A (a freeholder) leases land to B, B subleases it to C, and B then purchases A's reversion, the freehold estate (now vested in B) is deemed to be the reversion of C's sublease for the purpose of preserving the same incidents and obligations as would have affected B's reversion had there been no merger.

12.6 Disclaimer by Liquidator or Trustee in Bankruptcy

The liquidator of a company in liquidation, or the trustee in bankruptcy of an individual, may disclaim onerous property, which includes a lease. A disclaimer puts an end to the tenant's rights, interests and liabilities under the lease, but not necessarily to those of third parties. The issues are discussed at **14.8**.

12.7 Frustration

The doctrine of frustration has a limited application in leases. The Court of Appeal in *Denman* v *Brise* [1949] 1 KB 22 had held that, because a lease creates an interest in land, a lease of land could not be frustrated. There were, nevertheless, earlier dicta of two members of the House of Lords in *Cricklewood Property and Investment Trust Ltd* v *Leighton's Investment Trust Ltd* [1945] AC 221 to the effect that frustration might have a limited application, and this has since been supported by dicta in the House of Lords in *National Carriers Ltd* v *Panalpina (Northern) Ltd* [1981] AC 675.

In the *National Carriers* case, the tenants had a 10-year lease of a warehouse which was unusable for a period of up to 20 months because the only means of access to vehicles had been closed by the local authority. On the facts, the doctrine was held inapplicable because the period during which the premises could not be used was only a small proportion of the length of the lease. It might be inferred from this that a much longer interruption might have sufficed to frustrate the lease. Similarly, several of their Lordships in that case considered that a lease would be frustrated by the total destruction of the land demised. This might occur in coastal areas where land falls into the sea.

The mere destruction of the buildings on the land demised will not generally, however, cause the lease to be frustrated, because, in this case, the land itself remains. The same would appear to apply even if the premises leased comprised only the upper floors of a building which is totally destroyed. The tenant still retains a right to the use of the air space. In practice, of course, a well-drawn lease will provide for destruction through fire or other hazards by means of insurance.

If the doctrine of frustration is held not to apply to the event in question, the lease continues. In such a case, even if the premises are unusable, the tenant remains liable for the payment of rent during the remainder of the term. A tenant should therefore try to obtain a tenant's break clause exercisable in the event that the premises are destroyed or unusable.

12.8 Acceptance of Repudiatory Breach

Under general principles of contract law, if a breach of contract by one party indicates that that party intends no longer to be bound by it, the other may accept the repudiation and rescind the contract. In *Total Oil Great Britain Ltd* v *Thompson Garages (Biggin Hill) Ltd* [1972] 1 QB 318, the Court of Appeal considered that, because a lease creates an interest in land, a lease could not come to an end like an ordinary contract by repudiation and acceptance. This view has, however, recently been challenged.

In *Hussein* v *Mehlman* [1992] 2 EGLR 87, the landlord had let residential premises on a three-year assured shorthold tenancy. The premises were in a very bad state of repair — the bedroom ceiling had collapsed, the ceiling in the sitting-room was in a dangerous state, the outside toilet was unusable, and there were burst pipes and rising damp. The landlord refused to execute any repairs, and the tenant eventually vacated the premises and returned the keys. The landlord was in breach of the covenant to repair which is implied into certain short leases of dwellinghouses by the Landlord and Tenant Act 1985, s. 11. The assistant recorder at Wood Green county court relied, by analogy, upon the reasoning expressed in *National Carriers Ltd* v *Panalpina (Northern) Ltd* [1981] AC 675 in the context of frustration. He held that the landlord had committed a repudiatory breach of contract, and this had been accepted by the tenant's giving up possession and returning the keys. From that date, therefore, the lease had come to an end. Thus, although the tenant remained liable for the rent due up to that date, he was not liable for any further payments. He was also awarded damages for the discomfort and inconvenience which the breach had caused.

Although *Hussein* v *Mehlman* concerned a residential, rather than a commercial lease (to which the implied covenants in the Landlord and Tenant Act 1985 are inapplicable), the principle would appear to be applicable to leases in the commercial sector. The decision is a further indication of the trend to apply general principles of contract law to the law of leases; but it remains to be seen if the reasoning is accepted by a higher court. If the repudiatory breach were committed by the tenant, it would need to be established whether the landlord would need where appropriate to serve a notice under the Law of Property Act 1925, s. 146, before being permitted to re-enter the premises.

In the [illegible] case [illegible] [illegible] [illegible] [illegible] to 20 [illegible] [illegible] [illegible] [illegible] [illegible] [illegible] [illegible] [illegible] the [illegible] [illegible]. On the facts, [illegible] [illegible] [illegible] the period during which the premises [illegible].

The [illegible] [illegible] the building [illegible] [illegible] [illegible] [illegible] however, cause the [illegible] [illegible] [illegible] [illegible] [illegible] [illegible] [illegible] [illegible] even if the premises [illegible].

THIRTEEN

TERMINATION OF THE LEASE BY FORFEITURE

In the event of a breach of covenant by a tenant, the landlord may have a choice of remedies:

(a) an action for a monetary sum (i.e. arrears of rent or mesne profits, or damages for breach of covenant);
(b) distress (for rent arrears), which was discussed at **9.5**;
(c) forfeiture, which brings the lease to an end.

In recessionary times, forfeiture is generally a less attractive prospect for landlords, who may not be able to relet the premises for some time, and may not be able to obtain such favourable terms from a new tenant. Forfeiture may, conversely, benefit the tenant, who, free from the obligations of the lease, may be able to obtain a new lease elsewhere at a lower rent. Indeed, in exceptional circumstances, a tenant who is the only practical occupier of the demised premises may now even commit a breach of covenant in the hope that the landlord will forfeit the lease and then have no choice but to relet to the same tenant on terms more favourable to the latter (cf. *L.E. Grovewood Ltd* v *Lundy Properties Ltd* (15 October 1993 ChD unreported)).

It should be borne in mind from the outset that, even if the landlord seeks to forfeit the lease, the tenant may have a right to seek relief from forfeiture (see **13.4.6** and **13.5.2**). If a head lease is forfeited, any sublease falls with it. A sublessee, however, has a right to claim relief from forfeiture of the head lease: see **13.4.6.4** and **13.5.2.4**.

The landlord may seek to forfeit the lease only in respect of:

(a) a breach of covenant in a lease which contains an express proviso for re-entry in that event;

or

(b) a breach of a condition to which the lease is subject – the condition may be express or implied.

13.1 Express Proviso for Re-entry

There will usually be a proviso whereby the landlord reserves the right to terminate the lease upon the occurrence of specified events, often the breach of any of the tenant's covenants: see the examples in **13.1.4**. In the absence of an express proviso of re-entry, the landlord will be limited to other remedies for breach of covenant, such as an action for arrears of rent.

13.1.1 CONSTRUCTION

A proviso for re-entry is construed according to the intention of the parties. If the intention is not clear, however, any uncertainty is construed against the lessor. Thus a proviso which entitles the landlord to re-enter for breach of a positive covenant will not entitle it to re-enter for breach of a negative covenant, and vice versa.

13.1.2 EFFECT OF OCCURRENCE OF SPECIFIED EVENT

A breach of covenant which gives the lessor a right of re-entry does not itself bring the lease to an end. It merely gives the lessor the right to elect whether to forfeit the lease or to affirm (and perhaps sue only for a monetary sum, perhaps for arrears of rent or damages for breach of covenant). The right to forfeit may, however, be accidentally waived (see **13.6**), and the landlord must therefore take all precautions to avoid this.

13.1.3 WHERE LEASE CREATES TERM BEGINNING AT AN EARLIER DATE

It often happens that the term granted by a lease begins at a date earlier than that upon which the lease is executed (see **1.2.1.2**). The covenants contained in such a lease, and therefore the right to forfeit for their breach, are not, however, retrospective. Thus in one case the lease contained a covenant against the construction of buildings of less than a specified value. Before execution of the lease, but after the commencement of the term, the tenant constructed a building of a lesser value. The landlord's action to forfeit the lease for breach of covenant failed because the covenant took effect only from the execution of the lease: there had therefore been no breach of covenant (*Bennett* v *Kidd* [1926] NI 50). The landlord should therefore ensure that the lease is executed when the tenant's liability is intended to commence.

13.1.4 FORMS OF PROVISO FOR RE-ENTRY

13.1.4.1 For breach of tenant's covenants

Any well-drawn lease will therefore contain the appropriate proviso for re-entry; and the landlord should ensure that the proviso reserves the right of re-entry for breach, not merely of the covenant to pay rent, but of all covenants. A proviso to achieve this might appear in the following form:

> **Provided that if all or any part of the rent hereby reserved shall be unpaid for fourteen days after becoming payable (whether formally demanded or not) or if any of the tenant's covenants herein contained shall not be observed or performed then in any such case it shall be lawful for the landlord at any time thereafter to re-enter upon the demised premises or any part thereof in the name of the whole and thereupon the term hereby granted shall absolutely determine but without prejudice to any right of action or remedy by either party against the other in respect of any arrears of rent or any antecedent breach of any of the covenants herein contained.**

In regard to antecedent breaches, this proviso is even-handed between the landlord and the tenant. The landlord might prefer the following wording:

> **. . . but without prejudice to any claim by the landlord against the tenant for any antecedent breach of any of the tenants' covenants herein contained.**

13.1.4.2 For insolvency or other events

It is quite common for a lease to provide for re-entry, not merely upon breach of the tenant's covenants, but also in the event of the tenant's insolvency or upon other specified events which would indicate that the tenant is financially insecure (and therefore likely to default on future payments of rent). To include such events, the precedent of a proviso for re-entry in **13.1.4.1** would usually be extended by the inclusion of additional words before 'then in any such case', on the lines of the following:

> **or if the tenant for the time being shall become bankrupt or, being a company, shall enter into liquidation (whether compulsorily or voluntarily) save for the purposes of**

reconstruction or amalgamation or if the tenant for the time being shall enter into any arrangement or composition with his or its creditors or shall suffer any process of distress or execution on the tenant's goods to be levied . . .

13.2 Condition

Unlike a covenant, which defines the parties' rights and obligations under the lease, a condition affects the nature of the estate granted. Thus a lease may be granted subject to a condition precedent or (as is more common) a condition subsequent. The occurrence of the condition subsequent will give the landlord the right to re-enter even if no express proviso for re-entry is contained in the lease. Thus if a lease is stated to be, for instance,

subject to the condition that the lessee shall not sublet

the lessor may seek to forfeit the lease in the event of its breach even in the absence of any express proviso for re-entry. As will be seen, however, a s. 146 notice (see **13.4**) must still be served.

13.2.1 IMPLIED CONDITIONS

Some conditions need not be express, but will be implied into every lease. One such is a condition that the tenant must not deny the title of its landlord or do acts which are inconsistent with the landlord's title. If the tenant breaches such condition, the landlord has a right to determine the lease by re-entry. Before forfeiting the lease, the landlord must serve a notice under the Law of Property Act 1925, s. 146, in the usual way. Even where the tenant has disclaimed the landlord's title, the court is still empowered to grant relief from forfeiture (*W.G. Clark (Properties) Ltd* v *Dupre Properties Ltd* [1992] Ch 297, doubting dicta to the contrary in *Warner* v *Sampson* [1959] 1 QB 297, CA).

13.3 Effecting Re-entry

Re-entry can be effected either by simply taking physical possession, or by taking possession pursuant to an order of the court. In residential tenancies, re-entry by the landlord without a court order is a criminal offence (Protection from Eviction Act 1977, s. 2). This is not the case in non-residential tenancies; but physical re-entry even into business premises is unlawful unless peaceable. Thus it is an offence for any person, without lawful authority, to use or threaten violence for the purpose of securing entry into any premises where, to his knowledge, there is someone present on the premises opposed to entry (Criminal Law Act 1977, s. 6(1)).

Before the decision of the House of Lords in *Billson* v *Residential Apartments Ltd* [1992] 1 AC 494 (discussed **13.4.6.1**), it was thought that, in the case of forfeiture for breach of a covenant other than a covenant to pay rent, the right to relief from forfeiture was lost as soon as the landlord had re-entered, even if such re-entry was not pursuant to a court order. Where it could be effected, peaceable possession, being quicker and cheaper, was therefore often preferred by landlords. Their Lordships' decision that relief can be given after peaceable re-entry without a court order means, however, that peaceable re-entry will generally be less popular with landlords. From the landlord's point of view, therefore, it is now generally better in such circumstances to re-enter pursuant to a court order, as the landlord can thereafter be secure in its possession.

13.4 Forfeiture for Breach of a Covenant other than a Covenant to Pay Rent

This is governed by statute, the Law of Property Act 1925, s. 146. A statutory notice must be served as specified in s. 146(1):

> A right of re-entry or forfeiture under any proviso or stipulation in a lease for a breach of any covenant or condition in the lease shall not be enforceable, by action or otherwise, unless and until the lessor serves on the lessee a notice—
>
> (a) specifying the particular breach complained of; and
> (b) if the breach is capable of remedy, requiring the lessee to remedy the breach; and
> (c) in any case, requiring the lessee to make compensation in money for the breach;
>
> and the lessee fails, within a reasonable time thereafter, to remedy the breach, if it is capable of remedy, and to make reasonable compensation in money, to the satisfaction of the lessor, for the breach.

Any forfeiture made in pursuance of an invalid notice is void. Note that although para. (c) appears to oblige the lessor to ask for compensation, it has been held that a notice is not invalidated by its omission to request compensation (*Rugby School (Governors)* v *Tannahill* [1935] 1 KB 87). Furthermore, if the breach is irremediable (see **13.4.3**), the notice does not need to require it to be remedied (*Rugby School (Governors)* v *Tannahill*).

Forfeiture for non-payment of rent is expressly excluded by s. 146(11) from the procedure specified in s. 146(1). Rent for this purpose includes a service charge only if the lease provides that it is recoverable as rent. If the lease does not so provide, an action to forfeit for non-payment of a service charge is subject to the statutory procedure in s. 146, so that a statutory notice must first be served.

13.4.1 CONDITION FOR FORFEITURE ON BANKRUPTCY OR INSOLVENT LIQUIDATION OF LESSEE

13.4.1.1 Specified types of leases

By the Law of Property Act 1925, s. 146(9), the obligation to serve a statutory notice under s. 146(1) does not apply to a condition for forfeiture on the bankruptcy of the lessee or on taking in execution of the lessee's interest if contained in a lease of:

(a) agricultural or pastoral land;
(b) mines or minerals;
(c) a public house or beer-shop;
(d) a furnished dwellinghouse; or
(e) any property with respect to which the personal qualifications of the tenant are of importance for the preservation of the value or character of the property, or on the ground of neighbourhood to the lessor, or to any person holding under him.

In such instances, the landlord may therefore effect a forfeiture (either by an action for possession or peaceable re-entry) without serving the statutory notice. A common thread running through these exceptions is that they all involve circumstances where it could be important for the lessor to be able to regain possession swiftly (in the case of agricultural land, for instance, because there may be seasonable crops; in the case of mines, in the interests of safety) (*Hockley Engineering Co. Ltd* v *V & P Midlands Ltd* [1993] 1 EGLR 76).

Although the subsection refers to bankruptcy, this includes the insolvent liquidation of a corporation (Law of Property Act 1925, s. 205(1)(i) and *Horsey Estate Ltd* v *Steiger* [1899] 2 QB 79). It would nevertheless appear that para. (e) can apply only to a tenant who is an individual. It cannot apply to a corporate tenant, since a corporation lacks 'personal qualities' and cannot be considered a 'neighbour' (*Hockley Engineering Co. Ltd* v *V & P Midlands Ltd*). The 'importance' referred to in para. (e) is to be assessed objectively. 'If a lessor wishes to have a person with particular personal qualities as his lessee in a particular property he can achieve this . . . by choosing the tenant carefully and . . . by making sure that the tenant has no power whatever to assign or part with possession of the property' (per Judge Micklem (sitting as a judge of the High Court) in *Hockley Engineering Co. Ltd* v *V & P Midlands Ltd* at p. 79). From the landlord's point of view, this indicates the importance of an absolute covenant against assignment, underletting, or parting with possession.

13.4.1.2 Other leases

In other cases of forfeiture for bankruptcy, the Law of Property Act 1925, s. 146(10), requires a landlord to serve a s. 146 notice:

(a) if bringing the forfeiture action against the tenant within one year from the bankruptcy;
(b) if bringing the action against an assignee, where the lease was sold within one year from the bankruptcy.

This means that no s. 146 notice need be served on the bankrupt tenant for forfeiture more than one year from bankruptcy, nor on an assignee where the lease was sold more than one year from bankruptcy. Bearing in mind the similarity of the wording of this subsection to s. 146(9), it is to be assumed that it too applies to forfeiture upon an insolvent liquidation.

The effects of bankruptcy or insolvent liquidation of the tenant under a commercial lease are considered more fully in **chapter 14**.

13.4.2 SERVICE OF SECTION 146 NOTICE

The statutory notice under s. 146 must be served upon the lessee, and this is defined to include (*inter alia*) an original or derivative underlessee, and the persons deriving title under a lessee. A mortgagee, whether by subdemise or by legal charge, is thus included. It has nevertheless been held that service of one notice upon the lessee in possession, or upon a lessee with a subsisting lease, suffices (*Church Commissioners for England* v *Ve-Ri-Best Manufacturing Co.* [1957] 1 QB 238). Thus, if the lessor serves notice upon such person, it has complied with the section, and the tenant's mortgagee, for instance, has no right to be served (*Egerton* v *Jones* [1939] 2 KB 702). If there are joint lessees, all must be served (*Blewett* v *Blewett* [1936] 2 All ER 188).

An assignment of a lease validly vests the lessee's estate in the assignee, even if made in breach of a covenant against assignment (whether absolute or qualified) (*Old Grovebury Manor Farm Ltd* v *W. Seymour Plant Sales and Hire Ltd (No. 2)* [1979] 1 WLR 1397). Since the assignee becomes the lessee, it is the assignee upon whom the s. 146 notice must be served. Service upon the assignor is invalid: see also *Fuller* v *Judy Properties Ltd* [1992] 1 EGLR 75 discussed in **13.4.6.2**).

Except in the case of breach of a repairing covenant (**13.4.5**), service of the s. 146 notice may be made by leaving it at or sending it by registered post (or by recorded delivery) to the last known place of abode or business in the United Kingdom of the person served, or by leaving it or affixing it to land or buildings comprised in the lease (Law of Property Act 1925, s. 196(3) and (4); Recorded Delivery Service Act 1962, s. 1 and schedule).

Once the landlord has re-entered pursuant to a court order, it is too late for the tenant to seek relief from forfeiture. Thus, as stated by Slade LJ in *Export Clothing Service and Sales Ltd* v *Hillgate House Ltd* [1986] Ch 340, the purpose of the statutory notice is twofold: first, if the breach is remediable, to give the tenant an opportunity to put it right; and, secondly, to give the tenant an opportunity to apply to the court for relief (provision for which is made in s. 146(2)).

These factors are important in regard to the length of the notice which must be given. If the breach is remediable, the notice must be sufficient to give the tenant an opportunity to remedy it. If, however, the breach is irremediable, the notice may be relatively short. Ultimately, therefore, the period of notice depends on the circumstances of each case. In *Scala House and District Property Co. Ltd v Forbes* [1974] QB 575, the court held 14 days' notice sufficient in the case of an irremediable breach.

It has been held that, where the breach of covenant is irremediable (such as the breach of a covenant against assignment), a s. 146 notice may still be validly served even after the landlord has peaceably re-entered the premises (*Fuller* v *Judy Properties Ltd* [1992] 1 EGLR 75). The reason is that the tenant still has the opportunity to apply to the court for relief. The result would appear to be otherwise in the case of a remediable breach, such as the breach of a repairing covenant, where the re-entry would prevent the tenant from effecting the necessary repairs. In such a case, the landlord would need to vacate the premises prior to serving the statutory notice and complying with the Leasehold Property (Repairs) Act 1938.

If the landlord does re-enter the demised premises without serving the requisite s. 146 notice, the tenant may either bring an action for possession or (where it is possible) effect peaceable re-entry. The tenant may also sue the landlord for damages for trespass and for breach of the implied covenant for quiet enjoyment (see **1.5**).

13.4.3 REMEDIABLE AND IRREMEDIABLE BREACHES

At one time, the courts looked to see whether the breach itself was capable of remedy. Thus a breach of a covenant, for example, to build by a certain date, was treated as an irremediable breach (*Stephens* v *Junior Army and Navy Stores Ltd* [1914] 2 Ch 516 in which, on the facts, however, the breach was waived). The modern approach, however, is to look, not at the remediability or otherwise of the breach itself, but to the remediability of the harm done to the lessor. This was the view of Slade LJ in *Export Clothing Service and Sales Ltd* v *Hillgate House Ltd* [1986] Ch 340 at p. 355 who considered that, in the ordinary case, the breach of a promise to do something by a certain time can for practical purposes be remedied by the thing being done even out of time.

This modern approach means that most positive covenants are remediable (e.g. by performing the act covenanted to be performed, albeit late). Thus in the *Export Clothing* case it was held that the breach of a covenant to reinstate premises by a specified date was capable of remedy by the performance of the covenant together with payments of monetary compensation. Exceptionally, the breach of some positive covenants will be irremediable, such as a breach of a covenant to insure where the premises have since been destroyed by fire, since the loss to the lessor cannot be retrieved.

A breach of a negative covenant may be irremediable if it is once-for-all. Thus it was held in *Scala House and District Property Co. Ltd* v *Forbes* [1974] QB 575 that a breach of a covenant against assignment was an irremediable breach. Where the breach is of a continuing nature, such as a breach of a user covenant, or a breach of a covenant to repair, the issue is again whether the harm to the lessor can be retrieved. A breach of a covenant against using the premises for immoral purposes is more likely to be considered to be irremediable, since there may be a lasting taint (see *Rugby School (Governors)* v *Tannahill* [1935] 1 KB 87; also *Dunraven Securities Ltd* v *Holloway* (1982) 264 EG 709 (premises used as a sex shop)).

13.4.4 EXCUSABLE BREACH

The landlord is not entitled to forfeit if the tenant has a lawful excuse for non-compliance with its covenants in the lease. The concept of an excusable breach was recognised in *John Lewis Properties plc* v *Viscount Chelsea* [1993] 34 EG 116, where the leases in question, which had been granted in 1934, contained covenants by the tenants to redevelop various properties comprised in the leases at specified dates in the future. The tenants were not able to carry out the redevelopment scheduled for completion by 1987, however, because it would entail the demolition of a building which had been listed in 1969. Such statutory controls had not existed when the leases were entered into, and there was no reasonable prospect of listed building consent being obtained. The court accepted the tenants' argument that they had a lawful excuse for non-performance.

13.4.5 REPAIRING COVENANTS

Although s. 146 provides some protection for tenants in breach of covenant, the onus of bringing proceedings for relief under that section is still on the tenant. In the case of breaches of repairing covenants, this protection was considered inadequate. Thus, where the lessor is seeking to forfeit for breach of a repairing covenant, the tenant is given additional protection by two statutory provisions: the Landlord and Tenant Act 1927, s. 18(2), and the Leasehold Property (Repairs) Act 1938.

13.4.5.1 Landlord and Tenant Act 1927, section 18(2)

The Landlord and Tenant Act 1927, s. 18(2), is designed to ensure that the tenant is made aware of the service of a Law of Property Act 1925, s. 146, notice in respect of a breach of a repairing covenant. Merely posting the notice on the premises does not suffice. The subsection provides that a right of re-entry or forfeiture for breach of such a covenant is not enforceable, by action or otherwise, unless the lessor proves that the fact of service of the s. 146 notice was known either to the lessee, or to an underlessee (which underlessee reserved to the lessee only a nominal reversion), or to the person who last paid the rent due under the lease, and that a time reasonably sufficient to enable repairs to be executed has since elapsed. A person is, however, deemed to have knowledge if the notice was sent by registered post or by recorded delivery service (Recorded Delivery Service Act 1962, s. 1) to his last known place of abode in the United Kingdom. This can create problems if the lessee is outside the United Kingdom, has sublet, and receives the rent direct from his subtenants (see *Woodfall's Law of Landlord and Tenant*, 28th ed., release 28 (London: Sweet & Maxwell), vol.1, para. 17.139.

13.4.5.2 Leasehold Property (Repairs) Act 1938

The Leasehold Property (Repairs) Act 1938 was passed in order to put a stop to a common practice of the time which involved speculative builders buying small properties in some need of repair, and serving on the owners long schedules of dilapidations. The aim was to frighten the tenants into either buying the freehold at a high price, or into submitting to a higher rent. The 1938 Act shifted the onus of bringing proceedings on to the landlord. The statute originally applied only in the case of small houses, since it was tenants of such properties that it was designed to protect. The scope of the Act was, however, extended by the Landlord and Tenant Act 1954, s. 51. It does not apply to agricultural leases (Leasehold Property (Repairs) Act 1938, s. 7(1)), but is otherwise now of general application. Thus even business tenants are entitled to the protection which it affords.

The Leasehold Property (Repairs) Act 1938, s. 1, applies where the landlord serves a Law of Property Act 1925, s. 146, notice relating to breach of a repairing covenant contained in a lease for a term of at least seven years (Leasehold Property (Repairs) Act 1938, s. 7(1)), where, at the date of the service of the notice, at least three years of the term remain. In these circumstances, the landlord must inform the tenant in writing of the tenant's right to serve a counter-notice within 28 days. A tenant who serves a counter-notice in writing can claim the benefit of the Act. This means that the landlord may not take proceedings, by action or otherwise, to enforce any right of re-entry or forfeiture for the breach of the covenant, without the leave of the court. The court is, generally, the county court (s. 6(1)).

If the tenant does not serve a counter-notice, the leave of the court is not required. It is important to note that the counter-notice must be served by the tenant personally. Thus, a purported counter-notice served, for instance, by the tenant's mortgagee is ineffective (*Church Commissioners for England* v *Ve-Ri-Best Manufacturing Co. Ltd* [1957] 1 QB 238).

The leave of the court is not to be granted 'unless the lessor proves' that the requirements of at least one of five specified circumstances are met. The fifth of these is contained in para. (e): 'special circumstances which, in the opinion of the court, render it just and equitable that leave should be given'. Apart from this, however, the other circumstances all in essence require the lessor to prove 'that the immediate remedying of a breach of the repairing covenant is required in order to save the landlord from substantial loss or damage which the landlord would otherwise sustain' (per Lord Templeman in *Associated British Ports* v *C.H. Bailey plc* [1990] 2 AC 703).

Before the decision of the House of Lords in *Associated British Ports* v *C.H. Bailey plc*, it had been held that the landlord could discharge the burden of proof merely by bringing evidence to support a prima facie case (*Sidnell* v *Wilson* [1966] 2 QB 67). This and other earlier decisions were, however, overruled by the House of Lords in the *Associated British Ports* case, which held that 'proves' means on the balance of evidence, i.e. the normal civil standard of proof. This means that the battle between the landlord and the tenant on this issue is to be fought at this first stage, when the landlord seeks leave, rather than at the trial itself.

Examples of landlord's notice and tenant's counter-notice are set out in **Appendix 2**.

13.4.5.3 Urgent repairs

A problem arises if the repairs need to be effected urgently. In such circumstances, the landlord may not be able to afford the delay of having to serve a Law of Property Act 1925, s. 146, notice and go through the procedure of obtaining leave under the 1938 Act. One issue is whether the landlord can go ahead and effect the repairs, and then claim reimbursement from the tenant. This is dealt with at **10.2.4**. A problem, however, is that if the landlord does effect such repairs there is no longer a disrepair in respect of which the landlord can serve a s. 146 notice. Since the statutory notice is a prerequisite to the landlord's right to forfeit for such a breach, the result is that, even if the landlord is able to recover the cost of the repairs, it can no longer forfeit for the breach.

The landlord might, however, be able to argue that the tenant's breach is of such a serious nature that it comprises a repudiatory breach, and that the landlord elects to accept the repudiation. In these circumstances, it may be that no s. 146 notice need be served, and the lease terminates on the landlord's acceptance of the breach. The doctrine of repudiatory breach has found favour with the courts recently in a slightly different context, but remains undeveloped: see **12.8**.

13.4.6 RELIEF AGAINST FORFEITURE

In the case of forfeiture for breach of a covenant other than a covenant to pay rent, relief is provided in the Law of Property Act 1925, s. 146(2). This states:

> Where a lessor is proceeding, by action or otherwise, to enforce . . . a right or re-entry or forfeiture, the lessee may . . . apply to the court for relief; and the court may grant or refuse relief, as the court, having regard to the proceedings and conduct of the parties . . . and to all the other circumstances, thinks fit; and in case of relief may grant it on such terms, if any, as to costs, expenses, damages, compensation, penalty, or otherwise, including the granting of an injunction to restrain any like breach in the future, as the court, in the circumstances of each case, thinks fit.

Relief under the subsection is therefore available only where the lessor 'is proceeding, by action or otherwise'. What, then, does 'is proceeding' mean?

In *Pakwood Transport Ltd* v *15 Beauchamp Place Ltd* (1977) 36 P & CR 112, the Court of Appeal accepted that the tenant can apply for relief even before forfeiture proceedings have been instituted. This means that the tenant can apply (in its own action) as soon as a s. 146 notice has been served. It has also been held that, where the landlord, after service of the s. 146 notice, institutes proceedings and obtains a forfeiture order from the court, the tenant may still apply for relief before the landlord has gone into possession pursuant to that order, i.e. until the landlord has taken possession pursuant to such order, it is still 'proceeding' (*Quilter* v *Mapleson* (1882) 9 QBD 672, CA).

However, where the landlord has (after service of a s. 146 notice) instituted and obtained a forfeiture order from the court, and, pursuant to such order, has re-entered the premises, it is then too late for the tenant to apply for relief under s. 146(2). This was the decision in *Rogers* v *Rice* [1892] 2 Ch 170 (which, like *Quilter* v *Mapleson*, concerned the statutory predecessor of the Law of Property Act 1925, s. 146, namely the Conveyancing Act 1881, s. 14). The court there held that, in such circumstances, the landlord was no longer 'proceeding by action'.

13.4.6.1 Peaceable re-entry without court order

What, however, is the position if the landlord, instead of entering into possession with a court order, effects a peaceable re-entry without such order, i.e. after expiry of the s. 146 notice? The words 'or otherwise', in the expression 'is proceeding by action or otherwise', must refer to taking physical possession without a court order. The subsection therefore appears to give the tenant the right to apply for relief even after the landlord re-enters, whether pursuant to a court order or not. This was, indeed, the view of the court in *Pakwood Transport Ltd* v *15 Beauchamp Place Ltd* (1977) 36 P & CR 112, in which reliance was placed upon *Rogers* v *Rice* [1892] 2 Ch 170, and also of the lower courts in *Billson* v *Residential Apartments Ltd* [1992] 1 AC 494. The judgment of the Court of Appeal in *Billson,* not surprisingly, encouraged many landlords to take the route of peaceable re-entry without a court order, on the basis that this was a quicker and cheaper remedy than obtaining a court order, which nevertheless still enjoyed the same advantage of barring the tenant's right to relief under the subsection.

In the House of Lords in *Billson,* however, the decision of the lower courts was reversed. Their Lordships held that, where the landlord has not obtained a court order for possession, a tenant is still entitled to apply for relief under s. 146(2) even after the landlord has peaceably re-entered. Lord Templeman (with whose speech three of the other Law Lords agreed) said that 'is proceeding' can mean 'proceeds'. In his view, if the tenant were to lose the right to apply for relief as soon as peaceable re-entry were effected, the tenant would not be safe unless it applied for relief as soon as the s. 146 notice were served. He did not think that Parliament could have intended that the tenant's position should be worse if the landlord embarks on 'the dubious and dangerous' method of determining the lease by re-entry, than if the landlord effects forfeiture by court order.

The effect of the speeches of the House of Lords in the *Billson* case has been to reduce the number of instances in which landlords seek to effect a forfeiture merely by taking physical possession, because peaceable re-entry does not bar the tenant's right to apply for relief. Lord Goff of Chieveley, in his speech in *Billson,* nevertheless envisaged that a tenant who delays applying for relief too long after peaceable re-entry will find itself debarred from obtaining it. The difficult issue, however, is precisely what length of delay will bar a claim for relief. The tenant will no doubt have a reasonable time, but what this is will ultimately depend upon all the circumstances of the case.

As a result of *Billson,* a peaceable re-entry by the landlord without a court order validly determines the tenant's legal estate under the lease; but the tenant nevertheless retains a right to seek relief under s. 146(2). The right to relief from forfeiture under the subsection is treated as equitable in nature, and is therefore lost if, before the tenant makes such application for relief, the landlord's reversion comes into the hands of a bona fide purchaser of the legal estate without notice of the right to apply for relief (*Fuller* v *Judy Properties* [1992] 1 EGLR 75). It is therefore in the tenant's interests to prevent this occurring by making an application to the court for relief and registering the pending land action in the register of pending actions (Land Charges Act 1972, s. 5(1)). A pending land action does not bind a purchaser without express notice unless it is for the time being so registered (Land Charges Act 1972, s. 5(7)).

13.4.6.2 Willingness of court to grant relief

Even where a third-party purchaser has in good faith acquired a legal estate without notice, relief may still be granted provided that the third party is not thereby prejudiced. Thus in *Fuller* v *Judy Properties Ltd* [1992] 1 EGLR 75 the tenant, whose lease still had eight years to run, had assigned it to the defendants in breach of a fully qualified covenant against assignment without the consent of the landlord, the plaintiff. The defendants paid the tenant-assignor a premium of £30,000. The plaintiff peaceably re-entered without a court order and shortly after granted a new lease of the same premises to H Ltd for a term of 16 years at a rent, and at a premium of £16,000. H Ltd was a bona fide purchaser of a legal estate without notice of the defendants' right to seek relief. The Court of Appeal considered that, because the defendants had paid a sizeable premium for their assignment, it would be inequitable to deny them relief from forfeiture. Such relief could not, however, lose H

Ltd its priority. Relief was therefore granted on the basis that the defendants were retrospectively put into the position of immediate reversioners on H Ltd's lease. They were therefore entitled to the premium that H Ltd had paid to the plaintiff. The defendants would continue to have to pay the plaintiff the rent under their own lease; but they were entitled to receive the rent under H Ltd's lease.

Where the breach is remediable, the court will usually be willing to grant relief to a tenant prepared to remedy the breach and pay damages. Furthermore, recent decisions indicate a greater willingness than earlier cases to grant relief even where the breach of covenant is irremediable and deliberate (see *Fuller* v *Judy Properties Ltd* in which there had also been an attempt to conceal the breach from the plaintiffs). Where, however, the covenant breached is one against user of the premises for immoral purposes, relief will be granted only rarely (*British Petroleum Pension Trust Ltd* v *Behrendt* (1985) 52 P & CR 117).

The court also has jurisdiction to grant relief in respect of a part of the premises only. This was established in *GMS Syndicate Ltd* v *Gary Elliott Ltd* [1982] Ch 1, where A leased premises to B, who sublet part to C. C used the part sublet to it for immoral purposes in breach of the covenant in the head lease. A sought to forfeit B's lease, but the court granted B relief in respect of that part of the property which had not been sublet to C.

The court cannot force a tenant who has applied for relief to accept it. In *Fuller* v *Judy Properties Ltd* the proposed relief was acceptable to the defendants because they had already been refused planning permission to use the premises for their intended purpose.

13.4.6.3 A residual equitable relief outside the statute?

There is no general equitable jurisdiction to grant relief from forfeiture for breaches of covenant other than a covenant for the payment of rent (*Hill* v *Barclay* (1810) 16 Ves Jr 402). However, in *Abbey National Building Society* v *Maybeech Ltd* [1985] Ch 190 the court invoked the equitable jurisdiction to grant relief to the tenant's mortgagee after the landlord had re-entered pursuant to a court order for breach of a covenant to pay a contribution to the maintenance of the building in question (such sum not being expressed to be recoverable as rent). There may therefore remain an equitable jurisdiction to relieve after re-entry pursuant to a court order where there has been breach of a covenant to pay a sum of money other than rent (such as a service or maintenance charge, or insurance premiums) where such sums are not expressed to be recoverable as rent. The scope and status of the *Maybeech* decision is, however, uncertain. It has not been overruled; on the other hand it was not followed in *Smith* v *Metropolitan City Properties Ltd* [1986] 1 EGLR 52. It may therefore be that any equitable relief was entirely superseded by the statutory relief of s. 146 (*Official Custodian for Charities* v *Parway Estates Developments Ltd* [1985] Ch 151).

13.4.6.4 Relief for sublessees

Whilst the tenant's sublessee or mortgagee is a person who may be served with a notice under the Law of Property Act, s. 146, service under the section can be effective even if the tenant's sublessee or mortgagee is not served. A tenant's mortgagee or underlessee is in a weaker position than the tenant itself. A prospective mortgagee should insist upon a clause in the mortgage which obliges the lessee to notify the mortgagee immediately should it receive any notice under s. 146.

One general safeguard for the holders of derivative interests does, however, exist. The landlord must endorse upon the writ seeking forfeiture, the names and addresses of any underlessees or mortgagees of whom it is aware, and must send such persons a copy of the writ. This applies whether the action is brought in the High Court (Rules of the Supreme Court 1965, ord. 6) or in the county court (County Court Rules 1981, ord. 6). If such persons are not served, they may, according to *Abbey National Building Society* v *Maybeech Ltd*, apply for relief even after the landlord has re-entered pursuant to a court order; but, as has been pointed out, it is not clear whether this decision is good law. A prospective mortgagee should therefore take what steps it can to protect itself so far as possible by ensuring that the mortgage contains a covenant by the lessee-mortgagor to inform the mortgagee immediately of certain events such as the receipt of any statutory notices or the assignment of the reversion. Since it depends upon the tenant's compliance, however, such a covenant is of limited value.

Where the lessor is proceeding to forfeit the lease, an underlessee may apply to the court for relief under Law of Property Act 1925, s. 146(4). Since the opening words of this subsection are similar to those used in subsection (2), it would appear that the relief under subsection (4) also remains available after a re-entry without a court order (cf. *Billson* v *Residential Apartments Ltd* [1992] 1 AC 494, see **13.4.6.1**). Under subsection (4), the court may make an order vesting in the underlessee all or part of the property comprised in the lease upon such conditions as the court may think fit. This means that the relief takes the form of a new lease granted directly to the party seeking relief, thus creating privity of both contract and estate between such party and the lessor. The applicant cannot, however, obtain a lease for a term longer than it had under its original sublease (s. 146(4)).

For the purposes of the Law of Property Act 1925, s. 146(4), an underlessee includes a mortgagee of the lessee's interest, even if the mortgage is by legal charge (s. 87(1) and *Grand Junction Co. Ltd* v *Bates* [1954] 2 QB 160). It also includes an equitable chargee (*Ladup Ltd* v *Williams and Glyn's Bank plc* [1985] 1 WLR 851). A mortgagee who is granted relief must hold the new lease as a substituted security, i.e. subject to the mortgagor's (the erstwhile tenant's) equity of redemption (*Chelsea Estates Investment Trust Co. Ltd* v *Marche* [1955] Ch 328).

For further discussion of relief under the Law of Property Act 1925, s. 146(4), see **13.5.2.4**.

13.4.6.5 Relief from forfeiture for bankruptcy or insolvent liquidation

Since relief in this case is based entirely upon the Law of Property Act 1925, s. 146, no relief from forfeiture for bankruptcy or insolvent liquidation is available where the service of a s. 146 notice is dispensed with by s. 146(9) and (10) (see **13.4.1**). This means, for instance, that a bankrupt tenant's trustee in bankruptcy must apply for relief or sell the lease within one year of the bankruptcy. The statutory right of sublessees and chargees to apply for relief from forfeiture under s. 146(4) is, however, preserved by the Law of Property (Amendment) Act 1929, s. 1.

13.5 Forfeiture for Breach of a Covenant to Pay Rent

As in the case of forfeiture for breach of other covenants, a landlord is not entitled to forfeit the lease for breach of the covenant to pay rent unless the lease reserves to the landlord a right of re-entry for breach, or unless the lease is conditional upon the payment of the rent.

Forfeiture for breach of a covenant to pay rent is not subject to the procedure laid down in the Law of Property Act 1925, s. 146(11). Rather it is subject to a special statutory regime.

13.5.1 DISPENSING WITH FORMAL DEMAND FOR RENT

At common law, a landlord cannot re-enter unless it has first made a formal demand for rent. The requirements of a formal demand are very exacting: the demand must be made by the landlord or its agent at the place specified by the landlord for payment, or on the demised premises. It must be made before sunset on the last day for payment, and may relate only to the sum due in the last rental period.

However, the lease may (and every well-drawn lease will) dispense with the requirement of a formal demand for rent. The condition or proviso for re-entry will contain a form of words to the effect that the lease is to determine even if no formal demand for rent has been made. The expression commonly used (and which appears in the precedent set out at **13.1.4.1**) is: **'whether formally demanded or not'**. If the lease does not contain these words or other words to this effect, a formal demand may nevertheless be dispensed with if an action for possession is brought at a time when specified circumstances appertain. If the action is brought in the High Court, these requirements are (in essence) that at least a half year's rent is in arrear, and there are insufficient goods on the premises available for distress to satisfy the amount due (Common Law Procedure Act 1852, s. 210). If the action is brought in the county court, the requirements are broadly the same (County Courts Act 1984, s. 139(1)).

13.5.2 RELIEF AGAINST FORFEITURE

The procedure for obtaining relief depends upon whether the landlord brings an action for possession in the High Court or in the county court, or whether the landlord simply effects a peaceable re-entry without a court order.

13.5.2.1 Landlord brings action in the High Court

In the High Court, the position is governed by the Common Law Procedure Act 1852, ss. 210 to 212, and by the Supreme Court Act 1981, s. 38.

The Common Law Procedure Act 1852, s. 212, provides a form of automatic relief. Under it, the forfeiture proceedings are to be discontinued if the tenant or his assignee, before the trial of the action, pays the lessor or into court all the arrears and costs. If the proceedings are so discontinued, the old lease continues. It has been held, however, that the section applies only if the rent is at least one half year in arrear (*Standard Pattern Co. Ltd* v *Ivey* [1962] Ch 432).

Where the Common Law Procedure Act 1852, s. 210, applies, the tenant, his assignee and all other persons deriving title under him, have six months from the landlord's entry under a court order during which they may pay the rent arrears and costs and apply for relief. At the end of this time, any application for relief is barred. It would appear that relief under this section (like that under s. 212) is available only where the rent is at least one half year in arrear. Relief under s. 210 essentially circumscribes the original equitable jurisdiction. Equity regards the proviso for re-entry merely as a security for the payment of the rent, and is usually willing to grant relief if the tenant pays off the rent arrears and costs. For this reason, the conduct of the parties is generally irrelevant: thus even a long record of late payment of rent is insufficient in most cases to deny the tenant relief. The relief, being based upon equitable principles, remains, however, discretionary: thus relief will not be granted if it would damage the interest of a bona fide purchaser of the legal estate without notice.

Since forfeiture is complete when the landlord has re-entered pursuant to a court order, relief under s. 210 takes the form of a new lease.

Where the circumstances specified under ss. 210 to 212 do not apply (as, for instance, where less than one half year's rent is in arrear), relief remains available under the purely equitable jurisdiction (Supreme Court Act 1981, s. 38(1)). This section in effect preserves for the High Court the same jurisdiction to grant relief from forfeiture for non-payment of rent as was formerly enjoyed by the Court of Chancery. In practice, this purely equitable jurisdiction has been used most frequently in cases of peaceable re-entry and it is therefore discussed further in **13.5.2.3**).

13.5.2.2 Landlord brings action in the county court

Where the lessor's action for forfeiture is brought in the county court, the relief is specified in the County Courts Act 1984, s. 138. The section provides both for automatic and for discretionary relief.

If the lessee pays into court not less than five clear days before the return day all the rent in arrear with costs, the action ceases, and the lessee holds the land according to the lease without any new lease (s. 138(2)).

If no such payment is made, and the court considers that the lessor is entitled to forfeit, the statute provides for a deferred order. Thus the court must order possession of the land to be given to the lessor at the expiration of such period, not being less than four weeks from the date of the order, as the court thinks fit, unless within that period the lessee pays into court all the rent in arrears and costs (s. 138(3)). The period of postponement may be extended at any time before possession is recovered (s. 138(4)). If within the postponement period the lessee pays into court all the rent in arrear and costs, he holds the land according to the lease without any new lease (s. 138(5)). The foregoing relief is therefore automatic.

If, however, the lessee does not make such payment within this period, the order is enforceable in the prescribed manner and, so long as it remains unreversed, the lessee is, subject to prescribed qualifications, barred from all relief (s. 138(7)). The qualifications are twofold. First, if the lessor has not yet recovered possession in pursuance of the order, the court may, under s. 138(8), extend the period of postponement referred to in subsection (4). Secondly, if the lessor has so recovered possession, the lessee may, within six months thereafter, apply to the court for relief; and the court may, if it thinks fit, grant to the lessee such relief, subject to such terms and conditions, as it thinks fit (s. 138(9A)). A lessee granted relief under subsection (9A) holds the land according to the lease without any new lease (s. 138(9B)).

Payment into court by a stranger (i.e. by someone other than the lessee, its underlessee or mortgagee) is not a payment for the purposes of this section (*Matthews* v *Dobbins* [1963] 1 WLR 227).

A lessee who does not apply for relief within the six months specified in subsection (9A) is barred from all relief — not merely in the county court (under the County Courts Act 1984), but also in the High Court (under both the Common Law Procedure Act 1852, ss. 210 to 212, and the High Court's inherent equitable jurisdiction) (*Di Palma* v *Victoria Square Property Co. Ltd* [1986] Ch 150).

13.5.2.3 Landlord peaceably re-enters without court order

In these circumstances, the tenant may seek relief in the High Court, which has an inherent equitable jurisdiction to grant relief (*Howard* v *Fanshawe* [1895] 2 Ch 581). It is a condition for the granting of such relief that there is readiness on the part of the person seeking it to pay the arrears within such time as the court thinks fit. There is no statutory time-limit, but the claim must be made with reasonable promptitude. In practice, the court uses the six-month period prescribed by the 1852 Act as a guide. The court will also consider whether, in the event of delay, the greater hardship would be suffered by the lessor (were relief to be granted) or by the lessee (were it to be denied) (*Thatcher* v *C.H. Pearce & Sons (Contractors) Ltd* [1968] 1 WLR 748 at p. 756, where an application for relief was permitted even though it had been made six months and four days after re-entry).

Alternatively, the lessee may apply for relief to the county court, which may grant such relief as could have been granted by the High Court. The application for relief must be brought within six months of the re-entry (County Courts Act 1984, s. 139(2)); *Lovelock* v *Margo* [1963] 2 QB 786. Any application for relief after six months can therefore be brought only before the High Court.

13.5.2.4 Relief from forfeiture for underlessees

As in cases of forfeiture for breach of covenant other than a covenant to pay rent, the landlord must notify any underlessees (including mortgagees) of whom it is aware of pending forfeiture proceedings: see **13.4.6.4**. A sublessee or mortgagee ought therefore to take all possible steps to ensure that the landlord is made aware of its interest, as suggested in **13.4.6.4**.

In cases of relief from forfeiture for arrears of rent, sublessees and mortgagees may be able to claim the benefit of either or both of two separate statutory provisions for relief.

First, where the circumstances in the Common Law Procedure Act 1852, s. 210, apply, it is specifically provided that the section does not bar the right of a mortgagee of the lease who is not in possession and who, within six months of the re-entry, pays all the arrears of rent and the costs and damages sustained by the lessor, and who performs all the lessee's covenants.

Secondly, the relief to underlessees and mortgagees conferred by the Law of Property Act 1925, s. 146(4), is exceptional, since it extends to forfeiture proceedings for non-payment of rent. Under this subsection, an underlessee (which includes a mortgagee) may apply to have the property subject to the lease (or part of it) vested in the underlessee upon such conditions as the court thinks fit: see further **13.4.6.4**. An equitable chargee may also apply for relief under this provision (*Ladup Ltd* v *Williams and Glyn's Bank plc* [1985] 1 WLR 851).

If the landlord's action is in the county court, the right to relief afforded to a lessee by the County Courts Act 1984, s. 138, extends to an underlessee (County Courts Act 1984, s. 140), and this includes a mortgagee. It would therefore appear that an underlessee may make the payments into court specified in s. 138(2), (5) and (7) (*United Dominions Trust Ltd* v *Shellpoint Trustees* [1993] 35 EG 121, Slade LJ). It is furthermore expressly provided that an application for relief under s. 138(9A) (i.e. within six months of the lessors recovering possession under the order) may be made by a sublessee; and on such application the court may make an order to vest the land in such person as lessee of the lessor for the remainder of the term or for such lesser term (s. 138(9C)). The relief provided by the statute is exclusive; and it has been held that the High Court has no inherent jurisdiction to relieve a mortgagee whose application is made after the statutory period of six months (*United Dominions Trust Ltd* v *Shellpoint Trustees*).

13.6 Waiver of Forfeiture

A landlord will lose the right to forfeit the lease if, after the tenant's breach, the landlord does an unequivocal act which affirms the continued existence of the lease. Common acts of affirmation are the demand for, acceptance of, or action to recover rent; but any act which indicates that the landlord is treating the lease as still subsisting will suffice, such as a distress for rent, or an entry by the landlord to effect repairs pursuant to a right in the lease. However, the landlord's agreement with a tenant's creditors to a voluntary arrangement whereby the lease is to be assigned does not cause a waiver (*Re Naeem* [1990] 1 WLR 48; and see **14.3.1**). The onus of proving waiver is on the tenant (*Matthews* v *Smallwood* [1910] 1 Ch 777).

A clause in a lease which provides that certain acts by the landlord are not to effect a waiver are void. Similarly, expressing a demand for rent to be 'without prejudice' is ineffective to prevent a waiver (*Segal Securities Ltd* v *Thoseby* [1963] 1 QB 889). By contrast, the use of such expression in negotiations between the parties is effective for this purpose (*Re National Jazz Centre Ltd* [1988] 2 EGLR 57.

Waiver can arise only if the landlord is aware that the breach has occurred. The landlord will have imputed to it the knowledge of its agents. Thus, in *Metropolitan Properties Co. Ltd* v *Cordery* (1979) 39 P & CR 10, the porter's knowledge of a subletting was imputed to the landlord, who was thereby held to have waived a right to forfeit for breach of a covenant against subletting. Constructive knowledge, however, will not be sufficient (*Official Custodian for Charities* v *Parway Estates Developments Ltd* [1985] Ch 151).

A waiver may arise even through a mere clerical error, such as a demand for rent sent out by the landlord's agents (*Central Estates (Belgravia) Ltd* v *Woolgar (No. 2)* [1972] 1 WLR 1048). It is therefore vital that the tenant's managing agents are instructed to put a stop on rent demands. Solicitors acting for landlords should apprise their clients of the importance of this.

If, however, the landlord has made it clear to the tenant that no more rent will be accepted, it appears that the mere processing of the payment by the landlord's bank will not effect a waiver, provided that the landlord repays the money without delay. In *John Lewis Properties plc* v *Viscount Chelsea* [1993] 34 EG 116, the tenant held properties of the landlord under three separate leases, two of which the landlord sought to forfeit for breach of covenant. The landlord informed the tenant that it would not accept further payments of rent under those two leases, but the tenant continued to send direct to the landlord's bank a single cheque in respect of all three leases, which was credited to the landlord's account. On each occasion the landlord returned that portion of the rent attributable to the two leases it was seeking to forfeit, and informed the tenant again that it would not accept such rent. Mummery J considered that a bank's processing of cheques was a purely administrative matter not involving business decisions, and that it was not necessary for the landlord to instruct its bank not to accept the cheques. In the circumstances, he was of the opinion that there had been no acceptance so as to constitute a waiver.

The facts of *John Lewis Properties plc* v *Viscount Chelsea* are somewhat special; but the decision lends tacit support to the view that where the tenant pays the rent by standing order, the mere crediting of the landlord's account with such payments is not *per se* an acceptance of them.

It should be noted that the statutory notice period prescribed by the Law of Property Act 1925, s. 146, is a preliminary to the right to forfeit. Thus, where the breach is of a covenant other than a covenant to pay rent, a landlord who has served the requisite notice is entitled to demand rent (apportioned where necessary) referable to the period up to the expiry of the notice. Similarly, where the Law of Property (Repairs) Act 1938 applies and the tenant has served a counter-notice, a landlord who is taking steps to obtain leave to proceed is entitled to continue to demand rent referable to the period until the leave is obtained. In these instances, the demand or acceptance of rent does not effect a waiver.

Furthermore, waiver will not occur by the demand for or acceptance of rent after the landlord has done an unequivocal act to indicate that it is treating the lease as at an end: the clearest instance of this is the institution of proceedings for possession. In effect, therefore, a breach of covenant by the tenant may be considered to give the landlord a right to elect to affirm the lease (by an act of waiver) or to treat it as at an end (by an action for possession). An election, once made, is irrevocable. The landlord needs, however, to exercise caution, because the acceptance of rent after the institution of possession proceedings may evidence the grant of a new tenancy.

13.6.1 THE EFFECT OF WAIVER

This depends on the nature of the breach. If breach is once-for-all, the waiver means that the right to forfeit in respect of that particular breach is for ever lost. Waiver does not, however, cause the covenant itself to be destroyed: waiver of one breach does not prevent the landlord from seeking to forfeit subsequently in respect of a further breach of the same covenant (Law of Property Act 1925, s. 148). Acceptance of rent over a long period, however, may evidence a release of the covenant breached (*Wolfe* v *Hogan* [1949] 2 KB 194; *City and Westminster Properties (1934) Ltd* v *Mudd* [1959] Ch 129).

If the breach is continuing, such as a breach of a repairing covenant, a waiver by the landlord, whilst precluding the landlord from forfeiting for the breach up to the date of the waiver, does not preclude the landlord from forfeiting for the breach thereafter. Furthermore, provided the continuing breaches are substantially the same as those which have been waived, no new statutory notice need be served in order to forfeit for the continuing breaches (*Penton* v *Barnett* [1898] 1 QB 276, CA; *Greenwich London Borough Council* v *Discreet Selling Estates Ltd* [1990] 2 EGLR 65, CA). The best explanation was that offered by John Colyer QC in argument in the latter case, namely, that what is waived is not the breach itself, but merely the right to forfeit in respect of the breach.

13.6.2 MESNE PROFITS

There may often be a considerable delay between the occurrence of the breach and the obtaining by the landlord of an order for possession. Although, subject as explained above, waiver may be caused by the demand for or acceptance of rent, the landlord is nevertheless entitled to demand and accept mesne profits. Indeed, an additional claim for mesne profits for the relevant period (i.e. for the period from the service of the writ for possession until the date of judgment or the date of the order for possession) is usually made in the action for possession. Mesne profits are payments for the mere occupation of the land. A demand for or acceptance of mesne profits does not therefore effect a waiver or evidence a grant of a new tenancy. The rent payable under the lease is good evidence of the value of the mesne profits which may be demanded.

The landlord must take care, before accepting payments tendered by the tenant, that it is not thereby waiving the right to forfeit. Whether the sums in question comprise mesne profits or rents is a matter of evidence. If the tenant offers payment as rent, the landlord cannot accept it as mesne profits (*Croft* v *Lumley* (1858) 5 E & B 648).

FOURTEEN

INSOLVENCY OF TENANT

The recession has led to the insolvency of many lessees of commercial premises, and the subject-matter of this chapter is therefore of particular current importance. This chapter does not aim to provide a comprehensive guide to insolvency law; rather it is designed to highlight the practical implications of a tenant's actual or impending insolvency during the running of a commercial lease, and the options which are available to the landlord in the variety of situations which can arise.

14.1 Lease Expressed to be Determinable upon Insolvency, etc.

An insolvent tenant is hardly a desirable tenant, since default in the payment of the rent is probable and there may be default in the performance of the other obligations in the lease. For this reason, most commercial leases contain an express proviso whereby the lease is determinable upon:

(a) the appointment of a receiver over the tenant's property;
(b) the tenant's entering into a composition or arrangement with its creditors;
(c) (in the case of an individual tenant) the tenant's bankruptcy; or
(d) (in the case of a company tenant) the appointment of a liquidator or administrator.

The occurrence of one of these events would then give the landlord the right to take steps to terminate the lease: see **13.1.4.2**. Such a proviso must, however, be express; it will not be implied (*Hyde* v *Warden* (1877) 3 ExD 72). Thus in the absence of an express provision, the landlord has no right to terminate the lease merely because the tenant is insolvent or is facing insolvency.

Breach of a proviso that the lease shall determine upon the appointment of a receiver, a trustee in bankruptcy, or a liquidator, is a once and for all and irremediable breach. If, however, the determining event is the tenant's 'insolvency', meaning an inability to pay his debts, the breach is a continuing one. Bankruptcy is regarded as an irremediable breach (*Civil Service Co-operative Society* v *McGrigor's Trustee* [1923] 2 Ch 347).

The landlord may also make the lease determinable upon the insolvency of a third party, such as a guarantor (*Halliard Property Co. Ltd* v *Jack Segal Ltd* [1978] 1 WLR 377) or an original tenant after assignment.

The mere vesting of the lease in a tenant's trustee in bankruptcy does not breach a covenant against assignment (whether absolute or qualified), since such event occurs by operation of law, not by the tenant's own act (*Re Riggs* [1901] 2 KB 16).

It should be remembered that the general rule of construction of forfeiture clauses applies, i.e. they are construed against the landlord: see **13.1.1**. Clear words must therefore be used if they are to be held effective in the particular circumstances.

In certain instances, forfeiture for the bankruptcy or insolvent liquidation of the tenant can proceed without service of a notice under the Law of Property Act 1925, s. 146: see **13.4.1**.

14.2 Courses of Action open to the Landlord

A tenant which is insolvent or which is facing insolvency may have already defaulted on the rent or other payments (e.g. a service charge), or have otherwise breached covenants in the lease, and the tenant's insolvency or other act may (if there is an express proviso to this effect) have made the lease determinable. The landlord has a range of courses of action depending upon the particular circumstances of the case. The landlord's position where an administrative or Law of Property Act receiver has been appointed is considered at **16.2**.

14.2.1 COURSES OF ACTION PRIMARILY DESIGNED TO RECOVER RENT OR DAMAGES

14.2.1.1 Threaten petition for winding up or bankruptcy

A creditor owed at least £750 may petition for a compulsory winding up (where the debtor is a company) or for bankruptcy (where the debtor is an individual) if the claim remains unsatisfied three weeks after serving a statutory notice in a prescribed form (Insolvency Act 1986, ss. 123 and 267). In some cases, therefore, the service by a landlord of a statutory demand might do the trick. In practice, however, the landlord, as an unsecured creditor, may not fare so well in an actual bankruptcy or winding up.

There is a risk that rent payments made by the tenant at a time when he is unable to pay his debts may be set aside as a fraudulent preference. To be so caught, the payments must be made shortly before bankruptcy or insolvency (which can be a period of up to two years) (Insolvency Act 1986, ss. 239, 240, 340 and 341). In practice, however, this is unlikely, since the test is whether the tenant had a desire to prefer a creditor, not whether a preference was a natural consequence of the payment. Where, therefore, the tenant pays the rent in order to avoid a forfeiture and so continue in business, the landlord would appear to be safe (*Re MC Bacon Ltd* [1990] BCC 78).

14.2.1.2 Distress

Provided there are sufficient goods on the premises, distress for rent arrears is generally preferable to an action to recover the rent. An important advantage is that distress gives the landlord a legal lien, which means that he is in a favoured position, somewhat like that of a secured creditor. Not surprisingly, however, the right to distrain in cases of bankruptcy, liquidation or administration, is hedged with restrictions.

There are two general matters a landlord should bear in mind:

(a) A judgment for rent arrears can be enforced only by court procedures, not by distress (*Chancellor* v *Webster* (1893) 9 TLR 568).
(b) If he intends to forfeit the lease, he should be wary that a distress (which is an affirmation of the lease) does not cause the right of forfeiture to be waived: see **13.6**.

14.2.1.3 Action for rent arrears

Where the remedy of distress proves inadequate, rent arrears may need to be recovered in an action. In practice, however, an action to recover rent arrears will generally not be advisable. First, where the tenant is already insolvent, permission to bring the action may be required, and will rarely be given: generally the court will authorise an action for a debt only where the debt was incurred after, and for the purpose of, bankruptcy, administration or winding up (*Re Atlantic Computer Systems plc* [1992] Ch 505). Secondly, even where an action can be brought, the costs (and delays) of bringing an action to recover arrears which may never be recoverable from an insolvent tenant will dissuade most landlords from suing. Thirdly, leave of the court may ultimately be required to enforce a judgment.

14.2.1.4 Action against earlier tenant or guarantor

This was discussed at **3.1.4, 6.1** and **6.4**. If G acts as guarantor for the obligations of the tenant, T, and T's liquidator or trustee in bankruptcy disclaims the lease, G ceases to be liable for breaches committed thereafter. This applies whether T is the original tenant, T1 (*Stacey* v *Hill* [1901] 1 KB 660), or an assignee, T2 (*Murphy* v *Sawyer-Hoare* [1993] 27 EG 127).

The position is different, however, if G acts as a guarantor for T1 and the disclaimer is effected by the liquidator or trustee in bankruptcy of an assignee, T2. In such a case, since (under general principles) T1 remains liable for future breaches (*Warnford Investments Ltd* v *Duckworth* [1979] Ch 127), so (probably) does G, its guarantor.

These principles are considered further at **14.8.3.2**.

14.2.1.5 Recovering rents of subleases

Under the Law of Distress Amendment Act 1908, a head landlord whose tenant is in arrears with the rent is entitled to serve a notice on subtenants requiring them to pay the rent direct to the head landlord. Such a notice is effective against the tenant's receiver; but in bankruptcy, liquidation or administration the position remains unclear: it may be that the court's leave is needed before such notice can be served.

14.2.1.6 Use of bank guarantee or rent deposit

If the landlord required the tenant to ensure that its bank provided a guarantee or performance bond for the payment of the rent up to a specified amount, the landlord may look to this for payment.

If the landlord obtained a rent deposit from the tenant, the landlord may be able to use this to make good the arrears. Where a tenant is bankrupt or in insolvent liquidation, however, the landlord will not be able to satisfy the arrears out of the deposit if the tenant retains a proprietary interest in it. Furthermore, if the deposit creates a charge and legal proceedings are needed to enforce it, the landlord may require the court's leave to do so under the statutory provisions to be examined in this chapter.

14.2.1.7 Tenant default indemnity

A landlord may be able to insure against losses in the event of the tenant's insolvency. The premiums would normally be recouped as a component of a service charge. Such insurance is, however, expensive and somewhat unusual.

14.2.1.8 Proving in the winding up or bankruptcy

Where the tenant is insolvent, the landlord may find it is reduced to proving in the winding up or bankruptcy. In the case of winding up, the landlord can prove for rent up to the date of the liquidation, which means (in the case of a compulsory winding up) the date of presentation of the petition (Insolvency Rules 1986, r. 4.92). In the case of bankruptcy, however, the landlord can prove for rent due up to the date of the bankruptcy order (Insolvency Rules 1986, r. 6.112). In each case, rent payable in arrear can be apportioned.

Rent which accrues subsequently is not proved in the winding up or bankruptcy; but the landlord might be able to claim that it is an expense of such process, and thereby secure payment ahead of the tenant's ordinary creditors.

Where the landlord's claim is unliquidated (such as for damages for the tenant's breach of a repairing covenant) its value can be estimated by the trustee in bankruptcy or liquidator (Insolvency Act 1986, s. 322(3); Insolvency Rules 1986, r. 4.86). If the landlord, pursuant to a right reserved in the lease, has entered the premises and performed the repairs (see **10.2.4**), the measure of the claim can be calculated precisely.

The landlord's claim may include interest, either where this is provided for in the lease, or under the general law (Judgments Act 1838, s. 17; Insolvency Rules 1986, r. 4.93 and r. 6.113).

14.2.1.9 Landlord's right to rent arrears out of execution by other creditors

If a tenant is in rent arrears, the landlord has a right to be paid out of the proceeds of execution levied against the tenant on behalf of another creditor under a court order in priority to the execution creditor itself. If the execution is pursuant to proceedings in the High Court, the landlord's right is defined and governed by the Landlord and Tenant Act 1709, s. 1. The sheriff is under a duty to deal with the landlord's claim (for up to one year's rent arrears) if he receives notice of it, from whatever source, before he has parted with the proceeds of sale. It is therefore in the landlord's interests to notify the sheriff of any arrears due. In the county court, the landlord's rights are to be found in the County Courts Act 1984, s. 102. The landlord must claim his right (in signed writing) within five days of the bailiff's seizure or removal of the goods. The only restriction upon the landlord's right to claim priority occurs in the case of the tenant's bankruptcy, and is considered at **14.6.8**.

14.2.1.10 Appointment of a receiver

The High Court has jurisdiction under the Supreme Court Act 1981, s. 37, to appoint a receiver in all cases in which it appears to the court just and convenient to do so. A landlord might seek the appointment of a receiver where the premises need continuous management, which the tenant is not attending to. This is particularly appropriate to premises which are sublet to numerous separate businesses, each subtenant paying a service charge.

14.2.2 COURSES OF ACTION RELATING TO THE PREMISES

14.2.2.1 Accept surrender

The landlord may be willing to accept a surrender from the tenant, particularly if the lease has premium value. If the surrender is for an undervalue, there is the risk that it may be set aside upon the application of the trustee in bankruptcy, liquidator or administrator if at the time the tenant could not pay his debts (see the Insolvency Act 1986, ss. 238, 339, 436 and 423).

As considered further below, dealings by the tenant after bankruptcy or insolvency may be void.

Where the tenant is bankrupt or an insolvent company, the surrender may be accepted from the trustee in bankruptcy or the liquidator, who will generally prefer surrender to disclaimer where the lease has premium value, since the consideration for the surrender swells the fund available to creditors.

A surrender ends the liability of the surrendering tenant, an original tenant, and any surety in regard to future obligations under the lease. Liability for existing breaches remains. However, a landlord who expressly releases the surrendering tenant from such liability will also be taken to have released earlier tenants and their sureties (*Deanplan Ltd* v *Mahmoud* [1992] 1 EGLR 79).

For a general discussion of surrender, see **12.4**.

14.2.2.2 Seek forfeiture

Forfeiture is generally less desirable for the landlord in a recession, since the property may be empty for some time before a new tenant can be found, and the rent payable under the new lease may be less than that payable under the old. If, however, this is not the case (perhaps because the landlord granted the lease at a premium and therefore took a reduced rent), forfeiture may still be advantageous. If, as often occurs in commercial lettings, the lease was granted at a rack-rent with no premium and subject to periodic reviews, such financial cushion is absent. In such circumstances, forfeiture may be less advantageous.

If the landlord seeks to forfeit, the tenant has a right to apply for relief; as does the tenant's mortgagee, sublessee or equitable chargee. If the tenant is bankrupt or in liquidation, the trustee in bankruptcy or liquidator has such right, which may be assigned, as a chose in action, to a purchaser. If the forfeiture was for bankruptcy or insolvent liquidation, any application for relief by the trustee or liquidator must be made within one year after the bankruptcy or liquidation (Law of Property Act 1925, s. 146(10)). See **13.4.1.2** and **13.4.6.5**.

A right to forfeit is not lost if a judgment creditor has in the meantime obtained a charging order absolute over the lease under the Charging Orders Act 1979.

14.2.2.3 Consent to an assignment

If the tenant can assign the lease, any capital sum received from the assignee may enable it to pay off the arrears. A tenant is more likely to be able to do this if it paid a premium on the grant of the lease and therefore pays less than a rack-rent. If the tenant has found a prospective assignee, the landlord (where the right to assign is qualified) may therefore prefer to give its consent to the assignment, rather than to forfeit and be left with a loss of rent before the premises can be relet.

14.2.2.4 Put tenant's trustee in bankruptcy or liquidator to an election to disclaim or not

It is clearly unsatisfactory for a landlord not to know whether the trustee or liquidator will disclaim the lease, since definite arrangements to relet cannot be made. The landlord can require a trustee or liquidator to disclaim (if at all) within 28 days after the service upon him of a notice. This is considered further at **14.8.2**.

14.2.2.5 Apply to have lease rescinded?

The court has power, on the application of the other contracting party, to discharge a contract entered into by a bankrupt on such terms as the court considers equitable (Insolvency Act 1986, s. 345). Any damages payable by virtue of the order are provable as a bankruptcy debt. A parallel power exists in regard to a company's contracts on a winding up (Insolvency Act 1986, s. 186). It might be arguable that this power is applicable to a lease, in which case the landlord could apply to the court for its discharge. There is no authority on the point. Since, however, a lease creates an interest in land, it is probably unlikely that this procedure is available to a landlord.

14.2.2.6 Compel surety to take a new lease

This is possible if the tenant's surety has covenanted with the landlord to take a new lease of the premises in his own name in the event of disclaimer of the lease by the tenant's trustee in bankruptcy or liquidator. Such a covenant imposes an independent primary liability on the surety and thus survives the disclaimer. From the landlord's point of view, it is desirable that the surety covenants to take a new lease from the date of the disclaimer: see **3.1.4.4** and **14.8.3.2**.

14.3 Options open to the Tenant

The tenant's options may, understandably, be somewhat limited. If insolvency is looming, a tenant may be able to fend it off by reorganising its business. Failing this, it may seek to raise funds to pay its creditors through a surrender (see **14.2.2.1**) or an assignment (see **14.2.2.3**). In a final attempt to stave off disaster, the tenant might seek to enter into a voluntary arrangement with its creditors. If this fails, there may be no alternative to the tenant but to petition for its own liquidation (see **14.7**) or bankruptcy (see **14.6**), or (where it is a corporate body) to petition for an administration order (see **14.5**).

14.3.1 VOLUNTARY ARRANGEMENTS

The law differs according to whether the tenant is an individual or a corporate entity.

14.3.1.1 Individual debtors

The Insolvency Act 1986 enables a tenant to obtain a short moratorium on actions against him, in order to give him time to put proposals to his creditors (s. 253). The tenant can apply to the court for an interim order (which lasts for 14 days unless extended by the court) nominating a person to act as trustee or supervisor of the arrangement. During the period of the order, no bankruptcy petition may be presented or proceeded with, and no other proceedings or execution can proceed without the leave of the court (s. 252). During this period, therefore, the landlord cannot bring proceedings against the tenant, e.g. for forfeiture or for arrears of rent (*Re Naeem* [1990] 1 WLR 48). The landlord may, however, recover rent arrears by distress (*McMullen & Sons Ltd* v *Cerrone* [1993] EGCS 108).

The creditors' meeting is convened to consider the debtor's proposals for dealing with the debts. Votes at the creditors' meeting are weighted according to the size at the date of the meeting of each creditor's debt. Claims for unliquidated or unascertained sums are, however, disallowed. The voting power of the debtor's lessor will therefore clearly include the amount of rent then accrued due; but whether it includes a sum in respect of future rents is unclear: see McLoughlin, *Commercial Leases and Insolvency*, (London: Butterworths, 1992), p. 4.

Approval of the resolution requires a majority of more than three-quarters in value of the creditors voting on it. A vote by a lessor in favour of a voluntary arrangement that involves the assignment of the lease does not waive an existing right of forfeiture (*Re Naeem*). The outcome of the voting is reported to the court. If the resolution is rejected, the interim order ceases, so that the moratorium ends. If the resolution is accepted, the arrangement binds all creditors who had notice of the meeting and were entitled to vote, whether they did so or not.

14.3.1.2 Corporate debtors

A somewhat similar procedure for voluntary arrangements exists where the debtor is a company (see Insolvency Act 1986, ss. 1 to 7), but with the important difference that in this case there is no statutory moratorium. For this reason, the procedure is little used on its own and is really more appropriate in conjunction with an administration order, where there is a statutory moratorium.

14.4 Options open to a Mortgagee

An institutional lender which has advanced funds to the tenant will invariably have taken steps to secure its own position, whether by taking a mortgage or floating charge, or by obtaining guarantors, or both. An important remedy for a mortgagee is the appointment of a receiver. This is considered in the discussion of secured lending in **chapter 16**.

14.5 Administration of a Company

The process of administration, which is in practice quite popular, was introduced in the 1980s to enable an attempt to be made to rescue a company in the hope of avoiding liquidation. An administrator is appointed by a petition to the court made by the company, by any of its directors or creditors, or by a clerk of a magistrates' court (Insolvency Act 1986, s. 9).

If the court considers that the company is unable to pay its debts but that a specified purpose (including the survival of the company or a better realisation of its assets than in winding up) will be achieved, it may make an administration order. This appoints an administrator, who has all the powers of management of the company from the date of the order. Conversely, from that time the powers of any administrative receiver (see **16.2.1**) cease.

The administrator is the agent of the company and may do all things necessary for the management of the company's affairs (Insolvency Act 1986, s. 14 and sch. 1). The administrator must prepare proposals to give effect to the purpose of the administration order, and these must be put to a creditors' meeting. If the proposals are approved (which requires an ordinary majority) the court is informed. If they are rejected, the court may discharge the order or make any other order (Insolvency Act 1986, s. 24).

14.5.1 FROM PRESENTATION OF PETITION TO MAKING OF ORDER

During this period, by the Insolvency Act 1986, s. 10(1), except with leave of the court:

(a) no steps may be taken to enforce any security over the company's property,
(b) no other proceedings, execution or other legal process may be commenced or continued against the company or its property, and
(c) no distress may be levied against the company or its property.

It is unclear whether this catches the service of a notice under the Law of Distress (Amendment) Act 1908. As previously mentioned, the court is unlikely to give a landlord the requisite leave, e.g. to forfeit the lease, to sue or to distrain for rent arrears due at the presentation of the petition.

If, at the time of the petition, there is an administrative receiver of the company, no leave is required unless and until the person who appointed such receiver consents to the making of the order (Insolvency Act 1986, s. 10(3)).

14.5.2 FROM THE MAKING OF THE ORDER

As the tenant company's agent, the administrator is not personally liable for the rent or upon the other covenants in the lease. He is, furthermore, under no general obligation as administrator to pay the rent. He does, however, have a discretion to pay it; and, in exercising this discretion, he must act responsibly and take all the circumstances into account. If the aim of the administration order was to preserve the company as a going concern, which entails its being able to pay its outgoings, the administrator ought to pay the rent as it falls due, i.e. as an expense in the administration. Even if the order was made with a view to winding up, the administrator ought to pay over to the landlord any rents received from subtenants, at least up to the value of the rent under the head lease (*Re Atlantic Computer Systems plc* [1992] Ch 505).

The tenant company itself remains liable for the rent during the period of administration. Therefore, if the administrator declines to pay, the landlord may wish to bring an action to forfeit the lease or for the rent (or both), or to distrain. The landlord, however, faces two difficulties.

First, the moratorium on actions and distress against the company and its property continues after the order has been made, unless the administrator consents or the court gives leave (Insolvency Act 1986, s. 11(3)(d)). Peaceable re-entry by the landlord has been held to require leave within s. 11(3), as being either the enforcement of a 'security' over the company's property, or a 'legal process' (*Exchange Travel Agency Ltd* v *Triton Property Trust plc* [1991] 2 EGLR 50). If the landlord applies for leave, the court may, as a condition of refusing it, order the administrator to pay the rent. An order for costs can be made in the landlord's favour if the administrator refuses unreasonably (*Re*

Atlantic Computer Systems plc [1992] Ch 505). For a discussion of the approach of the court in deciding whether to grant leave (or to refuse it upon terms) under s. 11(3), see *Re Atlantic Computer Systems plc* [1992] Ch 505 at pp. 541–4.

Secondly, even if leave is obtained, the landlord may not be able to enforce the terms of the lease against the company.

14.6 Bankruptcy

14.6.1 BANKRUPTCY PETITION

Various persons may present a petition for bankruptcy, including the debtor personally (Insolvency Act 1986, s. 264). A creditor with a liquidated debt or debts of at least £750 may petition for bankruptcy if there is no reasonable prospect of the debtor paying (s. 267). A secured creditor cannot present a petition for the secured part of the debt without first surrendering the security (s. 269). Any disposition made by the debtor between the presentation of the petition and the making of the order is void. Following the presentation of the petition, the official receiver may be appointed to manage the property pending the making of a bankruptcy order (s. 286).

14.6.2 BANKRUPTCY ORDER

If a bankruptcy order is made, the debtor becomes an undischarged bankrupt. Until a trustee in bankruptcy is appointed, the official receiver manages the property, and will generally seek to preserve it instead of selling it.

If a trustee in bankruptcy is to be appointed, the official receiver must call a meeting of creditors within 12 weeks of the bankruptcy order. Upon appointment, all the bankrupt's property is automatically vested in the trustee, without the need for any conveyance or assignment. Certain basic personal and business items are, however, excluded.

The trustee in bankruptcy's function is to get in, realise and distribute the bankrupt's estate (Insolvency Act 1986, s. 305(2)). For this purpose, the trustee has a variety of statutory powers, including the power to carry on the bankrupt's business (s. 314 and sch. 5).

A trustee in bankruptcy in occupation of land is the occupier and liable to pay non-domestic rates, even after disclaiming (*Re Lister* [1926] Ch 149).

14.6.3 DISTRIBUTION OF ASSETS

The trustee in bankruptcy cannot dispose of property free from any specific charge to which it is subject. Thus the mortgagee of a bankrupt tenant has a wide range of choices available, including leaving the charge as it is, valuing or selling the security and suing for the balance, applying to the court for a sale, or putting the trustee to an election whether to exercise the power to redeem the charge at the value placed upon it. In this last instance, the trustee in bankruptcy has six months in which to redeem.

The trustee in bankruptcy is, nevertheless, empowered to redeem the charge at the value which the mortgagee has specified, giving the mortgagee 21 days in which to revalue. Alternatively, and with specified exceptions, the trustee may offer the security for sale.

Subject to the rights of mortgagees, the bankrupt's estate is distributable in the following order: bankruptcy expenses, pre-preferential debts (including, if the bankrupt is deceased, reasonable funeral and testamentary expenses), preferential debts, ordinary debts, interest on debts, and postponed debts. If any surplus remains, it is paid to the bankrupt.

14.6.4 LANDLORD'S POSITION AFTER PRESENTATION OF PETITION

The requirement that the debt be liquidated means that, whilst a landlord can bring a petition where sufficient rent is in arrear, it cannot petition for damage caused by a breach of, say, a tenant's repairing covenant, without first obtaining judgment for a sum in damages.

14.6.5 LANDLORD'S POSITION BETWEEN PETITION AND BANKRUPTCY ORDER

14.6.5.1 Execution of judgment

A landlord who obtained judgment against the tenant before the presentation of the petition may levy execution against the bankrupt's property. The landlord may not retain the benefit of the execution, however, unless it was complete before the making of the bankruptcy order (Insolvency Act 1986, s. 346). Even if execution was so completed, the landlord will not be entitled to its benefit if the sum raised by the sale exceeds £500 and, within 14 days of the sale, the sheriff is informed of the presentation of the petition in bankruptcy.

The court has an overriding power to permit the landlord to retain the benefit of the execution, but the court will exercise this power only in exceptional circumstances (s. 346(6)). Where the landlord is not entitled, the benefit of the execution passes to the trustee in bankruptcy.

14.6.5.2 Other actions

The landlord may bring an action for forfeiture, rent arrears, or breach of covenant, or he may levy distress; but the court may stay any action, execution or legal process against the debtor or the debtor's property (Insolvency Act 1986, s. 285(1)). The subsection does not include distress; but whether it includes the service of a notice under the Law of Distress (Amendment) Act 1908 is unclear.

A landlord who distrains does not thereby lose the right to prove in the bankruptcy (s. 347(10)); but it would appear that, once a landlord has lodged proof for arrears due before bankruptcy, those arrears (as opposed to arrears which accrue after bankruptcy) cannot later be distrained for.

14.6.6 AFTER THE MAKING OF A BANKRUPTCY ORDER

After the bankruptcy order has been made, the Insolvency Act 1986, s. 285(3), provides that no creditor may, in respect of a debt provable in the bankruptcy:

(a) bring legal proceedings against the property or person of the bankrupt without the leave of the court and upon such terms as the court may impose; or

(b) have any remedy against the bankrupt's person or property (which therefore includes levying of execution).

These restrictions do not, however, apply to an action for forfeiture (*Ezekiel* v *Orakpo* [1977] QB 260).

The landlord has a right to distrain for rent accrued due before the commencement of the bankruptcy, but only for a maximum of six months' such rent (s. 347(1)). Where a bankruptcy order is made within three months of a distress, the goods distrained are charged with the payment of preferential debts which cannot be met out of the bankrupt's estate (s. 347(3)).

These restrictions do not affect a secured creditor, which remains entitled to enforce its security.

The lease of a bankrupt tenant is vested in the trustee in bankruptcy. This means that, unless the lease is disclaimed, the trustee is liable for the rent accruing due and in respect of the other lessor's obligations from the date of vesting. The trustee is, however, generally entitled to an indemnity for such payments out of the bankrupt's estate. If the trustee does not disclaim, the landlord has a right (without the leave of the court) to distrain for the rent which accrues due after the commencement of the bankruptcy (s. 347(9)).

14.6.7 EFFECT OF TRUSTEE IN BANKRUPTCY'S DISCLAIMER

The trustee in bankruptcy may disclaim the lease. Since the law of disclaimer is broadly the same in the case of bankruptcy and insolvent liquidation, it is dealt with at **14.8**.

14.6.8 RESTRICTIONS ON LANDLORD'S PRIORITY OVER EXECUTION CREDITORS

If a tenant against whom execution has been levied is adjudged bankrupt before notice of the landlord's claim has been served on the sheriff or bailiff (see **14.2.1.9**), the landlord's claim is restricted to six months' rent, and does not extend to rent payable in respect of the period after the notice is served (Insolvency Act 1986, s. 347(6)). The landlord does not need the leave of the court to exercise this right.

14.7 Company Liquidation

14.7.1 VOLUNTARY AND COMPULSORY WINDING UP

A voluntary liquidation takes place at the behest of the company's members who may appoint a liquidator (where the company is solvent) or leave it to the creditors to appoint one (where the company is insolvent). The liquidator can manage the company's business so far as is necessary for the winding up and must pay the company's debts in the correct order of priority. A voluntary winding up commences at the time of the passing of the resolution for voluntary winding up (Insolvency Act 1986, s. 86).

Compulsory winding up by the court takes place on a number of grounds: one of these is if the company is unable to pay its debts. A company is deemed unable to pay its debts if (*inter alia*) it fails to pay, within three weeks of a written demand from a creditor, a debt of at least £750. A compulsory winding up commences at the time of the presentation of the petition for winding up (s. 129(2)). Public creditors are responsible for the lion's share of such winding-up orders. Some 55 per cent of these in London are for VAT debt, and another 10 per cent are brought by the Inland Revenue.

Certain dealings by the company with its property before liquidation are liable to be set aside: these comprise dealings at an undervalue or which prefer some creditors over others. The assignment of a lease at an undervalue might be set aside on this ground.

14.7.2 BEFORE COMMENCEMENT OF WINDING UP

In respect of rent accrued due before the commencement of the winding up, the landlord may put in a claim as an unsecured creditor. If the rent is payable in arrear, the landlord is entitled (under the Apportionment Act 1870) to apportion the rent in respect of the periods before and after the commencement of the winding up. Apart from putting in a claim, the landlord has the usual remedies for rent accrued due before the commencement of the winding up (forfeiture, distress, or action); but these are subject to the following statutory restrictions.

14.7.2.1 Voluntary winding up

(a) If the landlord has obtained judgment against the tenant company, then provided he completes execution before the resolution for voluntary winding up is adopted, he can retain the fruits of the execution, unless: (i) the execution is not complete at the time the landlord receives notice of a meeting to propose a resolution for a voluntary winding up (Insolvency Act 1986, s. 183); or (ii) a notice of the adoption of the winding-up resolution is served on the sheriff (s. 184). In these two cases, the sheriff must pay the proceeds of execution to the liquidator. A sheriff who levies execution for a judgment of more than £500 must keep the proceeds for 14 days to allow for notice of winding up to be served.

(b) The adoption of a winding-up resolution does not preclude the landlord from bringing an action for forfeiture, for rent or for breaches of other covenants, or from distraining. But the liquidator or any contributory or creditor may apply to the court, which has power (*inter alia*) to stay or restrain any proceedings under ss. 112 and 126. This evidently includes the power to stay a distress.

14.7.2.2 Compulsory winding up

(a) If the landlord has previously obtained judgment for the arrears and execution is completed before the presentation of the petition, the landlord can retain the benefit of the execution (Insolvency Act 1986, s. 183). An exception is where the execution is for a sum exceeding £500 and a notice of the presentation of the petition is served on the sheriff within 14 days. If execution is not complete by the date the petition is presented, the landlord loses the benefit of the execution. The court has an overriding power (exercised only in exceptional cases) to allow the execution creditor to retain the benefit of the execution.

(b) Where distress is effected within three months of a compulsory winding-up order, the goods distrained are charged with the payment of the company's preferential debts which cannot be met out of the company's property (s. 176).

(c) Between presentation of the petition and the making of a winding-up order, no leave is required to bring an action for forfeiture, for rent or for other breaches of covenant; but the company, a creditor or a contributory, may apply to the court to have any action or proceeding stayed (s. 126).

Subject to the rights enjoyed by secured creditors (which are broadly similar to those in a bankruptcy), the liquidated company's debts are paid in the following order: liquidation expenses, preferential debts, ordinary debts, interest on debts, postponed debts. Any surplus is paid to the shareholders. A landlord's debt for rent accrued due before winding up ranks merely as an ordinary debt.

14.7.3 AFTER COMMENCEMENT OF WINDING UP

Unless and until the lease is disclaimed or the company itself is dissolved, the company (despite being in liquidation) remains liable under the lease. The liquidator, being the company's agent, is not personally liable under the lease; and this is so, it would seem, even where the liquidator applies to have the lease vested in him or her under the Insolvency Act 1986, s. 145.

14.7.3.1 Restrictions on actions

In a compulsory winding up, after a winding up order has been made or a provisional liquidator appointed, no action may be brought or proceeded with against the company or its property without the leave of the court (Insolvency Act 1986, s. 130(2)). This has been held to include a distress (*Re Memco Engineering Ltd* [1986] Ch 86). If, however, the distress was begun before the commencement of the winding up, the landlord will generally be allowed to complete it. In the case of an action for rent arrears, leave would not usually be given. (A mortgagee, by contrast, can still enforce its security.) It is unclear whether a notice under the Law of Distress (Amendment) Act 1908 or peaceable re-entry by the landlord fall within the scope of the subsection.

14.7.3.2 Rent as liquidation expense

The landlord cannot claim in the liquidation for rent accruing due after the winding up has commenced, but he may have a better chance of recovering it as a liquidation expense under r. 4.218 of the Insolvency Rules 1986, which lists under 16 paragraphs, the order of priority of payment of such expenses.

Paragraph (a): 'the expenses properly chargeable or incurred by the official receiver or liquidator in preserving, realising or getting in any of the assets of the company'. The rent will fall within this paragraph if the liquidator retains the lease and actively seeks to sell or surrender it. Similarly, a payment of the rent by the liquidator in order to prevent a forfeiture ranks as an expense in preserving the lease (*Re Linda Marie Ltd* [1989] BCLC 46). A payment of a service charge may similarly rank as an expense of the liquidation; but not a claim for breach of other terms of the lease.

Paragraph (m): 'necessary disbursement' of the liquidator in the course of his administration. Even if the liquidator does not take active steps to sell or surrender the lease, but merely retains it, the landlord may be able to claim that the rent falls within this paragraph (*Re Linda Marie Ltd* [1989] BCLC 46). Such a claim ranks before the liquidator's remuneration (para. (o)). This argument might also be used even where the liquidator disclaims the lease, to recover the rent due in the period between the commencement of the winding up and the disclaimer. The statutory order of priority can be varied by order of the court.

Leave may be given for a landlord to distrain for rent which accrues due after liquidation if it is an expense of the liquidation.

14.8 Disclaimer

A trustee in bankruptcy or liquidator can disclaim onerous property. This includes property which might give rise to a liability to pay money or perform burdensome acts. This means that most leases rank as onerous property and can therefore be disclaimed. A lease can be disclaimed not merely during its contractual term but also during the period of holding over under Part II of the Landlord and Tenant Act 1954. Generally, a disclaimer does not require the leave of the court. Furthermore, unless the landlord puts the trustee in bankruptcy or liquidator to an election, there is no time-limit.

A tenant who is an assignee of the lease may have covenanted, in the licence to assign, to observe and perform the covenants in the lease for the residue of the term. The provisions of such a covenant are inextricably tied in with the assignment and the lease itself. Therefore the trustee in bankruptcy of such an assignee cannot disclaim the licence alone: if he or she purports to do so, this will operate as a disclaimer of the lease as well (*MEPC Ltd* v *Scottish Amicable Life Assurance Society* [1993] 36 EG 133, CA).

If the liquidator of a company does not disclaim the lease and the company is wound up, the lease will vest in the Crown as *bona vacantia* (Companies Act 1985, s. 654). The Crown also has a right to disclaim within a statutory period (Companies Act 1985, s. 656).

14.8.1 FORM OF DISCLAIMER

Disclaimer of a lease is made by filing in court a written notice in prescribed form and by serving copies on the landlord, and upon any subtenants and other persons under a liability in respect of the premises — such as an original (and in some cases an intermediate) tenant, and any sureties.

14.8.2 PUTTING TRUSTEE OR LIQUIDATOR TO ELECTION

A landlord or other person interested in the property can put the trustee or liquidator to an election by serving on him a notice requiring disclaimer to be made (if at all) within 28 days. The trustee or liquidator may apply to court for an extension of this time. By putting the trustee or liquidator to election, the landlord can shorten the period of uncertainty, and so perhaps relet the premises at an earlier date.

14.8.3 EFFECT OF DISCLAIMER

14.8.3.1 As between the landlord and the insolvent tenant

Disclaimer of a lease determines, as from the date it is made, the rights, interests and liabilities of the tenant (whether a bankrupt or an insolvent company) in respect of the lease. This means that the landlord needs to prove rents due until the date of disclaimer in the bankruptcy or liquidation. Disclaimer accelerates the landlord's reversion; thus the trustee or liquidator should remove any tenant's fixtures before disclaimer, otherwise the landlord will be entitled to them.

In the case of bankruptcy, disclaimer operates retrospectively to discharge a trustee in bankruptcy from personal liability back to the date of the commencement of the bankruptcy (Insolvency Act 1986, s. 315). Furthermore, unless the trustee has breached a term of the lease, he or she cannot be required to pay for the occupation of the premises for the period between the date of his or her appointment and the date of disclaimer. Arguably, however, the landlord might recover the rent accruing due between the appointment of the trustee in bankruptcy and the disclaimer as an expense of the bankruptcy: see **14.6.3**.

14.8.3.2 As between the landlord and third parties

Disclaimer does not affect the rights and liabilities of third parties, except so far as is necessary for the purpose of releasing the bankrupt person or insolvent company from liability.

The position of a third party — such as an earlier tenant or a surety — depends upon whether, after disclaimer, the landlord takes possession. It seems that the landlord can only sue a third party for future rent if, after disclaimer, the landlord does not take possession.

If the insolvent tenant is an assignee of the lease, the landlord can sue the original tenant for future rents falling due even after the disclaimer by the assignee's trustee or liquidator (*Warnford Investments Ltd* v *Duckworth* [1979] Ch 127). On the same principle, it would seem that a surety of the original tenant will similarly remain liable for future rents.

If, however, the insolvent tenant is the original tenant, then under the rule in *Stacey* v *Hill* [1901] 1 KB 660, the disclaimer also ends the secondary liability of the tenant's surety. The distinction between *Warnford Investments Ltd* v *Duckworth* and *Stacey* v *Hill* is hard to justify, and it has been suggested that the rule in *Stacey* v *Hill* is in need of review: see McLoughlin, *Commercial Leases and Insolvency* (London: Butterworths, 1992), pp. 148–9. It was, however, applied in *Murphy* v *Sawyer-Hoare* [1993] 27 EG 127, which establishes that where the insolvent tenant is an assignee, the disclaimer also ends the secondary liability of the assignee's surety.

A surety's liability will continue in respect of primary and independent obligations, but clear words are required to indicate that the obligations are primary and independent (*Murphy* v *Sawyer-Hoare*). A covenant by the surety to take a new lease in the event of disclaimer by the tenant's trustee in bankruptcy or liquidator is by its nature an independent primary liability, and thus survives (see **3.1.4.4**).

If the lease disclaimed is a head lease, it remains in existence in order to enable the subtenant to remain in possession during the remainder of the term of the sublease. The sublease will fall if the head lease is forfeited, but the subtenant does have the right to seek relief. Thus in practice the subtenant will have an incentive to ensure that the covenants in the head lease, including the covenant to pay rent, are complied with. If the lease disclaimed is subject to a mortgage, the mortgagee is in a similar position.

14.8.4 VESTING ORDERS

Any person who claims an interest in the disclaimed lease, or who is under any liability in respect of it which will not be discharged by the disclaimer, may apply to the court for an order that the lease be vested in an appropriate person (Insolvency Act 1986, ss. 181 and 320). The application must be made within three months of the applicant becoming aware of the disclaimer (Insolvency Rules 1986, r. 4.194 and 6.186). Thus, for instance, a landlord could apply for the lease to be vested in a subtenant or a surety, or a subtenant or a surety could apply to have the lease vested in itself. An application from a person with a derivative interest (i.e. a subtenancy or a mortgage) to have the lease vested in itself will have priority over a similar claim by a surety (*Re AE Realisations (1985) Ltd* [1988] 1 WLR 200). The court will not usually make a vesting order except on the basis that the person in whom the lease is to be vested takes on the same liabilities as the insolvent company was subject to at the commencement of the winding up, or as the bankrupt at the date of presentation of the petition (Insolvency Act 1986, ss. 182(1) and 321(1)).

In a liquidation, if the landlord (or another party) applies to have the lease vested in a subtenant or a mortgagee, the subtenant or mortgagee has the right to elect whether to take the lease or to be excluded from all interest in the property (Insolvency Act 1986, s. 182(4)). The court will normally specify a time-limit. If no subtenant or mortgagee is willing to have a vesting order in its favour, the court is empowered to vest the lease in any person who is liable to perform the obligations in the lease — such as an original tenant or a surety.

In a bankruptcy, if no person is willing to accept a vesting order on the basis of taking on the same liabilities as the bankrupt or an assignee, the court is similarly empowered to vest the lease in someone who is liable on the obligations in the lease (Insolvency Act 1986, s. 321).

FIFTEEN

TERMINATIONS AND RENEWALS UNDER THE LANDLORD AND TENANT ACT 1954, PART II

15.1 Scope of the Landlord and Tenant Act 1954, Part II

Many business tenants enjoy a measure of security of tenure which is conferred upon them by the Landlord and Tenant Act 1954, Part II. Under the Act, a tenant occupying premises for business purposes has a basic right to renew the lease at the end of the contractually agreed term. In the absence of agreement between the parties as to the terms of a new lease, the terms can be set by the court. The landlord can, however, oppose a renewal of the lease on specified statutory grounds. If the landlord successfully opposes a renewal, the tenant will be denied a new tenancy, but (depending upon the particular ground or grounds of opposition established) the landlord may be required to pay compensation to the tenant for disturbance. If matters are not settled before the expiry of the contractually agreed term, the tenancy is continued by the statute, and there is a statutory procedure for the settling of an interim rent. Even if the tenant is denied a new tenancy, the court will generally allow the tenant to continue in possession under the continuation tenancy for a few months to give the tenant time to make other arrangements.

In order to obtain the protection of Part II, a tenant must satisfy three requirements: there must be a tenancy; the whole or part of the premises must be occupied by the tenant; and the occupation must be for the purposes of the tenant's business, or for those and other purposes (Landlord and Tenant Act 1954, s. 23(1)).

15.1.1 TENANCY

Part II applies only to leases, not to licences. It does not apply to a tenancy at will (*Hagee (London) Ltd* v *AB Erikson and Larson* [1976] QB 209 (see **1.2.3**)). A sublease falls within the scope of part II, even if it was granted in breach of a covenant against subletting without the landlord's consent (*D'Silva* v *Lister House Development Ltd* [1971] Ch 17). An agreement for a lease is also protected (Landlord and Tenant Act 1954, s. 69(1), meaning of 'tenancy').

15.1.2 OCCUPATION

The tenant must occupy the premises. Premises can be occupied even if there is no building: thus a field used as a car park was held to be occupied (*Bracey* v *Read* [1963] Ch 88). But a right of way does not comprise 'premises', and it cannot be 'occupied' (*Land Reclamation Co. Ltd* v *Basildon District Council* [1979] 1 WLR 767).

So long as the occupation is genuine, it can be through a third party in a representative capacity — which is essential where the tenant is a company. Thus occupation could be through the tenant's managing agent or employee. An employee who has to leave the premises for a short time may nevertheless remain in occupation if stock or other property is left on the premises (*I and H Caplan Ltd* v *Caplan (No. 2)* [1963] 1 WLR 1247).

15.1.2.1 Subletting

Difficulties can arise where the tenant sublets the premises. First, the subletting may not comprise a business. Secondly, there is the problem of occupation.

A tenant who sublets the entire premises comprised in the lease cannot be in occupation, and so cannot take the benefit of the protection of Part II.

The position of a tenant who has sublet only a part of the premises demised can be more complex. A tenant who sublets regularly may be able to establish that the subletting is itself a business. The problem of occupation, however, remains. The tenant may be treated as in occupation only of the part retained, but generally not of the part sublet. Thus a tenant who sublets different units in an office block to different tenants will not be treated as in occupation of the whole of the premises merely because it retains possession of the common parts. If, however, the tenant can establish that it retains a sufficient degree of control over the premises, it may be able to show that it remains in occupation for the purposes of its business. Thus in *Lee-Verhulst (Investments) Ltd* v *Harwood Trust* [1973] QB 204, the tenant's business comprised the letting of residential flats. The tenant's employees and agents had access to all parts of the building in order to provide services, and this was held sufficient to show that the tenant was in occupation.

The tenant will not be in occupation, however, unless it acts as the manager of a business actively earning profits by the provision of accommodation, facilities and services, and devotes time to that purpose. Thus the mere passive receipt of rents does not qualify (*William Boyer and Sons Ltd* v *Adams* (1975) 32 P & CR 89).

It should be noted that each resident in the *Lee-Verhulst* case had exclusive occupation of his or her own flat for the purposes of the Rent Acts: the decision therefore indicates that occupation by the residents is not incompatible with occupation by the tenant. A more restrictive approach was, however, applied in *Graysim Holdings Ltd* v *P and O Property Holdings Ltd* [1993] 1 EGLR 96 (noted Haley [1993] JBL 478), where the tenant converted an empty shell of a building into a market hall which it rented out to 35 different stallholders. The tenant chose the stallholders, laid down the opening hours, paid for advertising, retained control over the common parts, and (for a service charge) provided lighting, heating and the services of a superintendent. It did not, however, retain any keys to the stalls, and had no right to enter them, and these points proved fatal to its claim to be in occupation of the entire premises for the purposes of the Act. The judge considered that the stallholders had exclusive possession of their stalls, and that they were therefore the only occupiers. Since the hallmark of a tenancy is exclusive possession, it follows from the decision that no tenant can ever be in occupation of premises which it has sublet — a result which, if correct, has startling implications for tenants who have sublet units in offices or shopping centres. It is suggested that the broader 'control' test advocated in earlier cases is preferable to that applied in *Graysim*.

15.1.2.2 Occupation for the purposes of a business

The requirement of the Landlord and Tenant Act 1954, s. 23(1), is that the premises are occupied 'for the purposes of a business carried on by him or for those and other purposes'. It is therefore not necessary that the business itself is carried on on the premises. Even occupation for an ancillary purpose suffices if it is necessary for the business. In *Chapman* v *Freeman* [1978] 1 WLR 1298 a hotel owner took a lease of a cottage near the hotel in order to house some of the hotel staff. Although it was conceded that the hotel owner was in occupation of the cottage, it was held that he was not in occupation for the purpose of his business: it may have been convenient for the staff to live in the cottage, but it was not necessary. See also *Methodist Secondary Schools Trust Deed Trustees* v *O'Leary* [1993] 1 EGLR 105.

Incidental business user (such as that of a businessman or businesswoman who takes work home in the evenings) is insufficient to bring the tenancy within Part II. Where there is mixed residential and business user (such as a shop with a flat above, or a dentist's residence part of which is used for a surgery), the tenancy falls within Part II only, not within the legislation protecting residential tenants. If the lease contains a user clause restricting the use of the premises to business purposes, a tenant who ceases business user loses thereby the protection afforded by Part II; even if such tenant thereafter occupies the premises as his or her residence, the protection afforded to a residential tenant will not be acquired. Conversely, even if the landlord has not consented to the change of use, a residential tenant who begins substantial business user may gain the protection of Part II (*Cheryl Investments Ltd* v *Saldhana* [1978] 1 WLR 1329, CA).

15.1.3 BUSINESS PURPOSES

For the purposes of Part II, 'business' includes a trade, profession or employment, and any activity carried out by a body of persons whether corporate or unincorporate (Landlord and Tenant Act 1954, s. 23(2)). Thus for this purpose the activities of managing a hospital have been held to comprise a business (*Hills (Patents) Ltd* v *University College Hospital Board of Governors* [1956] 1 QB 90). A members' tennis club has also been held to be a business within Part II (*Addiscombe Garden Estates Ltd* v *Crabbe* [1958] 1 QB 513). The dumping of waste, however, has been held not to comprise a business for the purposes of the Act on the ground that the activity in question must be in the nature of a trade, profession or employment (*Hillil Property and Investment Co. Ltd* v *Naraine Pharmacy Ltd* (1979) 39 P & CR 67, CA).

15.1.4 EXCLUSIONS

Certain types of leases are excluded from the scope of Part II. These are:

(a) an agricultural holding (Landlord and Tenant Act 1954, s. 43(1)(a));
(b) a mining lease (s. 43(1)(b));
(c) a service tenancy (s. 43(2));
(d) a short lease, i.e. a tenancy granted for a term certain not exceeding six months (unless the lease contains provision for extending it beyond six months, or the tenant has been in occupation for a period which, together with any period during which the tenant's predecessor was carrying on the tenant's business, exceeds 12 months) (s. 43(3)).

The last exclusion is designed to encourage landlords awaiting, for instance, redevelopment, to let the premises on a temporary basis.

Furthermore, the protection of Part II is available only to a lessee, not to a licensee. The essential characteristic of a lease is exclusive possession. Although *Street* v *Mountford* [1985] AC 809 concerned letting in the residential sector, nothing said by their Lordships in that case suggests that lettings of business premises are to be treated differently. Thus exclusive possession for a term at a rent creates a lease, even if the parties call it a licence: see further **1.1.4**.

Leases of on-licensed premises were formerly excluded from Part II, unless the sale of food or other non-intoxicating items comprised a substantial proportion of the business. This is, however, no longer the case: tenancies of on-licensed premises entered into on or after 11 July 1989 are now within the scope of Part II (Landlord and Tenant (Licensed Premises) Act 1990, s. 1(1)). Tenancies granted, or contracted to be granted, before that date, also gain the protection of Part II if they were not terminated before 11 July 1992 (s. 1(2) and (3)). The effect of this three-year period of grace for lessors of licensed premises was that many lessee publicans had their existing leases terminated before 11 July 1992 and were effectively compelled to take on new leases on less favourable terms.

15.1.5 CONTRACTING OUT

Any agreement relating to a tenancy to which Part II applies is void so far as it precludes the tenant from making an application or request for a new tenancy (Landlord and Tenant Act 1954, s. 38(1)).

This renders void, for instance, an agreement to surrender made pursuant to an offer-to-surrender clause (*Allnatt London Properties Ltd* v *Newton* [1984] 1 All ER 423, CA): for a detailed discussion see **12.4.4.1**. Such an agreement is valid, however, if the approval of the court (usually the county court) is obtained pursuant to an application made by the landlord and the tenant jointly (s. 38(4)). In *Hagee (London) Ltd* v *AB Erikson and Larson* [1976] QB 209, Lord Denning MR said that the county court always approves such applications where the agreement is made by business people properly advised by their lawyers.

If it is intended to exclude Part II, the lease must be granted conditionally upon the court's leave being obtained. The condition should be expressed; but, if it is not, the court may be able to infer that the agreement is conditional upon such consent (*Cardiothoracic Institute* v *Shrewdcrest Ltd* [1986] 1 WLR 368, discussed at **1.4**). If the grant is unconditional, the tenant will gain the protection of Part II, even though the lease envisages that an application is to be made (*Essexcrest Ltd* v *Evenlex Ltd* (1987) 55 P & CR 279, in which the lease contained blanks to be completed later regarding, *inter alia*, the date of the order).

Even if the court's approval is given, Part II is not excluded unless the contracting-out provision is contained in or endorsed on the lease or other document as the court may specify (s. 38(4)). In *Tottenham Hotspur Football and Athletic Co. Ltd* v *Princegrove Publishers Ltd* [1974] 1 WLR 113, however, the tenant went into occupation following an order of the court, but without the lease having been executed. It was nevertheless held that the Act had been effectively excluded because the tenant held under an agreement for a lease, which did include the exclusionary term. It has, however, been pointed out that, in view of the Law of Property (Miscellaneous Provisions) Act 1989, s. 2, this result may not apply to similar tenancies entered into after 26 September 1989 (Evans and Smith, *The Law of Landlord and Tenant*, 4th ed. (London: Butterworths, 1993), at p. 380).

An example of an application to the court to exclude Part II of the Act is contained in **Appendix 3**.

15.2 The Statutory Protection

15.2.1 THE CONTINUATION TENANCY

Section 24(1) of the Landlord and Tenant Act 1954 provides that a tenancy protected by Part II of the Act 'shall not come to an end unless terminated in accordance with the provisions of this part of this Act'. Thus, unless brought to an end by one of the methods permitted by Part II, a fixed-term tenancy continues even though the contractually agreed term has expired or has been prematurely determined by, for instance, the landlord's exercise of a break clause: see **12.3.1**. Similarly, unless brought to an end by one of the methods permitted by Part II, a periodic tenancy continues even though terminated at common law by the landlord's notice to quit. See further **15.2.2.1**.

The continuation tenancy under s. 24(1) is of uncertain duration, and so would be void at common law. It is, however, validated by the statute. The continuation tenancy does not create any new form of interest in the tenant but it prolongs the tenant's estate, subject to a statutory variation as to the mode of determination (*H.L. Bolton Engineering Co. Ltd* v *T.J. Graham and Sons Ltd* [1957] 1 QB 159; *GMS Syndicate Ltd* v *Gary Elliott Ltd* (1980) 41 P & CR 124). This means that, during the period of the continuation tenancy (often referred to as the period of holding over) the tenant, by virtue of retaining an estate in the land, may assign the tenancy. Similarly, the landlord may seek to forfeit the lease for breach of covenant or condition in the usual way. It was recently held by the Court of Appeal that the 'tenancy' continued by s. 24(1) is the tenancy only of the person holding over. If that person is an assignee, the original tenant will not, in the absence of express words in the lease, be liable for breaches committed by the assignee during the period of holding over (*City of London Corporation* v *Fell* [1993] QB 589; see further **6.1.1.2**).

The usual rule is that a tenant who purports to grant a sublease for a term which exceeds the duration of the tenant's own lease will be taken to have made an assignment. This principle does not, however, apply where the tenant is entitled to the protection of s. 24. Thus in *William Skelton and Son Ltd* v *Harrison & Pinder Ltd* [1975] QB 361, such a tenant (in error) purported to grant an underlease for a period which expired one month after his own contractually agreed term. It was held that this did indeed take effect as an underlease rather than as an assignment, because s. 24 conferred upon the tenant the right to hold over, which thereby supported the underlease.

15.2.2 TERMINATION OF A PART II PROTECTED TENANCY

There are six methods by which a tenancy protected by Part II may be terminated. The first three of these are methods provided for in the Act itself, namely:

(a) landlord's notice (s. 25);
(b) tenant's request for a new tenancy (s. 26);
(c) tenant's notice (s. 27).

The last three, by contrast, are methods of termination at common law, but are treated by s. 24(2) as methods of terminating a Part II protected tenancy, namely:

(d) tenant's notice to quit;
(e) surrender;
(f) forfeiture.

It should be noted that only the first two methods, i.e. (a) and (b), may lead to a new tenancy.

15.2.2.1 Landlord's notice

The landlord may terminate a tenancy within Part II of the Landlord and Tenant Act 1954 by giving the tenant a notice in the prescribed form, or in a form substantially to the like effect. The notice must be in writing, and it must specify the date at which the tenancy is to come to an end (the date of termination) (s. 25(1)). The prescribed form is set out in the Landlord and Tenant Act 1954 Part II (Notices) Regulations (SI 1983/133), as amended.

The notice must be generally given not more than 12 months nor less than six months before the date of termination specified in the notice (s. 25(2)). This requirement is subject to the following:

(a) In the case of a tenancy which (apart from Part II) could have been terminated by notice to quit, the date of termination specified in the notice must not be earlier than the earliest date on which, apart from Part II, the tenancy could have been brought to an end by the landlord's notice to quit (s. 25(3)(a)). Notice to quit means a notice to terminate a tenancy given in accordance with its provisions (s. 69(1)). Such a tenancy includes, therefore, not merely a periodic tenancy, but also a fixed-term tenancy terminable by the landlord's notice in accordance with a break clause. Furthermore, if the tenancy itself requires more than six months' notice to quit, the maximum period for giving notice is six months longer than the specified period of notice to quit (s. 25(3)(b)). This means that, if the tenancy requires the landlord to give the tenant nine months' notice to quit, the landlord must give notice under s. 25 not more than 15 months, nor less than nine months, before the termination date.

(b) In the case of any other tenancy (i.e. a fixed-term tenancy with no landlord's break clause), the date of termination specified in the notice must not be earlier than the date on which, apart from Part II, the tenancy would have come to an end by effluxion of time (s. 25(4)).

A landlord who wishes to terminate the lease must therefore comply both with any requirements for termination specified in the lease or laid down by common law, and also with the procedure laid down by s. 25. If the lease requires the landlord to serve a notice to terminate it (e.g. by means of a break clause), a single notice will suffice if it is capable of complying (and does in fact comply) both with the lease and with s. 25(1) (*Keith Bayley Rogers and Co.* v *Cubes Ltd* (1975) 31 P & CR 412). See further **12.3.1**. In some circumstances, however, a landlord may prefer to exercise a break clause without serving a s. 25 notice, such as where the landlord anticipates being able to establish a ground of opposition in the future: see Lewison, *Drafting Business Leases*, 4th ed. (London: Longman, 1993), p. 56.

The landlord's notice under s. 25 must also:

(a) require the tenant, within two months after the giving of the notice, to notify the landlord in writing whether or not the tenant will be willing to give up possession at the date of termination (s. 25(5)); and

(b) state whether the landlord would oppose an application to the court under Part II for the grant of a new tenancy; and, if so, it must also state on which of the grounds mentioned in s. 30 the landlord would do so.

Notice under s. 25 can be given only by the 'competent' landlord. This is not necessarily the tenant's immediate landlord. It will be the tenant's immediate landlord (L) if L either owns the freehold or has a tenancy which will not expire within the next 14 months. If neither of these requirements is met, the competent landlord will be L's landlord if that person satisfies either of these requirements. This process is repeated, as necessary, until the competent landlord is identified: (s. 44(1)).

A tenant who wishes to obtain a new tenancy must, within two months, serve on the landlord a counter-notice unequivocally expressing unwillingness to give up possession (s. 29(2)). A tenant who does serve such a counter-notice is entitled to apply for a new tenancy under s. 24(1). If the parties can agree swiftly on the terms of the new tenancy, the current tenancy ends on the date that the parties agree that the new tenancy is to commence (s. 28).

Failing agreement, a tenant who wishes to obtain a new tenancy must file an application to the court (either the High Court or the county court) not less than two nor more than four months after the landlord's s. 25 notice is given (s. 29(3)).

If, however, the tenant does not serve such a counter-notice, the tenancy will end on the termination date specified in the landlord's notice. The tenant, moreover, loses the right to apply to the court for the grant of a new tenancy (s. 29(2)).

15.2.2.2 Tenant's request for a new tenancy

The tenant may request a new tenancy either:

(a) in the counter-notice where the landlord has served a notice under s. 25 (see **15.2.2.1**); or
(b) when the tenant terminates the tenancy under s. 26.

A tenant is entitled to request a new tenancy under s. 26 only if it has a fixed-term tenancy exceeding one year, or a term of years certain and thereafter from year to year (s. 26(1)). Subject to this, a periodic tenant cannot apply for a new tenancy under s. 26. A tenant may not request a new tenancy under s. 26 if the landlord has previously served a s. 25 notice (in which case the tenant's request must be in the counter-notice); or if the tenant has given notice to quit or notice to terminate the tenancy under s. 27 (s. 26(4)).

The tenant's notice must be in the prescribed form and must be served on the competent landlord as defined in s. 44(1) (see **15.2.2.1**). The notice must suggest the terms of the new tenancy:

(a) The property. This need not be the entire premises comprised in the existing lease.

(b) The length of the term. In one case a tenant who held under a seven-year lease did not expressly specify the term of the proposed new lease; but he did specify that the other terms should be the same as those of his existing tenancy. It was held that this implied a request for a new tenancy of seven years, and that the tenant's notice was therefore valid (*Sidney Bolsom Investment Trust Ltd* v *E. Karmios and Co. (London) Ltd* [1956] 1 QB 529, CA).

(c) The date the new tenancy is to commence. This must be not less than six and not more than 12 months after the making of the request (s. 26(2)). The date so specified for the commencement of the new tenancy will also be the date upon which the old tenancy comes to an end. Thus a tenant cannot apply for a new tenancy more than 12 months before the termination of the existing tenancy. If the tenant terminates a tenancy by serving a notice under a break clause, this ranks as a notice to quit and the tenant loses the statutory right to apply for a new tenancy under the Act.

It has, however, been held that a tenant may exercise a break clause, not by the service of a notice to quit, but by the service of a request for a new tenancy under s. 26 (*Scholl Manufacturing Co. Ltd* v *Clifton (Slim-Line) Ltd* [1967] Ch 41, CA). This means that, in a market where rents are falling, a tenant might choose to exercise a break clause by the service of a s. 26 request in the expectation that the market rent settled under the new tenancy will be lower than that payable under its existing tenancy. Lewison suggests that landlords can prevent this by ensuring that a tenant's break clause obliges the tenant to give more than 12 months' notice. Since the new tenancy suggested in a s. 26 request must commence within 12 months after the making of the request, the tenant cannot then exercise the break clause by requesting a new tenancy (Lewison, *Drafting Business Leases*, 4th ed. (1993), at pp. 56–7).

(d) The rent.
(e) Other terms. These will usually be stated to be the same as those of the current tenancy.

The landlord may oppose the request for a new tenancy by serving a counter-notice within two months of the tenant's request for a new tenancy (s. 26(6)). (The landlord must be informed of this right in the tenant's request.) The counter-notice must indicate upon which of the statutory grounds of opposition in s. 30 the landlord will rely (s. 26(6)).

The tenant must apply to the court for a new tenancy not less than two nor more than four months after making the request for a new tenancy (s. 29(3)).

The time-limit imposed on the tenant by s. 26 may, however, be waived by the landlord's conduct. This occurred in *Bristol Cars Ltd* v *RKH (Hotels) Ltd* (1979) 38 P & CR 411, where the landlord initially indicated that it would not oppose a new tenancy, failed to serve a counter-notice under s. 26(6), and applied for an interim rent on the basis that the tenancy was continuing.

15.2.2.3 Tenant's notice

The tenant may terminate a fixed-term tenancy at the end of the term by giving to the immediate landlord notice in writing not less than three months before the expiration of the fixed term. Such notice will not be effective, however, if it is given before the tenant has been in occupation in right of the tenancy for one month (s. 27(1)).

When a fixed-term tenancy is continuing by virtue of s. 24, the tenant may bring it to an end on any quarter day by giving not less than three months' notice in writing to the immediate landlord. Such notice cannot be given unless the tenant has been in occupation in right of the tenancy for one month (s. 27(2)).

15.2.2.4 Tenant's notice to quit

A tenant who serves a notice to quit loses any protection afforded by Part II. A notice to quit includes a notice to quit served by a periodic tenant, or a notice to terminate a fixed-term tenancy served by a tenant under a break clause (see definition of 'notice to quit' in s. 69(1)). A tenant's notice to quit is not, however, effective to terminate the tenancy unless the tenant has been in occupation in right of the tenancy for one month (s. 24(2)(a)). This is clearly designed to ensure that any notice to quit is given willingly.

15.2.2.5 Surrender

A tenant who surrenders the tenancy loses the protection of Part II unless the instrument of surrender was executed before, or in pursuance of an agreement made before, the tenant had been in occupation in right of the tenancy for one month (s. 24(2)(b)).

15.2.2.6 Forfeiture

If the tenancy, or a superior tenancy, is forfeited, the tenant loses the protection of Part II. Even if the landlord has obtained judgment for possession, however, the tenant retains the protection of Part II (and may thus apply for a new tenancy) so long as an application for relief is pending (*Meadows* v *Clerical, Medical and General Life Assurance Society* [1981] Ch 70).

15.2.3 INTERIM RENT

Because the continuation tenancy prolongs the tenant's estate, subject to a statutory variation of the mode of determination, its terms are the same as those of the contractual tenancy which has been terminated. In the case of the rent payable, this could work hardship on the landlord, who would thereby lose (during a period of rising rents) the benefit of a higher rent during the period of holding over. The Landlord and Tenant Act 1954 therefore provides that the landlord may apply to the court for the determination of an 'interim rent' (s. 24A). Such application may be made if the landlord has given a s. 25 notice to terminate the tenancy, or if the tenant has made a request for a new tenancy under s. 26. The tenant, it should be noted, cannot apply for an interim rent (and so cannot seek to take advantage of a general fall in rents).

The interim rent must be one which it would be reasonable for the tenant to pay while the tenancy continues by virtue of s. 24 (s. 24A(1)). In determining the interim rent, the court must have regard to the rent payable under the terms of the tenancy (s. 24A(3)). Subject to this, however, the interim rent is to be determined in accordance with the provisions contained in s. 34(1) and (2) on the basis that a new tenancy from year to year of the whole of the premises comprised in the tenancy is granted to the tenant by order of the court. This means that the interim rent is essentially to be the open market rent payable by a yearly tenant holding under the terms of the tenancy (other than those relating to rent) and disregarding the matters specified in s. 34 (see **15.2.6.3**).

The fiction of a notional yearly tenancy means that the interim rent is generally lower than the final rent which may ultimately be fixed for a new tenancy. Although the court must have regard to the rent payable under the old lease, it is not clear how this regard operates. Thus in *English Exporters (London) Ltd* v *Eldonwall Ltd* [1973] Ch 415 and *Fawke* v *Viscount Chelsea* [1980] QB 441, CA, the court said that the method was to assess the market value of an annual tenancy in accordance with s. 34 and then discount the rent by reference to the existing rent level. This approach was adopted in *Ratners (Jewellers) Ltd* v *Lemnoll* (1980) 255 EG 987, where it led to a tempering of the market value of an annual tenancy by 20 per cent. In *Regis Property Co. Ltd* v *Lewis and Peat Ltd* [1970] Ch 695, however, the judge considered that the old rent was relevant only so far as it was of evidential value in calculating the market value of the notional annual tenancy.

An interim rent determined under s. 24A is payable from the date on which the proceedings were commenced or the date specified in the landlord's notice or the tenant's request, whichever is the later (s. 24A(2)).

15.2.4 THE STATUTORY GROUNDS OF OPPOSITION

There are seven statutory grounds upon which the landlord (either in his s. 25 notice, or in his counter-notice under s. 26(6)) may oppose an application under s. 24(1) for a new tenancy. These grounds are set out in paras (a) to (g) of s. 30(1).

There is an important difference between the grounds set out in paras (a), (b), (c) and (e) on the one hand, and those set out in paras (d), (f) and (g) on the other. Paragraphs (a), (b), (c) and (e) set out circumstances upon which the tenant 'ought not' to be granted a new tenancy. These words mean that, even if the landlord can make out a ground in one of those paragraphs, the court has a discretion whether to order the grant of a new tenancy. By contrast, if the landlord establishes a ground of opposition under paras (d), (f) or (g), the court has no discretion — it is obliged to refuse an application for a new tenancy.

15.2.4.1 Paragraph (a): breach by the tenant of a repairing obligation

The landlord must show that there is an existing breach (i.e. one which exists at the date of the service of the landlord's notice or counter-notice) and that it is so serious that (in the words of para. (a)) 'the tenant ought not to be granted a new tenancy'. The court will take into account past breaches, as well as any undertaking by the tenant to effect the necessary repairs (*Lyons* v *Central Commercial Properties (London) Ltd* [1958] 1 WLR 869, CA).

15.2.4.2 Paragraph (b): persistent delay by the tenant in paying rent

Persistent delay means that there must have been delay over a period. The court will take into account the number of times there has been delay, the length of the delays and the reasons for them, and the steps which the landlord needed to take to recover payment. The court will also consider how the landlord might be protected against future delays in rent payments, e.g. by requiring the tenant to pay a security deposit (*Hopcutt* v *Carver* (1969) 209 EG 1069, CA and *Rawashdeh* v *Lane* [1988] 2 EGLR 109, CA).

15.2.4.3 Paragraph (c): other substantial breaches of obligations under the tenancy or any other reason connected with the tenant's use or management of the holding

The court will look at the seriousness of the breach, whether it is remediable, and whether it has been waived by the landlord. The second part of the paragraph is wider than the first. Thus it could include the case where the tenant merely proposed to breach, for instance, a user clause. It has also been held to include an intended user which, although not in breach of the tenant's covenants in the lease, would contravene a planning enforcement order (*Turner and Bell* v *Searles (Stanford-le-Hope) Ltd* (1977) 33 P & CR 208, CA).

15.2.4.4 Paragraph (d): availability of suitable alternative accommodation

This ground is that the landlord has offered and is willing to provide or secure alternative accommodation for the tenant. The terms of the alternative accommodation must be reasonable having regard to the terms of the current tenancy and all other relevant circumstances. Furthermore, the accommodation and the time at which it is available must be suitable for the tenant's requirements (including the need to preserve goodwill) having regard to the nature and class of the business and to the situation and extent of, and facilities afforded by, the holding.

As mentioned above (at the beginning of **15.2.4**), this ground is not discretionary (*Betty's Cafés Ltd* v *Phillips Furnishing Stores Ltd* [1957] Ch 67).

If the tenant rejects an offer which the court finds reasonable within the paragraph, so that the tenant's application for a new tenancy is withdrawn, the tenant may still accept the landlord's offer if it remains open. There is no obligation on a landlord, however, to keep such offer open. A tenant who therefore rejects what is found to be a reasonable offer might find that it has been withdrawn, and so will be forced to vacate the premises: see Yates and Hawkins, *Landlord and Tenant Law*, 2nd ed. (London: Sweet & Maxwell, 1986), pp. 695–6.

15.2.4.5 Paragraph (e): in the case of a subtenancy of part, that possession is required for letting or disposing of the property as a whole

Because the circumstances in this paragraph are somewhat special, it is relied upon only rarely. It is relevant only where the 'competent landlord' within s. 44 (see **15.2.2.1**) is not the tenant's immediate landlord. Thus where L, a freehold owner, has leased business premises to T, who has in turn sublet part to S, if S applies for a new tenancy when T's lease has 14 months or less to run, the person to whom the request must be made is L. L may seek to rely on para. (e) because of needing possession in order to dispose of the premises as a whole, e.g. by reletting or sale. Under the paragraph, L must show that the aggregate of the rents which would be reasonably obtainable on separate lettings of the holding and the remainder of the property would be substantially less than the rent which would be reasonably obtainable on a letting of the property as a whole. The landlord will have difficulty in showing this unless T's lease ends very shortly after S's sublease.

15.2.4.6 Paragraph (f): the landlord intends to demolish or reconstruct

This ground is that, on the termination of the current tenancy, the landlord intends to demolish or reconstruct the whole or a substantial part of the premises comprised in the holding or to carry out substantial work of construction on the holding or part of it, and that he could not reasonably do so without obtaining possession of the holding.

The landlord must therefore establish two things: intention and the need for possession. The landlord is not required to bring evidence of a detailed scheme of development or to have entered into contracts, nor is it obliged to show that every potential obstacle in the way has been removed. It is enough to establish that the scheme has a reasonable prospect of fulfilment and that general arrangements in regard to planning permission, finance and building have been dealt with (*Capocci* v *Goble* [1987] 2 EGLR 102, CA). The intention must be shown at the date of application to the court (*Betty's Cafés Ltd* v *Phillips Furnishing Stores Ltd* [1959] AC 20). If, therefore, the landlord has a subsequent change of mind, there is nothing the tenant can do, unless it can prove misrepresentation or concealment of material facts, in which case the court may award the tenant compensation for damage or loss (s. 55(1)).

Because a tenant who is refused an order for a new tenancy is generally given a period of a few months after the hearing before being required to vacate, the landlord does not need to show an intention to demolish or reconstruct immediately. It is sufficient if there is an intention to do so some three or four months after the hearing. Even an intention to start within one year may suffice; but in no case can the landlord secure possession before the date upon which he expresses his intention to start work (cf. s. 31(2)).

Reconstruction means rebuilding, and the words 'demolish or reconstruct' are construed conjunctively. A substantial interference with the existing premises is required. The mere landscaping of a field without buildings was held not to comprise 'reconstruction' for this purpose (*Botterill* v *Bedfordshire County Council* [1985] 1 EGLR 82). Works of reroofing, rewiring and the installation of central heating, were held not to comprise a substantial work of construction within this paragraph (*Barth* v *Pritchard* [1990] 1 EGLR 109).

If the existing lease already entitles the landlord to enter the premises to carry out the works, the landlord is unlikely to be able to rely on para. (f) because it would not then need to obtain possession from the court: see Yates and Hawkins, *Landlord and Tenant Law*, 2nd ed. (London: Sweet & Maxwell, 1986) p. 699.

Originally a landlord could rely on this ground even though it needed possession for only a short period, or of only a part of the premises. This was, however, changed by the insertion of s. 31A into the Landlord and Tenant Act 1954 by the Law of Property Act 1969. This states that a landlord cannot rely on para. (f) if:

(a) the tenant agrees to the inclusion in the new tenancy of a term giving the landlord access and other facilities for carrying out the work intended, and that, as a result, the landlord could reasonably carry out the work without obtaining possession and without interfering to a substantial extent or for a substantial time with the tenant's business user; or

(b) the tenant is willing to accept a tenancy of an economically separable part (defined in s. 31A(2)) of the holding, and either the foregoing paragraph is satisfied with respect to that part or possession of the remainder would be reasonably sufficient to enable the landlord to carry out the intended work (s. 31A(1)).

Whether interference within (a) is substantial is a matter of fact: it has been held that works which would close the tenant's business for two weeks were not a substantial interference (*Cerex Jewels Ltd* v *Peachey Property Corporation plc* [1986] 2 EGLR 65, CA); whereas works which entailed closure for 12 weeks were (*Blackburn* v *Hussain* [1988] 1 EGLR 77). Furthermore, although s. 31A is clearly intended to be for the benefit of the tenant, the tenant is not entitled to waive the requirement that the works will not substantially interfere with its business user (*Redfern* v *Reeves* (1978) 37 P & CR 364).

15.2.4.7 Paragraph (g): the landlord intends to occupy the premises himself

The landlord must show that, on the termination of the current tenancy, he intends to occupy the holding for the purposes, or partly for the purposes, of a business to be carried on by him therein, or to reside there.

A landlord is not entitled to rely on para. (g), however, if its interest, or an interest which has merged into that interest, was purchased or created within five years of the termination of the current tenancy, and at all times since such purchase or creation the holding has been comprised in a business tenancy within s. 23(1) (s. 30(2)). For this purpose, any business carried on by a company in which the landlord has a controlling interest (as there defined) is treated as a business to be carried on by him (s. 30(3)).

Where the landlord's interest is held in trust, the intention of any of the beneficiaries to occupy for the purposes specified in para. (g) suffices (s. 41(2)). Where the landlord's interest is held by a member of a group of companies, the intended occupation of the landlord for the purposes of a business to be carried on by him includes the intended occupation by any member of the group for the purposes of a business to be carried on by that member (s. 42(3)(a)).

The requisite intention for this paragraph is similar to that required for para. (f), i.e. in this instance a firm intention to occupy within a reasonable time. Where the occupation will require planning permission, the landlord must have applied for it and show a reasonable prospect that this will be obtained (*Gregson* v *Cyril Lord Ltd* [1963] 1 WLR 41, CA). As under para. (f), the relevant date for the existence of that intention is the date of the hearing.

The landlord must intend to occupy the premises; but this does not have to be personal occupation — it may be through an agent (*Skeet* v *Powell-Sheddon* [1988] 2 EGLR 112, CA). It should be noted that the intention must be to occupy 'the holding'. This means that a landlord who intends to demolish the buildings which comprise the holding cannot come within para. (g) (*Nursey* v *P. Currie (Dartford) Ltd* [1959] 1 WLR 273, CA).

15.2.5 WHERE NO NEW TENANCY IS ORDERED

15.2.5.1 Landlord establishes opposition under any ground

If the landlord establishes a ground of opposition under any ground in s. 30, the court may not order a new tenancy (s. 31(1)). The continuation tenancy does not, however, come to an end immediately. It will continue for a limited period. The date specified for termination in the landlord's s. 25 notice or the date specified for the commencement of the new tenancy in the tenant's s. 26 request (as the case may be) will not necessarily be the date upon which the tenancy will end.

If, following the service of such notice or request, an application to the court is made under Part II, then, unless the termination date in the notice or the commencement date of the new tenancy in the request is later, the tenancy will end three months from the date the application is finally disposed of (s. 64(1)). An application is finally disposed of only after the expiration of any time for appeal (s. 64(2)). Since the period for appeal from judgment is currently four weeks, this means that, in the absence of an appeal being lodged, the tenancy will end four months after judgment.

If, however, the termination date in the notice or the date for the commencement of the new tenancy in the request is later than the period specified in s. 64, the tenancy will end on that later date.

15.2.5.2 Special provisions relating to grounds (d), (e) and (f)

If the landlord's opposition is based solely upon, or includes, one or more of grounds (d), (e) or (f), then, even though the landlord fails to establish opposition under one of those three grounds, the tenant may still fail to obtain a new tenancy. This will occur where the court would nevertheless have been satisfied of any of those three grounds if the date of termination specified in the landlord's request or the date of the commencement of the new tenancy in the tenant's request had been later (but not more than one year later). In such circumstances, the court must make a declaration to this effect specifying such later date, but without making an order for a new tenancy (s. 31(2)(a)). If the tenant takes no action thereafter, the tenancy will simply terminate as indicated in **15.2.5.1**. The tenant can, however, postpone the termination of the existing tenancy. Thus, if within 14 days from the declaration the tenant requires, the court must substitute the later date (specified in its declaration) as the date of termination (s. 31(2)(b)).

15.2.5.3 Misrepresentation or concealment

If the court refuses an order for the grant of a new tenancy and it subsequently appears that the court was induced to refuse the grant by misrepresentation or concealment of material facts, the court may order the landlord to pay the tenant compensation for his damage or loss thereby sustained: s. 55(1). Thus a landlord who, for instance, successfully opposed a renewal of the tenancy by falsely claiming an intention to occupy the premises under ground (g) could be made to pay compensation. The section will not, however, enable the tenant to claim compensation where the landlord genuinely had such an intention at the date of the hearing and merely had a change of mind subsequently.

15.2.5.4 Compensation for disturbance

A landlord who successfully opposes the grant of a new tenancy on grounds (a), (b), (c) or (d) does not have to pay compensation to the tenant. The rationale is evidently that the first three grounds are based on the tenant's own fault, and the fourth involves the tenant declining an offer of reasonable alternative accommodation.

Compensation is, however, payable if the landlord successfully opposes a tenant's application to the court for a new tenancy under grounds (e), (f) or (g), and upon no other ground. Similarly, compensation is payable if the landlord relies solely on grounds (e), (f) or (g) in its s. 25 notice, or in its counter-notice to a tenant's request for a new tenancy, and the tenant does not apply to the court for a new tenancy (s. 37(1)). These grounds, it should be noted, involve no fault or unreasonable conduct on the tenant's part.

Any compensation must be paid on the tenant quitting the holding (s. 37(1)). Compensation is calculated as the product of the appropriate multiplier and either the rateable value of the holding or twice the rateable value of the holding (s. 37(2)). The appropriate multiplier is specified in the Landlord and Tenant Act 1954 (Appropriate Multiplier) Order 1990 (SI 1990/363).

Twice the rateable value of the holding is used in this calculation if:

(a) during the whole of the 14 years immediately preceding the determination of the current tenancy, the premises have been occupied for the purposes of a business carried on by the occupier (or for those and other purposes); and

(b) if during that period there was a change in the occupier, the occupier immediately after the change was the successor to the business carried on by the immediately preceding occupier (s. 37(3)).

In any other case, the rateable value is used (s. 37(2)(b)).

Thus, for instance, successions to a business apart, a tenant who has occupied the premises for the purposes of a business for the previous 14 years obtains twice the compensation of a tenant who has occupied for a shorter period — even if this falls short of 14 years by only one day (*Department of the Environment* v *Royal Insurance plc* (1986) 54 P & CR 26).

It has been held that compensation received by a tenant under s. 37 is not liable to capital gains tax (*Drummond* v *Austin Brown* [1985] Ch 52, CA).

In limited circumstances, it is possible for the parties to contract out of the landlord's obligation to pay compensation under the section or to vary the amount of compensation payable. Such agreement is void, however, if:

(a) the tenant has been in occupation of the premises for the purposes of a business for five years preceding the date the tenant is to quit; or

(b) the tenant has been in business occupation for a lesser period, but is the successor to the business of the immediately preceding occupier, and their combined periods of business occupation total at least five years before the date the tenant is to quit (s. 38(2)).

In any other case, the agreement is valid (s. 38(3)).

15.2.6 TENANT OBTAINS NEW TENANCY

If the tenant has applied to the court under s. 24(1) for a new tenancy, then, unless the landlord establishes a statutory ground of opposition, or the circumstances stated in s. 31(2) apply (see **15.2.5.2**), the court must order the grant of a new tenancy on the terms there provided (s. 29(1)). If a tenant's application for a new tenancy is made following a landlord's s. 25 notice, such application is not to be entertained unless the tenant has duly notified the landlord that it will not be willing at the date of termination to give up possession (s. 29(2)).

The court has power to specify the terms of the new tenancy only insofar as they are not agreed between the parties themselves.

15.2.6.1 Property to be comprised in the new tenancy

In the absence of agreement between the parties, the court will order the grant of a new tenancy of the holding (s. 32(1)). 'The holding' means the property comprised in the tenancy, but excluding any part which is occupied neither by the tenant nor by the tenant's employee for the purposes of a business (s. 23(3)). This means that if the tenant has, for instance, sublet a part of the premises in circumstances such that it remains in occupation for the purposes of a business only of the remaining part, the court will order a new tenancy only of that remaining part. The court will designate the property which constitutes the holding by reference to the circumstances existing at the date of the order (s. 31(1)).

If the landlord opposed the grant of a new tenancy on ground (f), but the circumstances set out in s. 31A apply (including that the tenant is willing to accept a tenancy of an economically separable part), the order under s. 29 will be for the grant of a new tenancy of that part only (s. 32(1A)).

If the holding does not include all the property comprised in the current tenancy, the landlord may nevertheless require any new tenancy ordered to be granted to be a tenancy of the whole (s. 32(2)). If a landlord did not have this power, it might, for instance, by virtue of the Law of Property Act

1925, s. 139, become landlord of different tenants (including those who were previously sublessees) holding parts of the property comprised in the existing tenancy under different leases.

The tenant cannot be compelled to accept the landlord's offer of a lease of only part of the premises.

The order for a grant of a new tenancy under s. 29 will include 'rights enjoyed in connection with the holding', i.e. appurtenant rights such as easements, unless the parties agree otherwise or (in default of such agreement) the court otherwise determines (s. 32(3)).

15.2.6.2 Duration

An agreement between the parties on the duration of the new tenancy will be given effect to in the court order, whatever the term may be. In the absence of such agreement, the court will make an order for a term which it considers to be reasonable in all the circumstances, but in this case the court cannot make an order for the grant of a term certain of more than 14 years. The term ordered by the court begins on the termination of the current tenancy (s. 33).

Factors which the court will take into account in deciding upon the term include the term of the current tenancy (a longer term will rarely be ordered), the nature of the business and the comparative hardship between the parties. The court may also include a break clause in the new lease: as, for instance, where the landlord intends to redevelop the premises within a few years, but not within the period required to satisfy ground (f) of s. 30 (see **15.2.4.6**) (*National Car Parks Ltd* v *Paternoster Consortium Ltd* [1990] 1 EGLR 99). In a case where the redevelopment was likely to occur at the time of the tenant's retirement, however, the factor of comparative hardship was decisive against the inclusion of a landlord's break clause (*Becker* v *Hill Street Properties Ltd* [1990] 2 EGLR 78, CA).

15.2.6.3 Rent

In default of agreement between the parties, the court will determine the rent payable under the new tenancy as that at which, having regard to the terms of the tenancy (other than those relating to rent), the holding might reasonably be expected to be let in the open market by a willing lessor, but with specified matters being disregarded (s. 34(1)). This means that the other terms of the new tenancy will need to be settled (by the court, if the parties cannot agree) before the court is able to determine the rent (*O'May* v *City of London Real Property Co. Ltd* [1983] 2 AC 726, HL). There may be an open market even where there is only one lessor, provided there is a number of potential lessees (see *Air Canada* v *Heathrow Airport Ltd* (30 March 1993, county court, unreported) where the premises comprised an airport passenger lounge). Furthermore, a market can still be an open market even though most of the occupiers of the premises belong to a particular profession or engage in a particular trade. Thus in *Baptist* v *Trustees of the Honourable Society of Gray's Inn* (1993) 42 EG 287 (county court), Judge Owen held that there was an open market for lettings within the Inn, even though most of its occupants were barristers and that, since 1984, there had been no lettings other than to members of the Bar.

The statutory disregards are:

(a) any effect on rent of the fact that the tenant or the tenant's predecessors in title have been in occupation of the holding;
(b) any goodwill attached to the holding by reason of the carrying on there of the tenant's business (whether by the tenant or by a predecessor of such business);
(c) any effect on rent of certain types of improvements (defined in s. 34(2));
(d) any addition to the value of licensed premises attributable to the tenant's licence (s. 34(1)).

To be disregarded under para. (c), an improvement must be one carried out by the tenant for the time being and not in pursuance of an obligation to the immediate landlord. The improvement must, furthermore, be carried out either:

(a) during the current tenancy; or
(b) within 21 years of the application for a new tenancy, where the premises have since the improvement always been let on a tenancy within s. 23, and no tenant since such time has given notice to quit (s. 34(2)).

Suppose, therefore, that a business tenant (T) voluntarily effected improvements in 1955 and 1975, while tenant of L under lease 1, which expired in 1977. In determining the rent payable under the new lease (lease 2), the court will disregard both sets of improvements because they were both effected during the current tenancy. Let us now suppose that the term granted by the new lease expires in 1994. If T obtains a further renewal of the tenancy (lease 3) in 1994, the 1975 improvement will again be disregarded under paragraph (c), because it was effected within 21 years of the application for the new tenancy. The 1955 improvement, however, will not be disregarded, because it was carried out more than 21 years earlier.

Each party usually presents the evidence of a surveyor with experience in the valuation of business premises in the particular area. Where appropriate, such evidence will be supported by rental values for comparable properties. If there are no comparable properties, evidence of the profitability of the tenant's business may be taken into account (*Harewood Hotels Ltd* v *Harris* [1958] 1 WLR 108). In assessing the open market rent, the court is not restricted to considering a letting restricted to the use to which the tenant puts the property. It must also consider the most profitable use to which the premises, consistently with the user clause, could be put (*W.J. Barton Ltd* v *Long Acre Securities Ltd* [1982] 1 WLR 398). The state of repair of the premises is also a relevant factor in determining the market rent. If the landlord has breached a repairing covenant, this may reduce the market value of the premises for the purposes of the section, at least where the breach is a serious one (*Fawke* v *Viscount Chelsea* [1980] QB 441).

The court is specifically empowered to make provision for varying the rent, i.e. to include a rent review clause. It did not become common practice to insert rent review clauses in leases until the 1960s. Where such leases come up for renewal and the parties agree that a rent review clause should be inserted in the new lease, but not on its content, the court has power to order the insertion of a clause which provides for review downwards as well as upwards. This might be appropriate where there is specific evidence that rents in the area are likely to fall in the future (*Janes (Gowns) Ltd* v *Harlow Development Corporation* (1979) 253 EG 799). The county court in *Boots the Chemists Ltd* v *Pinkland Ltd* [1992] 2 EGLR 98, however, made an order including a downwards as well as upwards rent review clause even in the absence of such specific evidence. If the current lease already contains a rent review clause, however, the court will generally retain its terms in the order for the new tenancy: thus if the current lease provides for upwards-only review, so usually will the new (*Charles Follett Ltd* v *Cabtell Investments Ltd* [1986] 2 EGLR 76 no appeal on this point at [1987] 2 EGLR 88, CA; and (in the county court) *Blythewood Plant Hire Ltd* v *Spiers Ltd* [1992] 2 EGLR 103).

15.2.6.4 Other terms

In default of agreement between the parties, the other terms of the tenancy are such as may be determined by the court, which is to have regard to the terms of the current tenancy and to all relevant circumstances (s. 35). In practice, the terms of the new lease will be the same as those of the existing lease. This principle has been held applicable to the provision of guarantors. Thus where the original lease (for a term of one year) required the tenant to provide guarantors, the court held that a similar requirement should be inserted into the new (10-year) tenancy.

A variation in the terms, or the addition of new terms, will not generally be ordered unless the party seeking it can provide a convincing justification. Any variation to the benefit of one party must, moreover, be balanced by compensatory changes elsewhere. In *O'May* v *City of London Real Property Co. Ltd* [1983] 2 AC 726, (HL) the existing lease imposed an obligation on the landlord to repair. The landlord wished the new lease to contain a service charge (not provided for in the existing lease) to cover services and repairs in return for a small reduction in the rent. The House of Lords refused to insert such new terms. It held that such additional financial obligation could not be adequately compensated for in this way. The variation sought would benefit only the landlord, by quantifying a liability which, under the existing lease, was unquantifiable.

15.2.6.5 Carrying out the court's order

The landlord must execute the lease and can require the tenant to execute a counterpart (s. 36(1)). The court must revoke the order if the tenant applies for its revocation within 14 days of its being made. In this event, the current tenancy ceases to be one protected by Part II, and it continues for such period as the parties may agree, or the court shall determine is necessary to give the landlord a reasonable opportunity to relet or otherwise dispose of the property (s. 36(2)).

SIXTEEN

SECURED LENDING

16.1 Introduction

If a tenant borrows funds from an institutional lender to assist in the payment of a premium on the grant or assignment of a lease, or for other purposes connected with its business, the tenant will invariably be required to provide some form of security.

Such security could take the form of a mortgage over the lease itself or over other of the tenant's assets. These could, for instance, be plant and machinery or goods used in the tenant's business; or they could be other assets belonging to the tenant, such as the tenant's own home. If the tenant-borrower is a company, the lender may require a fixed security over the land, i.e. a legal charge of the leasehold title, and a floating charge over other assets used in the business. If the lease has little asset value (e.g. because it is granted at a rack-rent without a premium), the lender may require the company's directors to mortgage their personal assets, such as their own homes.

Security could also take the form of a personal guarantee provided by a third party — such as a director of a company or a parent or grandparent of a person setting up in business.

If the mortgage is of an existing lease, the prospective mortgagee should check the terms of the lease and ascertain whether there are any existing breaches of covenant. The mortgagee should also check to see if the lease contains a covenant by the tenant not to mortgage or charge the property. If the covenant against mortgaging or charging is a qualified one, the landlord's consent is not to be unreasonably refused (see the Landlord and Tenant Act 1927, s. 19(1)(a), and the Law of Property Act 1925, s. 86(1); see further **5.2**, **5.6.1** and **5.6.2**. A qualified covenant by the tenant against mortgaging or charging the lease might be as follows:

> **Not to mortgage or charge or permit or suffer to be mortgaged or charged all or any part of the demised premises without the prior written consent of the landlord.**

If the lender takes a legal charge over the tenant's lease, the lender (the mortgagee) will need to protect its position so far as possible against breaches by the tenant of the terms of the lease. If the landlord seeks subsequently to forfeit the lease, the mortgagee has a right to apply for relief; but the mortgagee will wish to have as early warning as possible of any default by the tenant. The mortgagee may not itself necessarily receive a copy of the Law of Property Act 1925, s. 146, notice: see **13.4.2**. The mortgage deed should therefore contain a covenant by the mortgagor to inform the mortgagee as soon as it receives service of notice under s. 146. This method is not, however, necessarily secure, and, although the landlord should inform a mortgagee of whom it is aware, of forfeiture proceedings, the mortgagee cannot be guaranteed to learn of them. See further, **13.4.6.4**, **13.4.6.5** and **13.5.2.4**. In any event, the mortgagee should be advised to notify the landlord in writing of its interest.

The position of a mortgagee in the event of the tenant's insolvency has been considered in **chapter 14**. See the discussion of the mortgagee's rights in the event of the tenant's bankruptcy (**14.6.3**), and particularly the effect of a disclaimer (**14.8.3.2**) and a vesting order (**14.8.4**).

The remainder of this chapter deals with the mortgagee's important right to appoint a receiver, and its impact on the rights of the parties to the lease.

16.2 Receivership

16.2.1 APPOINTMENT OF A RECEIVER

The tenant may have mortgaged the lease or other assets or both.

If the lease has been specifically mortgaged, a receiver appointed by the mortgagee to enforce such fixed charge is known as a 'Law of Property Act receiver', because he or she is subject, in addition to the provisions of the mortgage deed, to the provisions of the Law of Property Act 1925, s. 109. The appointment must be in writing.

If the tenant is a company, it may give a debenture creating a floating charge over its assets, including the lease. A receiver appointed to enforce a charge over all or substantially all of a company's assets is known as an 'administrative receiver'. Such a receiver is subject to the provisions contained both in the debenture creating the charge and in the Insolvency Act 1986.

Where more than one person has been appointed a receiver, it is important for the landlord to know whether the appointment is joint or several. The landlord should check, not merely the document making the appointment, but also the terms of the mortgage or debenture itself. If the mortgage makes provision for a joint appointment only, a purported joint and several appointment is invalid.

16.2.2 RECEIVER AS AGENT

The mortgage deed or debenture will usually create an express agency, and in practice the receiver will be stated to be the agent of the mortgagor. In the absence of express provision, a Law of Property Act receiver is deemed to be the agent of the mortgagor (Law of Property Act 1925, s. 109(2)); and an administrative receiver appointed under a debenture is deemed the agent of the company which granted it (Insolvency Act 1986, s. 44). The effect of the receiver being the agent of the mortgagor, rather than of the mortgagee, is that it is only the former who is liable for the receiver's defaults.

Although a receiver may be appointed as agent of a mortgagor company, such agency ceases upon a winding-up order or resolution for a voluntary winding up. Similarly, although a receiver may be appointed after the company has gone into liquidation, the receiver will not be agent of the liquidated company. Even after the company's liquidation, however, the receiver retains the powers of disposal conferred by the mortgage deed or debenture. Furthermore, if the receiver has already instituted proceedings in the name of a tenant company mortgagor, those proceedings may be continued even after the tenant has gone into liquidation. Thus in *Gough's Garages Ltd* v *Pugsley* [1930] 1 KB 615, the receiver was held entitled to continue an application to the court for a new lease (under the renewal provisions contained in the predecessor to the Landlord and Tenant Act 1954, Part II), even though the tenant had been compulsorily wound up since the receiver's action had been commenced.

A receiver in occupation of property as agent of an insolvent tenant would not appear to be itself liable to pay business rates (*Ratford* v *Northavon District Council* [1987] QB 357). A receiver may, however, be liable if the premises occupied are those of a tenant which is a company in liquidation (*Banister* v *London Borough of Islington* (1972) 71 LGR 239).

16.2.3 DUTIES OF A RECEIVER

The receiver's first duty is to the chargee who appoints him. Various duties arise in contract, equity and tort. Thus, in *Knight* v *Lawrence* [1991] 1 EGLR 143, a receiver was held liable in negligence to the mortgagee where, the mortgaged properties being let, he failed to serve on the tenants notices of rent review, thus reducing the price obtained when the properties were sold.

Subject to this, the receiver owes equitable duties to the tenant as mortgagor. In regard to managing the property, such duties are limited: the mortgagor can complain of fraud of *mala fides*, but not of other acts or omissions, unless these breach a term of his appointment (*Re B Johnson and Co. (Builders) Ltd* [1955] Ch 634, in the context of an administrative receiver). In regard to selling the property, the receiver must take reasonable care to obtain market value, this being the same standard of care as was laid down for mortgagees exercising their power of sale in *Cuckmere Brick Co. Ltd* v *Mutual Finance Ltd* [1971] Ch 949. The Privy Council has recently stated, obiter, that, in exercising its powers, an administrative receiver owes no duty of care to the company in tort (*Downsview Nominees Ltd* v *First City Corporation Ltd* [1993] AC 295). This suggests that prior cases (such as *American Express International Banking Corporation* v *Hurley* [1985] 3 All ER 564) which held that the receiver owes a duty of care in tort to a tenant's guarantor, may need to be reconsidered. Since, however, a guarantor could (through subrogation, see **3.1.4.1**) to the mortgaged property, a receiver might be held to owe a duty to such guarantor in equity.

A Law of Property Act receiver generally has extensive powers conferred expressly by the mortgage deed; apart from this, a receiver has the statutory powers conferred by the Law of Property Act 1925, s. 109. Under the section, the receiver has power to demand and recover all the income of which he or she is appointed receiver, by action, distress, or otherwise, and to give receipts for the same. An administrative receiver will similarly generally have extensive powers conferred expressly by the debenture, but otherwise has various statutory powers, including the power to make disposals, to insure, to carry on the company's business, and to grant leases (Insolvency Act 1986, s. 42 and sch. 1).

The receiver will dispose of or use the charged property in order to pay off the amount owed the chargee. A Law of Property Act receiver must apply any income from the property, and the proceeds of sale, in the order specified in the Law of Property Act 1925, s. 109(8). Such income, might comprise, for instance, rents from sublessees. The statutory order of application of payments is:

(a) rents, taxes, rates and other outgoings on the property;
(b) payments and interest on annual sums of prior mortgages;
(c) receiver's commission, insurance premiums payable under the mortgage deed, and proper repairs directed by the mortgagee;
(d) interest on principal moneys due under the mortgage;
(e) principal money due under the mortgage, if directed in writing by the mortgagee.

Any balance must be paid to the person who would otherwise have been entitled to the income of, or who is otherwise entitled to, the mortgaged property.

If the Law of Property Act receiver is given an express power of sale, it would appear that the application of the sale proceeds is governed instead by the Law of Property Act 1925, s. 105, i.e. discharge of prior mortgages, payment of costs of the sale, discharge of the mortgage money, interest and costs, and then to the person entitled to the mortgaged property.

An administrative receiver appointed under a floating charge must, if the company is not in the course of being wound up, pay preferential debts before discharging the principal or interest under the debenture (Insolvency Act 1986, s. 40(2)). Preferential debts include: debts due to the Inland Revenue, to Customs and Excise, social security and occupational pensions contributions, and up to four months' salary to employees.

16.2.4 POSITION OF THE LANDLORD

The tenant's receivership does not prevent its landlord from pursuing its remedies of forfeiture or distress, or from bringing an action for rent arrears, or for damages for breach of any other covenants in the lease. No leave is required to distrain goods subject to a floating charge or to bring an action for rent arrears. Furthermore, by serving a notice under the Law of Distress (Amendment) Act 1908, a head landlord is entitled to the subrents even against its immediate tenant's receiver (*Rhodes* v *Allied Dunbar Pension Services Ltd* [1989] 1 WLR 800).

Once a receiver has been appointed, however, the receiver has priority over a judgment debtor, even though the judgment debt was obtained before the receiver was appointed. Indeed, the receiver has priority even where the goods have already been seized by the sheriff. In this instance, therefore, the landlord has an additional reason for preferring to recover rent by means of distress rather than by action.

Provided the agency is disclosed, the receiver is not personally liable either, even in respect of a new lease which he or she enters into. In such circumstances, therefore, a receiver does not incur personal liability when renewing the lease under the provisions of the Landlord and Tenant Act 1954, Part II. Similarly, a receiver occupying the demised premises as the tenant's agent for the purpose of carrying on the tenant's business is not personally liable for the rent due under the lease (*Re Atlantic Computer Systems plc* [1992] Ch 505).

Although the receiver is generally the agent of the tenant, he or she is jointly liable with the tenant for any tort which is committed in the course of the agency. Thus, if in the course of realising the assets, the receiver damages the premises demised, the landlord could sue either or both of them for the tort of waste: see **7.1.3**.

APPENDIX 1

THE LAW SOCIETY STANDARD BUSINESS LEASES

The authors and publishers gratefully acknowledge the permission of the Law Society to reproduce the text of their two standard business leases, which were published by the Law Society in 1991.

1. Lease of Whole Building

THE LAW SOCIETY BUSINESS LEASE (WHOLE OF BUILDING)

DATE ______________________________

LANDLORD ______________________________

OF ______________________________

____

____

LETS TO

TENANT ______________________________

OF ______________________________

____

THE PROPERTY KNOWN AS

PROPERTY ______________________________

____

RESIDENTIAL ACCOMMODATION [WHICH INCLUDES

____

______________________________]

FOR THE PERIOD STARTING ON

LEASE PERIOD ______________________________

AND ENDING ON

____

FOR USE (EXCEPT ANY RESIDENTIAL ACCOMMODATION) AS

USE ALLOWED ______________________________

OR ANY OTHER USE TO WHICH THE LANDLORD CONSENTS (AND THE LANDLORD IS NOT ENTITLED TO WITHHOLD THAT CONSENT UNREASONABLY)

THE TENANT PAYING THE LANDLORD RENT AT THE RATE OF

RENT ______________________________ POUNDS

(£)

A YEAR BY THESE INSTALMENTS:

(A) ON THE DATE OF THIS LEASE, A PROPORTIONATE SUM FOR THE PERIOD STARTING ON

______________________________ TO

______________________________ AND THEN

(B) EQUAL MONTHLY INSTALMENTS IN ADVANCE ON THE

RENT DAYS ______________________________ DAY OF EACH MONTH

THE RENT MAY BE INCREASED (UNDER CLAUSE 8) WITH EFFECT FROM EVERY

RENT REVIEW DATES ______________________________ ANNIVERSARY OF THE START OF THE LEASE PERIOD

This lease is granted on the terms printed on pages 2 to 4, as added to or varied by any terms appearing on any attached continuation page

TENANT'S OBLIGATIONS

1 PAYMENTS

1. The tenant is to pay the Landlord:

1.1 the rent

1.2 the amount of every premium which the Landlord pays to insure the property under this lease, to be paid within 14 days after the Landlord gives written notice of payment (and this amount is to be paid as rent)

and the following sums on demand:

1.3 a fair proportion (decided by a surveyor the Landlord nominates) of the cost of repairing maintaining and cleaning:

party walls, party structures, yards, gardens, roads, paths, gutters, drains, sewers, pipes, conduits, wires, cables and things used or shared with other property

1.4 the cost of any works to the property which the Landlord does after the Tenant defaults

1.5 the costs and expenses (including professional fees) which the Landlord incurs in:

(a) dealing with any application by the Tenant for consent or approval, whether or not it is given

(b) preparing and serving a notice of a breach of the Tenant's obligations, under section 146 of the Law of Property Act 1925, even if forfeiture of this lease is avoided without a court order

(c) preparing and serving schedules of dilapidations either during the lease period or recording failure to give up the property in the appropriate state of repair when this lease ends

1.6 interest at the Law Society's interest rate on any of the above payments when more than fourteen days overdue, to be calculated from its due date

and in making payment under this clause:

(a) nothing is to be deducted or set off

(b) any value added tax payable is to be added.

2. The Tenant is also to make the following payments, with value added tax where payable:

2.1 all periodic rates, taxes and outgoings relating to the property, including any imposed after the date of this lease (even if of a novel nature), to be paid promptly to the authorities to whom they are due

2.2 the cost of the grant, renewal or continuation of any licence or registration for using the property for the use allowed, to be paid promptly to the appropriate authority when due

2.3 a registration fee of £20 for each document which this lease requires the Tenant to register, to be paid to the Landlord's solicitors when presenting the document for registration

3. USE

3. The Tenant is to comply with the following requirements as to the use of the property and any part of it and is not to authorise or allow anyone else to contravene them:

3.1 to use the property, except any residential accommodation, only for the use allowed

3.2 to use any residential accommodation only as a home for one family

3.3 not to do anything which might invalidate any insurance policy covering the property or which might increase the premium

3.4 not to hold an auction sale in the property

3.5 not to use the property for any activities which are dangerous, offensive, noxious, illegal or immoral, or which are or may become a nuisance or annoyance to the Landlord or to the owner or occupier of any neighbouring property

3.6 not to display any advertisements on the outside of the property or which are visible from the outside unless the Landlord consents (and the Landlord is not entitled to withhold that consent unreasonably)

3.7 not to overload the floors or walls of the property

3.8 to comply with the terms of every Act of Parliament, order, regulation, bye-law, rule, licence and registration authorising or regulating how the property is used, and to obtain, renew and continue any licence or registration which is required

4 ACCESS

4. The Tenant is to give the Landlord, or anyone authorised by him in writing, access to the property:

4.1 for these purposes:

(a) inspecting the condition of the property, or how it is being used

(b) doing works which the Landlord is permitted to do under clause 5.5(c)

(c) complying with any statutory obligation

(d) viewing the property as a prospective buyer or mortgagee or, during the last six months of the lease period, as a prospective tenant

(e) valuing the property

(f) inspecting, cleaning or repairing neighbouring property, or any sewers, drains, pipes, wires, cables serving neighbouring property

4.2 and only on seven days' written notice except in emergency

4.3 and during normal business hours except in an emergency

4.4 and the Landlord is promptly to make good all damage caused to the property and any goods there in exercising these rights

5 CONDITION

5. The Tenant is to comply with the following duties in relation to the property:

5.1 to maintain the state and condition of the property

5.2 to decorate the inside and outside of the property:

(a) in every fifth year of the lease period

(b) in the last three months of the lease period (however it ends) except to the extent that it has been decorated in the previous year

and on each occasion the Tenant is to use the colours and the types of finish used previously

5.3 to do the work to the property which any authority acting under an Act of Parliament requires

5.4 but the Tenant need not:

(a) alter or improve the property

(b) make good damage caused by an insured risk, except to the extent that the policy moneys have not been paid because of any act or default of the Tenant

5.5 if the Tenant fails to do any work which this lease requires him to do and the Landlord gives him written notice to do it, the Tenant is to:

(a) start the work within two months, or immediately in case of emergency, and

(b) proceed diligently with the work

(c) in default, permit the Landlord to do the work

5.6 not to make any structural alterations, external alternations or additions to the property

5.7 not to make any other alterations unless with the Landlord's consent in writing (and the Landlord is not entitled to withhold that consent unreasonably)

5.8 to keep any plate glass in the property insured for its full replacement cost with reputable insurers, to give the Landlord details of that insurance on request, and to replace any plate glass which becomes damaged

6 TRANSFER ETC.

6. The Tenant is to comply with the following:

6.1 the Tenant is not to share occupation of the property and no part of it is to be transferred, sublet or occupied separately from the remainder

6.2 the Tenant is not to transfer or sublet the whole of the property unless the Landlord gives written consent in advance, and the Landlord is not entitled to withhold that consent unreasonably

6.3 any sublease is to be in terms which are consistent with this lease, but is not to permit the sub-tenant to underlet

6.4 within four weeks after the property is transferred mortgaged or sublet, the Landlord's solicitors are to be notified and a copy of the transfer mortgage or sublease sent to them for registration with the fee payable under clause 2.3

7 OTHER MATTERS

7. The Tenant:

7.1 is to give the Landlord a copy of any notice concerning the property or any neighbouring property as soon as he receives it

7.2 is to allow the Landlord, during the last six months of the lease period, to fix a notice in a reasonable position on the outside of the property announcing that it is for sale or to let

7.3 is not to apply for planning permission relating to the use of alteration of the property unless the Landlord gives written consent in advance

8 RENT REVIEW

8.1 On each review date, the rent is to increase to the market rent if that is higher than the rent applying before that date

8.2 The market rent is the rent which a willing tenant would pay for the property on the open market, if let to him on the rent review date by a willing landlord on a lease on the same terms as this lease without any premium and for a period equal to the remainder of the lease period, assuming that at that date:

(a) the willing tenant takes account of any likelihood that he would be entitled to a new lease of the property when the lease ends, but does not take account of any goodwill belonging to anyone who had occupied the property

(b) the property is vacant and had not been occupied by the Tenant or any sub-tenant

(c) the property can immediately be used

(d) the property is in the condition required by this lease and any damage caused by any of the risks insured under clause 11 has been made good

(e) during the lease period neither the Tenant nor any sub-tenant has done anything to the property to increase or decrease its rental value, other than anything which the Tenant was obliged to do under the terms of this lease

8. 3 If the Landlord and the Tenant agree the amount of the new rent, a statement of that new rent, signed by them, is to be attached to this lease

8. 4 If the Landlord and the Tenant have not agreed the amount of the new rent two months before the rent review date, either of them may require the new rent to be decided by arbitration under clause 14.5

8. 5

(a) The Tenant is to continue to pay rent at the rate applying before the rent review date until the next rent day after the new rent is agreed or decided

(b) Starting on that rent day, the Tenant is to pay a new rent

(c) On that rent day, the Tenant is also to pay any amount by which the new rent since the rent review date exceeds the rent paid, with interest on that amount at 2% below the Law Society's interest rate

9 DAMAGE

9. If the property is damaged by any of the risks to be insured under clause 11 and as a result of that damage the property, or any part of it, cannot be used for the use allowed:

9. 1 the rent, or a fair proportion of it, is to be suspended for three years or until the property is fully restored, if sooner

9. 2 if at any time it is unlikely that the property will be fully restored within three years from the date of the damage, the Landlord (so long as he has not delayed the restoration) or the Tenant can end this lease by giving one month's notice to the other during the three year period, in which case

(a) the insurance money belongs to the Landlord and

(b) the Landlord's obligation to make good damage under clause 11 ceases

9. 3 a notice given outside the time limits in clause 9.2 is not effective

9.4 any dispute arising under any part of this clause is to be decided by arbitration under clause 14.5

LANDLORD'S OBLIGATIONS AND FORFEITURE RIGHTS

10 QUIET ENJOYMENT

10. While the Tenant complies with the terms of this lease, the Landlord is to allow the Tenant to possess and use the property without lawful interference from the Landlord, anyone who derives title from the Landlord or any trustee for the Landlord

11 INSURANCE

11. The Landlord agrees with the Tenant:

11. 1 the Landlord is to keep the property (except the plate glass) insured with reputable insurers to cover:

(a) full rebuilding, site clearance, professional fees, value added tax and three years' loss of rent

(b) against fire, lightning, explosion, earthquake, landslip, subsidence, heave, riot, civil commotion, aircraft, aerial devices, storm, flood, water, theft, impact by vehicles, damage by malicious persons and vandals and third party liability and any other risks reasonably required by the Landlord

so far as cover is available at the normal insurance rates for the locality and subject to reasonable excesses and exclusions

11. 2 and to take all necessary steps to make good as soon as possible damage to the property caused by insured risks except to the extent that the insurance money is not paid because of the act or default of the Tenant

11. 3 and to give the Tenant at his request once a year particulars of the policy and evidence from the insurer that it is in force

11. 4 and that the Tenant is not responsible for any damage for which the Landlord is compensated under the insurance policy

12 FORFEITURE

12. This lease comes to an end if the Landlord forfeits it by entering any part of the property which the Landlord is entitled to do whenever:

(a) payment of any rent is fourteen days overdue, even if was not formally demanded

(b) the Tenant has not complied with any of the terms in this lease

(c) the Tenant if an individual (and if more than one, any of them) is adjudicated bankrupt or an interim receiver of his property is appointed

(d) the Tenant if a company (and if more than one, any of them) goes into liquidation (unless solely for the purpose of amalgamation or reconstruction when solvent), or has an administrative receiver appointed or has an administration order made in respect of it

The forfeiture of this lease does not cancel any outstanding obligation of the Tenant or a Guarantor

13 END OF LEASE

13. When this lease ends the Tenant is to:

13. 1 return the property to the Landlord leaving it in the state and condition in which this lease requires the Tenant to keep it

13. 2 (if the Landlord so requires) move anything the Tenant fixed to the property and make good any damage which that causes

GENERAL

14 PARTIES' RESPONSIBILITY

14. 1 Whenever more than one person or company is the Landlord, the Tenant or the Guarantor, their obligations can be enforced against all or both of them jointly and against each individually

LANDLORD

14. 2 The Landlord includes the person who, at any particular time, has the right to receive rent under this lease

TENANT

14. 3 The Tenant includes the person who, at any particular time, is given the right by this lease to possess the property

SERVICE OF NOTICES

14. 4 The rules about serving notices in Section 196 of the Law of Property Act 1925 (as since amended) apply to any notice given under this lease

ARBITRATION

14. 5 Any matter which this lease requires to be decided by arbitration is to be referred to a single arbitrator under the Arbitration Acts. The Landlord and the Tenant may agree the appointment of the arbitrator, or either of them may apply to the President of the Royal Institution of Chartered Surveyors to make the appointment

HEADINGS

14. 6 The headings do not form part of this Lease.

Signed as a deed by/on behalf of the Landlord and delivered in the presence of:

....
Witness

....
Witness's occupation and address

....

Signed as a deed by/on behalf of the Landlord and delivered in the presence of:

....
Witness

....
Witness's occupation and address

....

Signed as a deed by/on behalf of the Landlord and delivered in the presence of:

....
Witness

....
Witness's occupation and address

....

GUARANTEE BOX

The terms in this box only take effect if a guarantor is named and then only until the Tenant transfers this lease with the Landlord's written consent. The Guarantor must sign this lease.

'Guarantor':

of

agrees to compensate the Landlord for any loss incurred as a result of the Tenant failing to comply with an obligation in this lease during the lease period or any statutory extension of it. If the Tenant is insolvent and this lease ends because it is disclaimed, the Guarantor agrees to accept a new lease, if the Landlord so requires, in the same form but at the rent then payable. Even if the Landlord gives the Tenant extra time to comply with an obligation, or does not insist on strict compliance with terms of this lease, the Guarantor's obligation remains fully effective.

THIS DOCUMENT CREATES LEGAL RIGHTS AND LEGAL OBLIGATIONS. DO NOT SIGN IT UNTIL YOU HAVE CONSULTED A SOLICITOR.

....
Landlord

....
Tenant

....
Guarantor

2. Lease of Part of Building

THE LAW SOCIETY BUSINESS LEASE (PART OF BUILDING)

DATE ______________________________

LANDLORD ______________________________

OF ______________________________

____

LETS TO

TENANT ______________________________

OF ______________________________

____

THE PROPERTY KNOWN AS

PROPERTY ______________________________

____

WHICH IS PART OF

BUILDING ______________________________

____

(WHICH, WHEN REFERRED TO IN THIS LEASE, INCLUDES ITS GROUNDS) FOR THE PERIOD STARTING ON

LEASE PERIOD ______________________________ **AND ENDING ON**

____

FOR USE AS

USE ALLOWED ______________________________

OR ANY OTHER USE TO WHICH THE LANDLORD CONSENTS (AND THE LANDLORD IS NOT ENTITLED TO WITHHOLD THAT CONSENT UNREASONABLY)

THE TENANT PAYING THE LANDLORD RENT AT THE RATE OF

RENT ______________________________ **POUNDS**

(£)

A YEAR BY THESE INSTALMENTS

(A) ON THE DATE OF THIS LEASE, A PROPORTIONATE SUM FOR THE PERIOD STARTING ON

______________________________ **TO**

______________________________ **AND THEN**

(B) EQUAL MONTHLY INSTALMENTS IN ADVANCE ON THE

RENT DAYS ______________________________ **DAY OF EACH MONTH**

THE RENT MAY BE INCREASED (UNDER CLAUSE 9) WITH EFFECT FROM EVERY ANNIVERSARY OF THE START OF THE LEASE PERIOD

RENT REVIEW DATES ______________________________

This lease is granted on the terms printed on pages 2 to 5, as added to or varied by any terms appearing on page 6 or any attached continuation page

TENANT'S OBLIGATIONS

1 PAYMENTS

1. The Tenant is to pay the Landlord:

1.1 the rent

1.2 the service charge in accordance with clause 3 (and this is to be paid as rent)

and the following sums on demand:

1.3 a fair proportion (decided by a surveyor the Landlord nominates) of the cost of repairing maintaining and cleaning:

party walls, party structures, yards, gardens, roads, paths, gutters, drains, sewers, pipes, conduits, wires, cables and things used or shared with other property

1.4 the cost of any works to the property which the Landlord does after the Tenant defaults

1.5 the costs and expenses (including professional fees) which the Landlord incurs in:

(a) dealing with any application by the Tenant for consent or approval, whether or not it is given

(b) preparing and serving a notice of a breach of the Tenant's obligations, under section 146 of the Law of Property Act 1925, even if forfeiture of this lease is avoided without a court order

(c) preparing and serving schedules of dilapidations either during the lease period or recording failure to give up the property in the appropriate state of repair when this lease ends

1.6 interest at the Law Society's interest rate on any of the above payments when more than fourteen days overdue, to be calculated from its due date

and in making payments under this clause:

(a) nothing is to be deducted or set off

(b) any value added tax payable is to be added.

2. The Tenant is also to make the following payments, with value added tax where payable:

2.1 all periodic rates, taxes and outgoings relating to the property, including any imposed after the date of this lease (even if of a novel nature), to be paid promptly to the authorities to whom they are due

2.2 the cost of the grant, renewal or continuation of any licence or registration for using the property for the use allowed, to be paid promptly to the appropriate authority when due

2.3 a registration fee of £20 for each document which this lease requires the Tenant to register to be paid to the Landlord's solicitors when presenting the document for registration

3 SERVICE CHARGE

3. The Landlord and the Tenant agree that:

3.1 the service charge is the Tenant's fair proportion of each item of the service costs

3.2 the service costs:

(a) are the costs which the Landlord fairly and reasonably incurs in complying with his obligations under clauses 12 and 13

(b) include the reasonable charges of any agent contractor consultant or employee whom the Landlord engages to provide the services under clauses 12 and 13

(c) include interest at no more than the Law Society's interest rate on sums the Landlord borrows to discharge his obligations under clauses 12 and 13

3.3 the Tenant is to pay the Landlord interim payments on account of the service charge within 21 days of receiving a written demand setting out how it is calculated

3.4 an interim payment is to be the Tenant's fair proportion of what the service costs are reasonably likely to be in the three months following the demand

3.5 the Landlord is not entitled to demand interim payments more than once in every three months

3.6 the Landlord is to keep full records of the service costs and at least once a year is to send the Tenant an account setting out, for the period since the beginning of the lease period or the last account as the case may be:

(a) the amount of the service costs

(b) the service charge the Tenant is to pay

(c) the total of any interim payments the Tenant has paid

(d) the difference between the total interim payments and the service charge

3.7 within 21 days after the Tenant receives the account, the amount mentioned in clause 3.6(d) is to be settled by payment between the parties except that the Landlord is entitled to retain any overpayment towards any interim payments he has demanded for a later accounting period

3.8 the Landlord is either:

(a) to have the account certified by an independent chartered accountant, or

(b) to allow the Tenant to inspect the books records invoices and receipts relating to the service costs

3.9 disagreements about the amounts of the service charge or the service costs are to be decided by arbitration under clause 17.5

4 USE

4. The Tenant is to comply with the following requirements as to the use of the building and any part of it, and is not to authorise or allow anyone else to contravene them:

4.1 to use the property only for the use allowed

4.2 not to obstruct any part of the building used for access to the property or any other part of the building

4.3 not to do anything which might invalidate any insurance policy covering any part of the building or which might increase the premium

4.4 not to hold an auction sale in the property

4.5 not to use any part of the building for any activities which are dangerous, offensive, noxious, illegal or immoral, or which are or may become a nuisance or annoyance to the Landlord or to the owner or occupier of any other part of the building or of any neighbouring property

4.6 not to display any advertisements on the outside of the property or which are visible from outside the property unless the Landlord consents (and the Landlord is not entitled to withhold that consent unreasonably)

4.7 not to overload the floors or walls of the property

4.8 to comply with the terms of every Act of Parliament, order, regulation, bye-law, rule, licence and registration authorising or regulating how the property is used, and to obtain, renew and continue any licence or registration which is required

5 ACCESS

5. The Tenant is to give the Landlord, or anyone authorised by him in writing, access to the property:

5.1 for these purposes:

(a) inspecting the condition of the property, or how it is being used

(b) doing works which the Landlord is permitted to do under clauses 6.8(c) or 13

(c) complying with any statutory obligation

(d) viewing the property as a prospective buyer, tenant or mortgagee

(e) valuing the property

(f) inspecting, cleaning or repairing neighbouring property, or any sewers, drains, pipes, wires, cables serving the building or any neighbouring property

5.2 and only on seven days' written notice except in emergency

5.3 and during normal business hours except in an emergency

5.4 and the Landlord is promptly to make good all damage caused to the property and any goods there in exercising these rights

6 CONDITION

6. The Tenant is to comply with the following duties in relation to the property:

6.1 to maintain the state and condition of the inside of the property

6.2 to decorate the inside of the property:

(a) in every fifth year of the lease period

(b) in the last three months of the lease period (however it ends) except to the extent that it has been decorated in the previous year

6.3 where the property has a shop front to maintain and decorate it

6.4 when decorating, the Tenant is to use the colours and the types of finish used previously

6.5 to do the work to it which any authority acting under an Act of Parliament requires

6.6 the inside of the property is to include all ceilings, floors, doors, door frames, windows, window frames and plate glass and the internal surfaces of all walls but is to exclude joists immediately above ceilings and supporting floors

6.7 but the Tenant need not:

(a) alter or improve the property

(b) make good damage caused by an insured risk, except to the extent that the policy moneys have not been paid because of any act or default of the Tenant

6.8 if the Tenant fails to do any work which this lease requires him to do and the Landlord gives him written notice to do it, the Tenant is to:

(a) start the work within two months, or immediately in case of emergency, and

(b) proceed diligently with the work

(c) in default, permit the Landlord to do the work

6.9 not to make any structural alterations or additions to the property

6.10 not to make any other alterations unless with the Landlord's consent in writing (and the Landlord is not entitled to withhold that consent unreasonably)

6.11 to keep any plate glass in the property insured for its full replacement cost with reputable insurers, to give the Landlord details of that insurance on request, and to replace any plate glass which becomes damaged

7 TRANSFER ETC

7. The Tenant is to comply with the following:

7.1 the Tenant is not to share occupation of the property and no part of it is to be transferred, sublet or occupied separately from the remainder

7.2 the Tenant is not to transfer or sublet the whole of the property unless the Landlord gives written consent in advance, and the Landlord is not entitled to withhold that consent unreasonably

7.3 any sublease is to be on terms which are consistent with this lease, but is not to permit the sub-tenant to underlet

7.4 within four weeks after the property is transferred mortgaged or sublet, the Landlord's solicitors are to be notified and a copy of the transfer mortgage or sublease sent to them for registration with the fee payable under clause 2.3

8 OTHER MATTERS

8. The Tenant:

8.1 is to give the Landlord a copy of any notice concerning the property or any neighbouring property as soon as he receives it

8.2 is to allow the Landlord, during the last six months of the lease period, to fix a notice in a reasonable position on the outside of the property announcing that it is for sale or to let

8.3 is not to apply for planning permission relating to the use or alteration of the property unless the Landlord gives written consent in advance

9 RENT REVIEW

9.1 On each rent review date, the rent is to increase to the market rent if that is higher than the rent applying before that date

9.2 The market rent is the rent which a willing tenant would pay for the property on the open market, if let to him on the rent review date by a willing landlord on a lease on the same terms as this lease without any premium and for a period equal to the remainder of the lease period, assuming that at that date:

(a) the willing tenant takes account of any likelihood that he would be entitled to a new lease of the property when the lease ends, but does not take account of any goodwill belonging to anyone who had occupied the property;

(b) the property is vacant and had not been occupied by the Tenant or any sub-tenant;

(c) the property can immediately be used;

(d) the property is in the condition required by this lease and any damage caused by any of the risks insured under clause 12 has been made good;

(e) during the lease period neither the Tenant nor any sub-tenant has done anything to the property to increase or decrease its rental value, other than anything which the Tenant was obliged to do under the terms of this lease

9.3 If the Landlord and the Tenant agree the amount of the new rent, a statement of that new rent, signed by them, is to be attached to this lease

9.4 If the Landlord and the Tenant have not agreed the amount of the new rent two months before the rent review date, either of them may require the new rent to be decided by arbitration under clause 17.5

9.5

(a) The Tenant is to continue to pay rent at the rate applying before the rent review date until the next rent day after the new rent is agreed or decided

(b) Starting on that rent day, the Tenant is to pay the new rent

(c) On that rent day, the Tenant is also to pay any amount by which the new rent since the rent review date exceeds the rent paid, with interest on that amount at 2% below the Law Society's interest rate

10 DAMAGE

10. If the property is or the common parts are damaged by any of the risks to be insured under clause 12 and as a result of that damage the property, or any part of it, cannot be used for the use allowed:

10.1 the rent, or fair proportion of it, is to be suspended for three years or until the property or the common parts are fully restored, if sooner

10.2 if at any time it is unlikely that the property or the common parts will be fully restored within three years from the date of the damage, the Landlord (so long as he has not wilfully delayed the restoration) or the Tenant may end this lease by giving one month's notice to the other during the three year period, in which case

(a) the insurance money belongs to the Landlord and

(b) the Landlord's obligation to make good damage under clause 12 ceases

10.3 a notice given outside the time limits in clause 10.2 is not effective

10.4 any dispute arising under any part of this clause is to be decided by arbitration under clause 17.5

LANDLORD'S OBLIGATIONS AND FORFEITURE RIGHTS

11 QUIET ENJOYMENT

11. While the Tenant complies with the terms of this lease, the Landlord is to allow the Tenant to possess and use the property without lawful interference from the Landlord, anyone who derives title from the Landlord or any trustee for the Landlord

12 INSURANCE

12. The Landlord agrees with the Tenant:

12.1 the Landlord is to keep the building (except the plate glass) insured with reputable insurers to cover

(a) full rebuilding, site clearance, professional fees, value added tax and three years' loss of rent

(b) against fire, lightning, explosion, earthquake, landslip, subsidence, heave, riot, civil commotion, aircraft, aerial devices, storm, flood, water, theft, impact by vehicles, damage by malicious persons and vandals and third party liability and any other risks reasonably required by the Landlord

so far as cover is available at the normal insurance rates for the locality and subject to reasonable excesses and exclusions

12.2 and to take all necessary steps to make good as soon as possible damage to the building caused by insured risks except to the extent that the insurance money is not paid because of the act or default of the Tenant

12.3 and to give the Tenant at his request once a year particulars of the policy and evidence from the insurer that it is in force

12.4 and that the Tenant is not responsible for any damage for which the Landlord is compensated under the insurance policy

13 SERVICES

13. The Landlord is to comply with the following duties in relation to the building:

13.1 to maintain the state and condition (including the decorations) of:

(a) the structure, outside, roof, foundations, joists, floor slabs, load bearing walls, beams and columns of the building

(b) those parts of the building which tenants of more than one part can use ("the common parts")

13.2 to decorate the common parts and the outside of the building every five years, using colours and types of finish reasonably decided by the Landlord

13.3 to pay promptly all periodic rates, taxes and outgoings relating to the common parts, including any imposed after the date of this lease (even if of a novel nature)

13.4 to pay or contribute to the cost of repairing, maintaining and cleaning party walls, party structures, yards, gardens, roads, paths, gutters, drains, sewers, pipes, conduits, wires, cables and other things used or shared with other property

13.5 to provide the services listed on page 5, but the Landlord is not to be liable for failure or delay caused by industrial disputes, shortage of supplies, adverse weather conditions or other causes beyond the control of the Landlord

14 FORFEITURE

14. This lease comes to an end if the Landlord forfeits it by entering any part of the property, which the Landlord is entitled to do whenever:

(a) payment of any rent is fourteen days overdue, even if it was not formally demanded

(b) the Tenant has not complied with any of the terms in this lease

(c) the Tenant if an individual (and if more than one, any of them) is adjudicated bankrupt or an interim receiver of his property is appointed

(d) the Tenant if a company (and if more than one, any of them) goes into liquidation (unless solely for the purpose of amalgamation or reconstruction when solvent), or has an administrative receiver appointed or has an administration order made in respect of it

The forfeiture of this lease does not cancel any outstanding obligation of the Tenant or a Guarantor

15 END OF LEASE

15. When this lease ends the Tenant is to:

15.1 return the property to the Landlord leaving it in the state and condition in which this lease requires the Tenant to keep it

15.2 (if the Landlord so requires) remove anything the Tenant fixed to the property and make good any damage which that causes

PROPERTY RIGHTS

16 BOUNDARIES

16.1 This lease does not let to the Tenant the external surfaces of the outside walls of the property and anything above the ceilings and below the floors

FACILITIES

16.2 The Tenant is to have the use, whether or not exclusive, of any of the following facilties:

the right for the Tenant and visitors to come and go to and from the property over the parts of the building designed or designated to afford access to the property, the rights previously enjoyed by the property for shelter and support and for service wires, pipes and drains to pass through them, and the right to park vehicles in any designated parking area subject to any reasonable rules made by the Landlord

16.3 The Landlord is to have the rights previously enjoyed over the property by other parts of the building for shelter and support and for service wires, pipes and drains to pass through it, and the right for the Landlord and his tenants and their visitors to come and go to and from the other parts of the building over the parts of the property designated for that purpose

GENERAL

17 PARTIES' RESPONSIBILITY

17.1 Whenever more than one person or company is the Landlord, the Tenant or the Guarantor, their obligations can be enforced against all or both of them jointly and against each individually

LANDLORD

17.2 The Landlord includes the person who, at any particular time, has the right to receive rent under this lease

TENANT

17.3 The Tenant includes the person who, at any particular time, is given the right by this lease to possess the property

SERVICE OF NOTICES

17.4 The rules about serving notices in Section 196 of the Law of Property Act 1925 (as since amended) apply to any notice given under this lease

ARBITRATION

17.5 Any matter which this lease requires to be decided by arbitration is to be referred to a single arbitrator under the Arbitration Acts. The Landlord and the Tenant may agree the appointment of the abitrator, or either of them may apply to the President of the Royal Institution of Chartered Surveyors to make the appointment

HEADINGS

17.6 The headings do not form part of this Lease

SERVICES

These are the services mentioned in clause 13.5 (delete or add as required)

Cleaning of the common parts

Lighting of the common parts

Heating of the common parts

Lift maintenance

Hot and cold water to wash hand basins in the common parts

Porterage

Fire extinguishers in the common parts

Heating in the property

Window cleaning for the building

Furnishing the common parts

Signed as a deed by/on behalf of the Landlord and delivered in the presence of:

....

Witness

....

Witness's occupation and address

....

Signed as a deed by/on behalf of the Tenant and delivered in the presence of:

....

Witness

....

Witness's occupation and address

....

Signed as a deed by/on behalf of the Guarantor and delivered in the presence of:

....

Witness

....

Witness's occupation and address

....

GUARANTEE BOX

The terms in this box only take effect if a guarantor is named and then only until the Tenant transfers this lease with the Landlord's written consent. The Guarantor must sign this lease.

'Guarantor':

of

agrees to compensate the Landlord for any loss incurred as a result of the Tenant failing to comply with an obligation in this lease during the lease period or any statutory extension of it. If the Tenant is insolvent and this lease ends because it is disclaimed, the Guarantor agrees to accept a new lease, if the Landlord so requires, in the same form but at the rent then payable. Even if the Landlord gives the Tenant extra time to comply with an obligation, or does not insist on strict compliance with terms of this lease, the Guarantor's obligation remains fully effective.

APPENDIX 2

A. Landord's notice to a tenant under the Law of Property Act 1925, s. 146, in respect of a breach of a repairing covenant to which the Leasehold Property (Repairs) Act 1938 applies.

To: Titanic Steel (Holdings) Ltd.
50 The Grove, Arden Street, Sheffield, S11 1PL [registered office]

4 March 1994

We, Rother & Co., of 9 Blue Boar Chambers, Chesterfield, as solicitors and agents for your landlord, Olympic (Nominees) plc, whose registered office is at 90 Illyria Crescent, Westminster, SW1F 2MW, hereby give you notice as follows:

1. A lease (the lease) made the twelfth day of November 1986 between yourselves, Titanic Steel (Holdings) Ltd (the tenant) (1) and Olympic (Nominees) plc (the landlord) (2) relating to the land and buildings known as 14–22 Industrial Road, Sheffield (the demised premises) contains a covenant binding upon you as follows:

> 16 (a) to keep in tenantable repair the interior of the demised premises and any additions and improvements thereto together with the window frames and fittings, sashcords and the sanitary apparatus and all sinks cisterns water pipes and drains in connection therewith

2. The above-mentioned covenant has been broken and the particular breaches complained of are committing or permitting the dilapidations specified in the schedule below.

3. We require you:

(a) to remedy the breaches specified within a reasonable time; and
(b) to pay compensation in money to the landlord for such breaches; and
(c) to pay all cost, charges, disbursements, fees and expenses incurred by the landlord in connection with the preparation and service of this notice.

4. If you fail to remedy the breaches specified within a reasonable time, the landlord will re-enter the premises pursuant to its right contained in clause 5 of the lease and will claim damages.

5. You have a right to serve a counter-notice claiming the benefit of the Leasehold Property (Repairs) Act 1938. Such notice must indicate that you claim the benefit of the Leasehold Property (Repairs) Act 1938. It must be in writing and served within 28 days of the service upon you of this notice. It may be served by leaving it at our offices at 9 Blue Boar Chambers, Chesterfield, or by sending it to that address in a letter sent either by registered post or by recorded delivery service.

APPENDIX 2

SCHEDULE

[listing dilapidations]

[signed]

Rother & Co.

B. Tenant's counter-notice to the above

To: Rother & Co.
9 Blue Board Chambers, Chesterfield

12 March 1994

As solicitors and agents of Titanic Steel (Holdings) Ltd, we give notice that in regard to the notice served by you upon it on 4 March 1994, our client claims the benefit of the Leasehold Property (Repairs) Act 1938.

[signed]

Carboys & Co.
24 Glass Street,
Jarbury JM3 3PM

APPENDIX 3

Originating application for an order authorising the exclusion of the Landlord and Tenant Act 1954, sections 24–28

IN THE BLANK COUNTY COURT
MATTER NO

IN THE MATTER OF SECTION 38(4) OF THE LANDLORD AND TENANT ACT 1954 AS AMENDED BY THE LAW OF PROPERTY ACT 1969

and

IN THE MATTER OF THE PROPOSED LEASE OF THE SECOND FLOOR OF 66 SWAN STREET, LEICESTER LE4 2AB

BETWEEN

GLEBE ENTERPRISES LTD	First Applicant
and	
RUTHWELL TRADING CO. LTD	Second Applicant

ORIGINATING APPLICATION

We, Glebe Enterprises Ltd of 22 Clougha Way, Clitheroe, Lancashire, and Ruthwell Trading Co. Ltd of 44 Oakley Way, Broadstairs, Kent, hereby jointly apply to the Court for an order in the following terms:

> UPON THE JOINT APPLICATION herein
> IT IS ORDERED that the Court do authorise the Applicants to enter into an agreement in the terms of Clause 7 of the draft lease attached hereto excluding in relation to the said lease the provisions of Sections 24 to 28 inclusive of the Landlord and Tenant Act 1954 (as amended).

The grounds upon which this Application is made are as follows:

1. The First Applicant is the proposed Landlord and the Second Applicant is the proposed tenant of the above named premises

2. The Applicants have both taken independent legal advice

3. The Second Applicant is aware of the rights that it is giving up in the making of this Application

4. The proposed lease is for a term of eighteen months and is on the terms that have been agreed between the parties herein on the assumption that vacant possession of the said premises will be yielded up to the First Applicant upon the expiration or sooner determination of the said term, which can be assured only if the Court authorises an agreement excluding in relation to the proposed tenancy the provisions of Sections 24 to 28 of the Landlord and Tenant Act 1954

5. Accordingly the First Applicant is unwilling to let the said premises other than on terms which exclude the provisions of Sections 24 to 28 of the said Act

6. (a) Both Applicants concur in the making of this Application as required by Section 38(4) of the said Act (as amended by Section 5 of the Law of Property Act 1969)

(b) It is not intended to serve any other person with notice of this Application. To the knowledge of the Applicants no other person is likely to be affected by the making of the proposed Agreement

(c) Both Applicants request and agree that the Blank County Court shall have jurisdiction in this matter

7. The address for service of the First Applicant is:

c/o Rother & Co
9 Blue Boar Chambers,
Chesterfield

8. The address for service of the Second Applicant is:

c/o Carboys & Co.
24 Glass Street,
Jarbury JM3 3PM

DATED this fifteenth day of March 1994

Signed ....

Title ....

For and on behalf of
Glebe Enterprises Ltd

Signed ....

Title ....

For and on behalf of
Ruthwell Trading Co. Ltd

To: The District Judge

INDEX

INDEX